SEMEIA 73

"READING WITH": AN EXPLORATION OF THE INTERFACE BETWEEN CRITICAL AND ORDINARY READINGS OF THE BIBLE

African Overtures

Guest Editors: Gerald West and Musa W. Dube
Board Editor:
Phyllis A. Bird

©1996
by the Society of Biblical Literature

Published by
SCHOLARS PRESS
P.O. BOX 15399
Atlanta, GA 30333-0399

Printed in the United States of America
on acid free paper

Contents

Contributors to this Issue v

An Introduction: How We Have Come to "Read With"
    Gerald West and Musa W. Dube 7

I. "READING WITH": THEORETICAL CONSIDERATIONS

1. Reading the Bible Differently: Giving Shape to the Discourse of the Dominated
    Gerald West 21

2. Race, Class, and Gender as Hermeneutical Factors in the African Independent Churches' Appropriation of the Bible
    Itumeleng J. Mosala 43

II. "READING WITH" SOUTH AFRICAN READERS

3. Confessional Western Text-Centered Biblical Interpretation and an Oral Residual Context
    Jonathon A. Draper 59

4. A Real Reader Reading Revelation
    Tim Long 79

III. "READING WITH" WOMEN

5. Readings of *Semoya*: Batswana Women's Interpretations of Matt. 15:21–28
    Musa W. Dube 111

6. Engaging Popular Religion: A Hermeneutical Investigation of Marian Devotion in the Township of Mphophomeni
    Megan Walker 131

IV. "READING WITH": INCULTURATION READERS

7. Bible Study in Africa: A Passover of Language
    John S. Pobee 161

8. Interpreting the Bible in African Contexts: Glasgow Consultation
   John Riches 181

9. The Parable of the Shrewd Manager (Lk 16:1–13): An Essay in the Inculturation Biblical Hermeneutic
   Justin S. Ukpong 189

V. DOING THEOLOGY WITH ORDINARY READERS

10. Work, the Bible, Workers, and Theologians: Elements of a Workers' Theology
    Albert Nolan 213

11. Old Testament Theology, for Whom?
    Gunther H. Wittenburg 221

VI. RESPONDENTS

Scholar and Ordinary Reader—More than a Simple Interface
   Bernard C. Lategan 243

Response to "Reading With..."
   Renita J. Weems 257

Biblical Scholars at the Interface Between Critical and Ordinary Readings: A Response
   Daniel Patte 263

A Response to "Reading With...": "Critical" and "Ordinary" Readings
   Teresia M. Hinga 277

CONTRIBUTORS TO THIS ISSUE

Jonathan Draper
  School of Theology
  University of Natal
  Private Bag X01
  Scottsville 3209
  South Africa

Musa W. Dube
  Dept. Of Theology and
  Religious Studies
  University of Botswana
  Private Bag 0022
  Gaborone
  Botswana

Teresia M. Hinga
  Department of Religious Studies
  De Paul University
  2320 North Kenmore Avenue
  Chicago, IL 60614

Bernard Lategan
  Faculty of Arts
  University of Stellenbosch
  Stellenbosch 7600
  South Africa

Timothy Long
  St. Bernard
  27 Ramushu Street
  Atteridgeville
  Pretoria
  South Africa

Itumeleng J. Mosala
  Department of Education
  Private Bag X895
  Pretoria 0001
  South Africa

Albert Nolan
  Contextual Publications
  P.O. Box 556
  Johannesburg 2001
  South Africa

Daniel Patte
  Department of Religious Studies
  Vanderbilt University
  Nashville, TN 37240

John Pobee
  World Council of Churches
  150 Route de Ferney
  1211 Geneva 2
  Switzerland

John Riches
  Department of Biblical Studies
  The University of Glasgow
  Glasgow G12 8QQ
  Scotland

Justin Ukpong
  Catholic Institute of West Africa
  P.O. Box 499
  Port Harcourt
  Nigeria

Megan Walker
  School of Theology
  University of Natal
  Private Bag X01
  Scottsville 3209
  South Africa

Renita J. Weems
  Vanderbilt Divinity School
  Nashville, TN 37240

Gerald West
  School of Theology
  University of Natal
  Private Bag X01
  Scottsville 3209
  South Africa

Gunther Wittenberg
  Kenosis Community
  P.O. Box 28172
  Haymarket 3200
  South Africa

An Introduction: How We Have Come to "Read With"

Gerald West, University of Natal
Musa W. Dube, University of Botswana

The often unruly, real reader is not usually welcome in the corridors of the academy among critical readers of the Bible (Moore: 90; see also Tracy), so it may be useful to tell how we have come to read the Bible with real readers.

Before we do so, we must be more specific about our use of terms. We use the term "ordinary readings" to refer to the interpretations of "ordinary readers" of the Bible. The term "reader" alludes to the well charted shift in hermeneutics towards the reader (Abrams: 8–29; Barton: 201–207; Lategan: 3–4; McKnight: 2–3; Eagleton: 119). Because most of the readings of this volume take place in Africa, our use of the term "reader" is metaphoric in that it includes the many who are illiterate, but who listen to, discuss, and retell the Bible.

The term "ordinary" is used in a general and a specific sense. The general usage includes all readers who read the Bible pre-critically. But we also use the term "ordinary" to designate a particular sector of pre-critical readers, those readers who are poor and marginalized. In most of the essays the particular usage usually takes precedence over the general. All of the essays are refreshingly clear about who exactly it is that biblical scholars are reading with.

Which brings us to the other "reader" in our title. "Critical readings" are the interpretations, whether exegetical or hermeneutical, a dubious distinction which we will not develop here, of readers who have been trained in use of the tools and resources of biblical scholarship. Thus, we use the term "critical" in the very specific sense that it has within biblical studies. Ordinary readers do have resources to read texts critically, but they do not have access to the structured and systematic sets of resources that constitute the craft of biblical scholars.

The term "reading with" will be explained more fully in the first essay, but it may be useful here to point to the properties of the interface. "Reading with" signifies a reading process in which the respective subject positions of ordinary, untrained readers and critical, trained readers are vigilantly foregrounded and in which power relations are structurally acknowledged. As we have said, who the reading subjects are is carefully specified in each essay.

And just as *who* is reading is clearly accounted, so too is *where* the readings take place. The readings are all African readings, as the subtitle indicates. We recognize that the readings are all "re-presentations" and we recognize that "Africanness" is a contested concept. The way in which we are introducing this volume is itself an attempt to problematize "representation" and notions of "Africanness." But, and this is important, the subtitle does not geographically delimit the discourse of the title. We would argue that the concept of "reading with" is as relevant to other contexts as it is to Africa. On reflection it might have been helpful to demonstrate this by including essays by those from other contexts who are also working in the interface between ordinary and critical readings of the Bible. Fortunately, the essays by the respondents (see, for example, the response by Patte) go some of the way to filling this gap.

The respondents make a substantial contribution to this volume in other respects too. While there have been many responses to this volume in its process of production, and we want to note the contributions of the two *Semeia* Board Editors for the volume, Vincent Wimbush and Phyllis Bird, only the four "official" respondents get to speak. They have chosen to speak in a variety of ways, Renita Weems and Teresia Hinga choosing to focus on certain selected areas of interest to them and their communities, and Bernard Lategan and Daniel Patte choosing to engage, in quite different ways, with the range of essays.

And there is a considerable range to be found in this volume. Some readers might argue that some of the essays do not belong in this journal; others might feel uncomfortable with parts of the volume. Some might suggest that we are doing nothing different from what is always done; while others might find what we are doing strange and inappropriately different. Our hope is that many will appreciate the broad-ranging character of this volume—as our respondents did, each in his or her own way.

Perhaps the best way we can introduce this volume is to give an account of how we, the editors, have come to "read with." The introductory comments so far, and the stories that are to follow, are an attempt, then, to foreground who we are and where we come from and what matters to us and our communities.

White, middle-class, males are groomed for greatness, particularly in the apartheid past of South Africa. We grow up expecting to be major players in the scheme of things. And even if we partially betray our race, class, and gender by struggling against apartheid and its legacy, we still expect to play a pivotal role in that struggle. This is a part of my, Gerald West's, story.

It was only when I briefly left South Africa in the mid-1980s, just as a State of Emergency had been declared, and spent time with black exiles, that my perspective and expectations were changed. Black South African exiles made two things abundantly clear to me. They made it clear that they were in no doubt that I should return to South Africa, because that was where I belonged; they could not, in fact, understand that there might be any other option. Their own experience of living in England was that of exile, and they simply assumed that this was my experience as well. But they also made it clear what my role on my return ought to be. Greatness was not my destiny; others would soon fulfill that role, and they would not be white. And yet, my black comrades maintained, I did have something to offer in our struggle for survival, liberation, and life. The resources and skills that I had obtained through my position of privilege, and at the the cost their oppression, should be made available to the struggle. I had a role, but the role was to wait for the call to serve, and then to serve.

My black comrades in exile then, and many other black colleagues, friends, and communities since, have asked me to make myself of use to them. I am still learning what it means "to be made use of," and I am discovering in the process that I am becoming partially constituted by my work with them. Work with poor and marginalized communities enables white middle-class male biblical scholars like me to be partially constituted by the experiences, needs, questions, and resources of such communities. This does not mean that my "whiteness," "middle-classness," and "maleness" cease to be the major factors that constitute me, but they are no longer the whole story. I will need to be reminded again and again that I am indeed substantially shaped by my "whiteness," "middle-classness," and "maleness," but I now know that I need not remain content always to be so.

In attempting to be made use of, I have found that the critical resources of biblical scholarship have something to offer to poor and marginalized readers of the Bible and much to learn from them. Critical ways of working with text is itself a contribution, as is the alternative access to the tradition that critical readings often offer. But if it is true, as Daniel Patte asserts, that our "critical interpretation is a praxis that is intrinsically ethical, because from its starting point to its concluding point it is structured by concerns for others (and the Other)" (Patte: 2), then I must continually choose to embrace the risk that comes with such an ethic, the risk of choosing to be partially constituted by particular communities of the poor and marginalized, those who have most often been the victims of dominant readings of the Bible, those who are most "other," even though such a choice is partial.

My essay says more of these things. Musa Dube will now speak.

A Long Walk in a Hall of Mirrors

The story of how I come to "read with ordinary readers" is about my long walk in a hall of mirrors. As a black Motswana African woman, I am indeed privileged to be admitted in this hall of magnificent mirrors; I have, nevertheless, struggled to see my image. Its mirrors occasionally give me a piece of what should be my face, and it is usually something undesirable. To walk in a hall of mirrors that resists reflecting one's own image is to belong to suppressed knowledges proper (Mosala: 50–51).

For me, therefore, to "read with ordinary readers" is not just to attempt to represent the reality of my face in the hall of strange mirrors, but mainly to knock at its illusive and exclusive glasses. This little gesture will remind us, "the critical biblical readers," of the diverse world outside the global structures of dominance. In this way, the term "ordinary readers" is also used to highlight the grind of global structures of dominance, which most Africans and Two-Thirds World people inhabit and which continue to define reality for them. I use globalization here to describe a process that is traceable to the Industrial Revolution, or even earlier, that stimulated the need for international markets, to the latest rise of multinational corporations and financial companies that have led to the enormous Two-Thirds World debts (see Lind: 30–43; Ngungi, 1993:60–74).

My long walk in the hall of exclusionary mirrors begins from the time I started school and learnt to chant, "Red says stop and green says go," where we had no traffic lights; from the time I went to high school and read so much English literature to the extent that reading a local novel was boring; and to the time I learnt the history of great heros such as Cecil John Rhodes' dream of building a railway from Cape to Cairo, and David Livingstone's determination to open up Africa for Commerce, Christianity, and Civilization. Beginning from then, to read has been to look into the mirror and see the face of someone else.

Yet, as I said, this is not to imply that in literature and history there is a lack of constructions of African faces. In history, there are always the strangely savage Shaka Zulus, who had to be subjugated in the interests of civilization, and the Good Kgamas, who voluntarily embraced the dreams of colonizing heroes. In short, one's image appears in relation to the dominant structures—furthering their interests through either physical death or mental death.

In literature, there are, in the likes of *Heart of Darkness*, Africans who are characterized as masses of loosely connected black limbs, eyes, hands; who are fiendish and who utter only incomprehensible sounds (Conrad:

59, 75–76). The characterization is usually sharply contrasted with the divine characteristics of the likes of Mr. Kurtz, of whom the narrator tells us "all Europe contributed to the making of Mr. Kurtz" (Conrad: 83). As a product of Europe, his character notably invokes the image of God: Mr. Kurtz is "A Voice" and at his death "it was as though a veil had been rent" (Conrad: 115–19).

William Shakespeare granted intelligible speech to a black character by maintaining that "when thou didst not, savage, know thine own meaning, but would gabble like a thing most brutish, I endowed thy purposes with words that made them known." That is, the colonized black people can only speak because the "civilized" have taught them a language. To this assertion, the Caliban of *The Tempest* responds accordingly: "You taught me language; and my profit of it is I know how to curse" (Shakespeare: 19). Needless to say, these faces are so undesirable that as a black African reader one naturally turns away to look again into the mirror for the images of intelligence, divinity, and civilization, usually represented by distant lands and people.

It took travelling to these distant lands to grasp fully that I have been admitted into a hall of mirrors that was hostile to my difference. I began to realize that I was caught in the grind of global structures that set the standard of what can be learnt and what should be excluded, what is acceptable and what is not (Tolbert, 1995: 347–361). In these distant lands, I easily discussed Shakespeare, Dickens, and Conrad with the literate people. But, they, more often than not, only knew nothing about my country and culture; they also openly held that colonialism was good for Africa.

I was also confronted by images of scantily dressed African children and working African women—children, I must say, that reminded me of the days when I happily played outside in the hot and dusty weather of Botswana, and women who reminded me of my mother, except that the pictures often had the epithet "twenty pence a month can feed an African child." I was forced to grasp the power of a camera writing someone else's story—a drama that thrives in the American movies and the media in general—and to realize that our standards of living are put on a selective scale that belittles them. On this scale of the West, we pass only as poor. Indeed, a picture of my own mother, weeding her own field and producing her own crops, can serve as proof of this devastating truth.

Yet the grind of structural globalization is not a mere misrepresentation, a distortion of facts, or a trifle that is best ignored. It is a construction that affects the political, social, and economic realities of this world. With the IMF, World Bank, global markets, and mega-media companies the lives of women, men, and children in the obscure corners of their worlds are drastically affected. Similarly, misrepresentation of differences is not purposeless. Its function is to subordinate and marginalize differences by imposing its own standards. Education, and so too biblical studies, is a major servant of these powers of dominance, or, as I have said, it is a hall of delicately constructed mirrors that selectively reflects certain images, excludes others, and misrepresents other realities.

What finally passes as critical and ordinary readings, therefore, closely reflects the global structures of dominance that defines, exports, and markets what is worthy of study and what is not. The so-called critical theories and methods of reading the Bible are thoroughly systematized cultural models of the West. These models are created and sustained by thousands of trained scholars through privileged institutions of financial donors, publishers, professional societies, universities, colleges, and seminaries (Bible and Culture Collective: 44). Insofar as it refers to Two-Thirds World readers, "ordinary readers" represents those who read from different cultural perspectives, those whose reading techniques are unrecognizable to the Western trained reader, and those who stand outside the hall of mirrors for whatever reasons, but whose standards are still defined and seen through the structures that subordinate and marginalize differences.

INTERCONNECTIONS: THE IMMEDIATE AND GLOBAL CONTEXTS

The concern for differences and the call for ethical interpretation among Western biblical scholars tends to focus within the boundaries of the West and within the biblical religious culture. It is as if biblical texts and its institutions exist in isolation of other cultures and other worlds. Also, it is as if the West exists, or has always existed, independent of other worlds. My story, and that of many Two-Thirds World people, however, constantly attests to interconnections and interdependence: it shows that the impact of Western structures grind too far for its scholars to exonerate themselves or to regard a "specific" or "particular" critical biblical practice to be adequate for the making of our contemporary world (Said: 326–36; Lind: 30–43; Ngungi, 1993:68–74).

By far and for too many centuries, biblical readers and institutions of the West have travelled around the world, interacting with various cultures and people. They have travelled together with colonial structures of exploitation and liberation movements. Similarly, the formerly colonized Two-Thirds World has engaged the West, both by gun and pen, to fight for their independence (Harlow: 31–74). In the post-independence era, the cultures, politics, and economies of the West and Two-Thirds World have become even more interconnected and interdependent through relations of the past and present. It seems, therefore, surprising that critical biblical readings, more often than not, have little or nothing to say concerning the interaction of biblical texts with world cultures and global structures of both the past and the present. Neither does one find critical theories of reading the Bible as one among many world cultures. How can we explain this silence?

Critical biblical studies makes indirect connections to its churches, its ordinary readers (referring here to the non-academic reader of the West) and the global structures of dominance of their countries. Critical biblical studies appears to be an engine running at its own will and service. The question of the Western Christian churches' association with the global structures of dominance seems to have no place in biblical studies. Does an American "critical biblical reader," for example, have anything to say about TV evangelists who, together with CNN news and "Days of Our Lives," buy themselves into many Two-Thirds World TV stations? Despite these indirect connections, the interelatedness of Western ordinary readings and powers of subjugation is tellingly expressed in the assertion of black South Africans: "When the white man came to our country he had the Bible and we had the land. The white man said to us, 'Let us pray.' After the prayer, the white man had the land and we had the Bible" (West: 21). Clearly, many African "ordinary readers" have made direct connections between colonial movements, biblical texts, and Western readers.

What, if any, are the ethical commitments of a Western critical academic biblical scholar concerning Western non-academic biblical readings that have inspired, justified, and accompanied modern colonialism and neo-colonialism? Given that the Two-Thirds World "ordinary readers" are the poor and marginalized men and women who work day and night to pay the IMF, what is the moral responsibility of critical readers and their readings to a world heaving under globalization? Where should critical biblical practice begin to address these issues? Among many other admirable efforts (see the anthologies of Segovia and Tolbert; Sugirtharajah), this volume's attempt to "read with ordinary readers" is indicative of an approach that probes the interconnections of our immediate and global power relations and how they inform, or should inform, our biblical practice.

As the readers will discover, authors of this volume offer various techniques of "reading with." For example, at the request of some "ordinary readers," West began to impart some of his academic skills to them while they also remolded his approach; Mosala set out to examine the nature of biblical hermeneutics in Black African Independent Churches (AICs); Draper's participatory mode of research engages student readers and students' participation and collection of the interpretations of Anglican church grassroots readings; Dube used both questionnaire and sermon analysis to learn from the reading techniques of Batswana (AICs) women; Walker examined how a biblical character, Mary the mother of Jesus, functions for women by participating in KwaZulu-Natal Marian devotions; Pobee offers a conversation between First World and African biblical studies by elucidating on hermeneutics of culture, socio-politics, mission, ecumenism, pluralism, gender, body, and silence; Riches gives a short report on a joint effort of some African and Western countries to integrate academic and popular biblical readings; Ukpong's inculturation approach reads the parable of the shrewd manager from the experience of his exploited Nigerian peasant farmers.

The examples of "reading with" offered by this volume are different, but they are generally marked by academic scholars who actively read with non-academic readers. It becomes clear that "reading with" involves examining various forms of power relations between the academy and the church, men and women, texuality and orality, poor and rich, black and white, immediate and global interconnections (see Lategan's response). In this way, the volume challenges Western biblical practitioners to identify and to acknowledge their reading partners as well as the purposes and impact of their readings (see Patte's and Weems' response).

To return to an earlier point, the dividing line between those who make direct connections (African "ordinary readers") and those who make indirect connections (Western critical biblical readers) indicates that it is imperative for "critical biblical readings" to be engaged with, and to be engaged by, ordinary readings from their immediate contexts and of their global counterparts for pedagogical reasons. Exploring how these interconnections foster oppression or liberation will contribute to moving "critical biblical studies" towards international biblical readings as well. As the story of Dube indicates, many international students who walk in the exclusionary hall of mirrors—a hall that is not only set up in the West but is effectively exported across the globe—experience boredom, nightmares, professional death, or loss of interest the moment they earn their certificates, because they hardly find the connections they are looking for. In this way, the exclusive powers of dominance maintain their hegemony. Moreover, this factor has serious implications for academic biblical pedagogy, as attested by Draper's study of oral versus literary readings.

The teaching of academic biblical studies has already made a significant shift towards interdisciplinary approaches. This shift needs to include examining the biblical text's close association with schools and departments of the military, anthropology, commerce, geography, novel, media, IMF, and natural history as institutions that engineer the global structures of dominance. This shift must involve examining how biblical texts have shaped the economic, political, and social policies of the world as well as the immediate context (see Mazrui: 1–9). It must encourage the current interdisciplinary efforts to be both specific and international. Above all, it must clarify how immediate contexts and global contexts have been molded, and how they should mold, critical biblical readings.

That the academic readings of Western centers pass as the standard critical biblical readings is undebatable. However, the cry against biblical textual violence, its suppression of diversity—be it gender, race, class, ethnicity, sexual and cultural orientations—and its alignment with global structures of dominance must finally be addressed by those concerned with reading for differences, for liberation, and for both immediate and global social justice. This volume's attempt to "read with ordinary readers," therefore, explores the making of our exclusive critical biblical practice, probes the power relations of our interconnections, and seeks to cultivate an academic biblical practice that is truly international. As we see it, "reading with ordinary readers" seeks to challenge any association or disassociation that serves any status quo. It challenges scholars to become even more socially engaged, more ethically committed by situating themselves within their immediate and global contexts.

Works Consulted

Abrams, M. H.
    1958   *The Mirror and the Lamp: Romantic Theory and the Critical Tradition*. New York: W. W. Norton.

Barton, J.
    1984   *Reading the Old Testament: Method in Biblical Study*. London: Darton, Longman, and Todd.

Bible and Culture Collective
    1995   *The Postmodern Bible*. New Haven: Yale University Press.

Conrad, Joseph
    1902   *Heart of Darkness*. New York: Bantam.

Eagleton, Terry
    1989   "Reception Theory." Pp. 119–27 in *Issues in Contemporary Critical Theory*. Ed. P. Barry. London: Macmillan.

Harlow, Barbara
    1987   *Resistance Literature*. New York: Methuen.

Lategan, Bernard C.
1984   "Current Issues in the Hermeneutic Debate." *Neotestamentica* 18:1–17.

Lind, Christopher
1995   *Something Is Wrong Somewhere: Globalization, Community and the Moral Economy of the Farm Crisis.* Halifax: Fernwood.

Mazrui, Ali
1990   *Cultural Forces in World Politics.* London: James Curry.

McKnight, Edgar V.
1985   *The Bible and the Reader: An Introduction to Literary Criticism.* Philadelphia: Fortress.

Moore, Stephen D.
1989   "Doing Gospel Criticism as/with a 'Reader'." *BTB* 19:85–93.

Ngungi, Thiongo
1986   *Decolonizing the Mind: The Politics of Language in African Literature.* London: James Curry.
1993   *Moving the Centre: The Struggle for Cultural Freedoms.* London: James Curry.

Patte, Daniel
1995   *Ethics of Biblical Interpretation: A Reevaluation.* Louisville, KY: Westminster/John Knox.

Said, Edward
1992   *Culture and Imperialism.* New York: Alfred A. Knopf.

Segovia, Fernando F. and Mary Ann Tolbert, eds.
1995   *Reading From This Place: Vol. 1. Social Location and Biblical Interpretation in the United States.* Minneapolis: Fortress.
1995   *Reading From This Place: Vol. 2. Social Location and Biblical Interpretation in Global Perspective.* Minneapolis: Fortress.

Shakespeare, William
1969   *The Tempest.* Cambridge: Cambridge University Press.

Shaw, Timothy M.
1996   "Africa in the Global Political Economy at the End of the Millennium: What Implications for Politics and Policies?" *Africa Today* 42: 7–30.

Sugirtharajah, R. S., ed.
1991   *Voices From the Margin: Interpreting the Bible in the Third World.* Maryknoll, NY: Orbis.
1993   *Asian Faces of Jesus.* Maryknoll, NY: Orbis.

Tolbert, Mary Ann
1995   "Christianity, Imperialism, and the Decentering of Privilege." Pp. 247–361 in *Reading From This Place: Vol. 2. Social Location and Biblical Interpre-*

tation in Global Perspective. Ed. Fernando F. Segovia and Mary Ann Tolbert. Minneapolis: Fortress.

Tracy, David
1987   *Plurality and Ambiguity: Hermeneutics, Religion, Hope.* San Francisco: Harper and Row.

Wylie, Dan
1991   "Autobiography as Alibi: History and Projection in Nathaniel Isaac's *Travels and Adventures in Eastern Africa (1836)*." Pp. 71–90 in *Current Writing: Text and Reception in Southern Africa*. Vol. 3. Durban: University of Natal.

I
"READING WITH": THEORETICAL CONSIDERATIONS

READING THE BIBLE DIFFERENTLY:
GIVING SHAPE TO THE DISCOURSES OF THE DOMINATED

Gerald West
University of Natal
South Africa

ABSTRACT

What happens when ordinary readers from poor and marginalized communities call on biblical scholars to serve them in their reading of the Bible? What role is there for the socially engaged biblical scholar? These and related questions are discussed, largely from the perspective of biblical scholars who have chosen to offer their resources and themselves to those who read the Bible differently.

INTRODUCTION

The Bible is a significant text in South Africa which has shaped and will continue to shape our history.[1] The story of the Bible in South Africa is complex and ambiguous: for most of the people in South Africa, many of whom are Christian, the Bible has been both oppressor and liberator; it has supported apartheid and struggled against apartheid; it stands against them and it stands with them.

The dilemma that confronts black South Africans in their relationship with the Bible is captured in the following well-known anecdote: "When the white man came to our country he had the Bible and we had the land. The white man said to us, 'Let us pray.' After the prayer, the white man had the land and we had the Bible." This anecdote clearly points to the central position that the Bible occupies in the process of oppression and exploitation. The anecdote also reflects the paradox of the oppressor and the oppressed sharing the same Bible and the same faith.

The narrative of the Bible in South Africa becomes even more complex when Desmond Tutu responds to the above anecdote after one of its

---

[1] The financial assistance of the Centre for Science Development of the Human Sciences Research Council towards this research is hereby acknowledged. Opinions expressed in this publication and conclusions arrived at are those of the authors and do not necessarily represent the views of the Institute for Research Development or the Human Sciences Research Council.

tellings by stating, "And we got the better deal." While Tutu's response would be and has been challenged, it does capture something of the reality of the Bible in South Africa—it plays a central role in the lives of many, particularly the poor and marginalized. The Bible is a symbol of the presence of the God of life with them.

Two recent studies have clearly demonstrated this. In discussing the construction of an indigenous theology of work, James Cochrane argues that besides being "the primary source of the Christian mythos," the Bible "is probably the only source of theology for most members of our churches. It is, as some have said, the people's book par excellence" (Cochrane, 1991:181). Cochrane's argument is based on and supported by The Institute for Contextual Theology's Church and Labour Project Research Group. The report of this group notes that perhaps "the most interesting question of all, given the response to it, was whether or not the Bible had any significance for workers, and if so, what kind of a meaning it could have." "The answers are astonishing," the report continues, "at least to anyone who might have thought that the general picture of a relatively high level of alienation from the Church would be echoed in this question." Not only did the research find that an effective eighty percent of respondents regarded the Bible as significant, "a very high positive evaluation in the light of all the other generally more negative data" concerning, for example, the relevance of the church, but that workers are deeply engaged with the Bible (ICT Church and Labour Project Research Group: 272). "Overall," the report concludes, "the most important conclusion to be drawn from this question is that the Bible is a rich source of interpretation for the worker's life, certainly of much greater significance than the liturgical and pastoral operations of the Church" (273).

In his research with the informal peri-urban shack community of Amaoti, Graham Philpott examines "how members of that community use and re-interpet the symbol of the kingdom of God to make meaning of and communicate their reality of poverty and oppression, of suffering and hope." He notes that "the re-interpretation of this symbol has emerged from a particular Bible study group which has met regularly over a four-year period to reflect on their involvement in the struggles of their community *in the light of the God who is revealed in the Bible* and in their community life" (Philpott, my emphasis). Philpott goes on to argue that "This reflection has equipped them better to *dialogue with and engage the oppressive reality* of their community, so that they can work against the forces of death and be involved in engendering life" (1993).

That the Bible is both a significant and an ambiguous text in the South African context raises serious questions for biblical scholars. In this essay I will explore some of these questions, particularly how biblical scholars can work together with ordinary people from poor and marginalized communities in reading the Bible and doing theology in our South African context.

A Deepening Interpretive Crisis

The Kairos Document, which emerged from the struggle against apartheid ten years ago, argued that "the crisis" in South Africa "impels us *to return to the Bible* and to search the Word of God for a message that is relevant to what we are experiencing in South Africa today" (17). In other words, the crisis that was shaking the foundations of our country was both political and interpretive. Wonderfully, we are emerging from our political crisis with a popularly elected democratic government. Unfortunately, our interpretive crisis is deepening.

As its subtitle intended, *The Kairos Document* was a "challenge to the church," as was the document produced a few years later, *The Road to Damascus: Kairos and Conversion*. Sectors of the church responded to these challenges, joining those who already were engaged in various ways in the struggle against apartheid. The church (like the synagogue, mosque, and temple) became a site of struggle. However, now that our political crisis has passed, there are worrying indications that, in the words of a prominent churchman, "the church must now go back to being the church." But surely we were most truly "church" in the streets of our struggle? While it is no longer necessary for the church to represent the liberation movements, as it was in decades of their bannings, this does not mean that the readings and theologies forged in the struggle ought to be abandoned in order to "go back to being the church," whatever this might mean.

Our struggle *against* apartheid demanded new readings and theologies of us. Our struggle *for* full liberation and life requires that we build on what we have learned. The present danger is that we do indeed "go back to being the church," even before we have adequately articulated the readings and theologies which we lived by in the days of struggle and which will enable us to go forward to full liberation and life. The "working" readings and theologies that resourced our struggle are in danger of being forgotten as the church sighs and begins to pick up the patterns of the past. This is our deepening interpretive crisis.

Political liberation in South Africa has created some "space" for the church, but just how that space is to be filled is a crucial question. Now is not the time to return to comfortable certainties; rather now is the time for the recognition and articulation of the subjugated and incipient resources of our struggle. Subjugated and incipient readings of the Bible and their related theologies have been resources for many, particularly for the poor and marginalized, and their struggle for full liberation and life is not yet over.

A Case Study In KwaZulu-Natal

During the latter half of the 1980s KwaZulu-Natal was at war. The United Democratic Front (UDF), which had been launched in 1983, was rapidly gaining support, organizing, and mobilizing throughout South Africa. With a mandate from the banned African National Congress (ANC), extensive affliation by a variety of community-based organizations, including sectors of the church, and strong and enabling local leadership, the UDF gained substantial grassroots support. However, in KwaZulu-Natal the growth of the UDF was not only opposed and obstructed by the state, as elsewhere, but also by Inkatha, who consider KwaZulu-Natal their traditional territory.

Inkatha responded to the UDF's growing support by embarking on an intimidating membership drive, particularly in those areas where the UDF was beginning to set up structures. Whenever and wherever people resisted being press-ganged into Inkatha membership violence followed.[2] Funded, trained, armed, transported, and supported by the apartheid state, Inkatha attempted to crush the UDF (Truluck). The violence this has generated is horrific, and every black family in the region has experienced terror and death.

One of the many cries to emerge from the violence was, as *The Kairos Document* demonstrates, a cry to reread the Bible in such a way as to discover the God of life in the midst of the forces of death. Received readings and theologies no longer made sense. The biblical and theological resources for those struggling with the God of life against the forces of death were not always apparent. Remarkably, this questioning brought Bible readers from poor and marginalized communities into dialogue with socially engaged biblical scholars at the university. Ours is a context in which biblical interpretations do matter; they do shape our world. As the South African context constantly reminds us, biblical interpretations have life and death consequences; they shape the type of response the state, the church, and ordinary people make to particular social realities.

Our initial response as biblical scholars to the dialogue was an overwhelming sense of the inadequacy and paucity of our resources in this context. And yet the community also helped us to recognize that we did

---

[2] This was the so-called "black on black violence" popularized by ignorant international media, and makes as much sense as speaking of the conflict in Bosnia as "white on white violence."

have resources which might be useful, provided we were willing to read the Bible and do theology *with* them. The result of our dialogue is an emerging interface in which socially engaged biblical scholars and poor and marginalized readers of the Bible do what we call "contextual Bible study."

Our work together is guided by the basic assumption that resources for a contextual reading of the Bible are to be found both in biblical studies and in poor and marginalized communities. The experience of similar initiatives in other contexts of crisis have demonstrated two potential problems which constantly recur in such an interface: biblical scholars either romanticize and idealize the contribution of the poor and marginalized or they minimize and rationalize that community's contribution (see Segundo). Both are problematic. "Listening to" presupposes the speaking voice of a wholly self-knowing subject free from ideology, while "speaking for" denies the subject status of the poor and oppressed altogether (Arnott: 125). We can only move beyond "speaking for" and "listening to" the poor and marginalized if we are willing to enter into a "speaking with" (Spivak; Arnott).[3]

Following Jill Arnott and Gayatri Spivak, I use the phrase "speaking with" to point to "the need to occupy the dialectical space between two subject-positions, without ever allowing either to become transparent" (Arnott: 125). This requires that biblical scholars remain constantly alert to, and interrogative of, our own positionality and that of our discourse partners, so as to ensure that the mediating process of representation remains visible. In other words, with Arnott and Spivak, I am arguing that "speaking with" takes seriously the subjectivity of both the biblical scholar and the ordinary poor and marginalized reader of the Bible, and all that this entails for their respective categories and contributions.

However, the power relations in the interface between the ordinary reader and the biblical scholar cannot be obliterated, and they must not be ignored. They must be foregrounded. Postmodern feminists like Arnott, Spivak, Elizabeth Ellsworth, and Audre Lorde emphasise the creative and constructive potential of "a genuinely dialectical interaction between two vigilantly foregrounded subject-positions" (Arnott: 127). Only then can we move beyond "speaking for" and "listening to" towards a place where difference enables. "Difference must be not merely tolerated, but seen as a fund of necessary polarities between which our creativity can spark like a dialectic. Only then does the necessity for interdependency become unthreatening" (Lorde: 112; Ellsworth: 319).

---

3 Spivak uses the phrase "speaking to," but I prefer the preposition "with."

Talk of an interdependency between biblical scholars and ordinary readers of the Bible from poor and marginalized communities can be threatening and unsettling in the corridors of the academy, and it certainly involves risk. But in the suffering and pain of KwaZulu-Natal we have come to recognize the necessity of interdependency and a need for "an ethic of risk" (Welch, 1985:26), which requires that we recognize the partiality of our particular choices *and* that we continue to struggle for full liberation and life. For us, reading the Bible and doing theology in this interface calls for dialogue and difference (West, 1994): "a speaking with" which vigilantly foregrounds both the readings and resources of biblical studies and the readings and resources of the poor and marginalized.

Conversion

Usually the connection between our work as biblical scholars and our life commitments is covert, and if our work is to be used by others, we want to remain in control. Clearly the interface I have outlined above, and to which I will return below, demands an overt connection between our biblical research and our social commitments, and that we risk allowing our work and ourselves to be used by others without our control. This requires something of a conversion "from below." Biblical scholars must be born "from below."

Implicit in my discussion so far are at least three threads within biblical studies which facilitate such a conversion. Liberation hermeneutics is probably the most obvious. While Western theologies have educated (and usually male) believers and non-believers as their primary dialogue partners, the primary interlocutors of liberation theologies are non-persons: uneducated believers, the poor, the exploited classes, the marginalized races, women, all the despised cultures (Frostin: 7–8). Liberation hermeneutics requires that cognizance of and commitment to the experience of these non-persons is a necessary condition for reading the Bible and doing theology (Frostin: 6; Schüssler Fiorenza, 1983:xxi). "The basic insight of liberation theologies and their methodological starting point is the insight that all theology knowingly or not is by definition always engaged for or against the oppressed" (Schüssler Fiorenza, 1984:45). Somewhat stridently liberation hermeneutics asks biblical scholars to make an option for the poor and marginalized.

A second, more polite, conversion-enabling thread is postmodernism. As Cornel West argues at length, postmodern points of view can serve as a useful springboard for a more engaged, even subversive, philosophical perspective.

This is so primarily because it encourages the cultivation of critical attitudes toward all philosophical traditions. This crucial shift in the subject matter of philosophers from the grounding of beliefs to the scrutiny of groundless traditions—from epistemology to ethics, truth to practices, foundations to consequences—can lend itself to emancipatory ends in that it proposes the tenuous self-images and provisional vocabularies that undergird past and present social orders as central objects of criticism.

West continues by arguing that this shift is particularly significant for "those on the underside of history" because "oppressed people have more at stake than others in focusing on the tenuous and provisional vocabularies which have had and do have hegemonic status in past and present societies" (West: 270–71).

The postmodern shift allows biblical scholars to abandon their quest for the certainty of "the right" reading in favour of the more humane concern for useful readings and resources—readings and resources that are a part of a discourse that takes seriously questions of ethics, practices, and effects. With its destabilizing of the interpretive process and its decentering of the interpretations of experts, postmodernism gives opportunity to the different subjectivities of others, including the poor and marginalized—the most "other."

The third thread is less obvious, but also offers a path for conversion. Reader response criticism, or reception hermeneutics, has introduced biblical scholars to a reader who is no longer perceived as a passive receiver of authorial or textual meaning, but who is now recognized as an active creator of meaning (see Lategan). While real ordinary readers of the Bible have never been fully admitted to the guild of "proper" readers (Moore), the logic of this approach demands their presence. The practice of "reading with" invites scholarly readers, and their allied "implied" readers and other surrogates (see Long's essay in this volume), to read the Bible with actual readers from poor and marginalized communities, even when many of these readers are only "readers" in a metaphorical sense.

While the ongoing process of conversion required by "reading with" demands continuing accountability to communities of the poor and marginalized, this "community consciousness" does not exclude our accountability as scholars to critical biblical research. A fundamentalism of the Left is not particularly useful (Mosala: 31), as I will argue below, in the struggle for full liberation and life, while a "critical consciousness" is useful.

Giving Shape to the Discourses of the Dominated

Experience in South Africa and Brasil in the interface constituted by "reading with," in which the subjectivities of both the socially engaged biblical scholar and poor and marginalized reader are vigilantly foregrounded and power relations are acknowledged and equalized, demonstrates the need for both "community consciousness" and "critical consciousness." The experiences, questions, needs, interests, as well as the readings and resources of the community, are the starting point of contextual Bible study, and socially engaged biblical scholars must allow themselves to be partially constituted by this reality (West, 1993:144; Welch, 1990:144). But what of the critical tools which are the trade of biblical scholars, do they have a role to play?

Remarkably, in contexts like Brasil and South Africa, biblical scholars are continually being "called" by ordinary readers of the Bible. Trust of intellectuals is reserved, however, only for those with whom the people choose to speak. The biblical scholars who are part of this "contextual Bible study process" are committed to doing biblical studies with and from the perspective of the poor and oppressed. So there has always been a clear recognition of their role as servants. Their contribution may be distinctive and different, but it is not in any way better or more significant. While not all of these biblical scholars are organic intellectuals, they all work closely with organic intellectuals.

But what is the usefulness of the socially engaged biblical scholar? Why is it that ordinary poor and marginalized readers of the Bible find their participation in the Bible reading process useful? Before I attempt an answer, we should shift perspective to more secure ground and consider the perspective of the socially engaged biblical scholar. How do they see their contribution? From their perspective, socially engaged biblical scholars involved in various liberation theologies agree in at least four crucial areas. They agree that the Bible must be read from the perspective of the poor and marginalized, that the Bible must be read *with* the poor and marginalized, that Bible reading is related to social transformation, and, significantly, that the Bible must be read critically.

While biblical scholars differ on the modes of critical reading to be used (West, 1995:131–73), some favouring historical-sociological modes (e.g. Mosala and Schüssler Fiorenza), others literary modes (e.g. Trible and Bal), and still others symbolic, thematic, and metaphoric modes (e.g. Schneiders and Croatto), the vital similarity is that all these modes of reading offer *a critical* reading of the Bible—they ask systematic and structured sets of questions of the Bible. Another important and related similarity of these different modes of reading is the concern that the appropriation of biblical elements, whether from behind the text, in the text, or in front of the text, is a *critical appropriation*. A critical reading and appropriation of the biblical text is the primary concern from the side of (organic) intellectuals involved in the interface between an engaged biblical studies with its socially committed trained readers of the Bible and ordinary poor and marginalized readers of the Bible.[4]

The historical and cultural struggles of the poor and marginalized must be the starting point of biblical interpretation in liberation hermeneutics. But clearly, in addition to this community consciousness a critical consciousness is also necessary. Why? So that, Per Frostin argues, the poor and marginalized can "create their own language" (10). Critical consciousness breaks the "culture of silence" created by their accommodation to the logic of domination.

When it comes to understanding the alleged silence of the poor and oppressed, we find thick and thin accounts of ideological hegemony. The thick version emphasizes the role of ideological state apparatuses, such as education systems, the church, and government structures, in controlling the symbolic means of production, just as factory owners monopolize the material means of production. "Their ideological work secures the active consent of subordinate groups to the social arrangements that reproduce their subordination" (Scott: 73).[5] The thin theory of hegemony makes less grand claims for the ideological control of the ruling class. What ideological domination does accomplish, according to this version,

> is to define for subordinate groups what is realistic and what is not realistic and to drive certain aspirations and grievances into the realm of the impossible, of idle dreams. By persuading underclasses that their position, their life-chances, their tribulations are unalterable and inevitable, such a limited hegemony can produce the behavioral results of consent without necessarily changing people's values. Convinced that nothing can possibly be done to improve their situation and that it will always remain so, it is even conceivable that idle criticisms and hopeless aspirations would be eventually extinguished. (Scott: 74)

But because "the logic of domination represents a combination of historical and contemporary ideological and material practices that are never completely successful, always embody contradictions, and are constantly being fought over within asymmetrical relations of power" (Giroux: xii), organic intellectuals, who can learn with the poor and marginalized while simultaneously helping them to foster modes of self-education and struggle against various forms of oppression, are able to point to the spaces, contradictions, and forms of resistance that raise the possibility for social struggle. However, and this is a key element of this position, oppressed people's accommodation to the logic of domination may mean that they actively resist emancipatory forms of knowledge offered by organic intellectuals (Giroux: xviii–xxiii).

---

4 This is clearest in the work of Mosala, Schüssler Fiorenza, and Gottwald.

5 For a detailed account of this phenomenon see Memmi.

Such accounts of ideological hegemony argue that "when oppressed people live in silence, they use the words of their oppressors to describe their experience of oppression. Only within the praxis of liberation and in dialogue with what Antonio Gramsci called 'organic intellectuals' is it possible for the poor to break this silence and create their own language" (Frostin: 10). So within liberation theologies, whether they be Latin American, black, womanist, or feminist, the role of the intellectual is crucial in breaking "the culture of silence"—in enabling a language.

But what if this analysis is inadequate and the poor and marginalized have not accommodated themselves to the logic of domination? What if they already have a language? These are questions that reflection on the contextual Bible study process in South Africa has begun to generate. James Scott's work on "domination and the arts of resistance" has been particularly useful here.

Scott problematises both thick and thin versions of ideological hegemony, and so too the role of the intellectual. In his detailed study of domination and resistance we find a more nuanced analysis, arguing that theories of hegemony and false consciousness do not take account of what he calls "the hidden transcript."

> Every subordinate group creates, out of its ordeal, a 'hidden transcript' that represents a critique of power spoken behind the back of the dominant. The powerful, for their part, also develop a hidden transcript representing the practices and claims of their rule that cannot be openly avowed. A comparison of the hidden transcript of the weak with that of the powerful and of *both* hidden transcripts to the public transcript of power relations offers a substantially new way of understanding resistance to domination. (Scott: xii)

The crucial point of Scott's detailed argument is that "the public transcript, where it is not positively misleading, is unlikely to tell the whole story about power relations. It is frequently in the interest of both parties to tacitly conspire in misrepresentation" (2). So social analysis which focuses on the public transcript, as most social analysis does, is focusing on the formal relations between the powerful and weak (13), but is not attempting to "read, interpret, and understand the often fugitive political conduct of subordinate groups" (xii). A focus on the hidden transcript, where it is accessible in the rumours, gossip, folktales, songs, gestures, jokes, and theatre of the poor and marginalized, or the more public infrapolitics of popular culture (198), reveals forms of resistance and defiance. "Unless one can penetrate the official transcript of both subordinates and elites, a reading of the social evidence will almost always represent a confirmation of the status quo in hegemonic terms" (90).

Put differently, in the words of the Ethiopian proverb with which Scott opens his study, "When the great lord passes the wise peasant bows deeply and silently farts." Theories of ideological hegemony look at the stage, the public transcript of the bowing peasant. Scott draws our attention to what is hidden, the silent fart, offstage.

Is there still not a case for Gramsci's notion of the dominated consciousness of subordinate groups? For Gramsci hegemony works primarily at the level of thought as distinct from the level of action (Gramsci: 333). Scott turns this around. He considers "subordinate classes *less* constrained at the level of thought and ideology, since they can in secluded settings speak with comparative safety, and *more* constrained at the level of political action and struggle, where the daily exercise of power sharply limits the options available to them" (91). So, he argues,

> subordinate groups have typically learned, in situations short of those rare all-or-nothing struggles, to clothe their resistance and defiance in ritualisms of subordination that serve both to disguise their purposes and to provide them with a ready route of retreat that may soften the consequences of a possible failure. (96)

This is because most protests and challenges, even quite violent ones, "are made in the realistic expectation that the central features of the form of domination will remain intact." Consequently, "most acts of power from below, even when they are protests—implicitly or explicitly—will largely observe the 'rules' even if their objective is to undermine them" (93). He believes "the historical evidence clearly shows that subordinate groups have been capable of revolutionary *thought* that repudiates existing forms of domination" (101). However, because the occasions on which subordinate groups have been able to act openly and fully on that thought are rare, the conflict will usually take "a dialogic form in which the language of the dialogue will invariably borrow heavily from the terms of the dominant ideology prevailing in the public transcript." So we must "consider the dominant discourse as a plastic idiom or dialect that is capable of carrying an enormous variety of meanings, including those that are subversive of their use as intended by the dominant" (102–3).

Given Scott's analysis, the role of the intellectual is less clear. Subordinate groups are already engaged in forms of resistance and already have a language. "The culture of silence" is a strategy and not the whole story. What is hidden is hidden for good reason, so any attempt to penetrate the disguise is dangerous. When dignity and autonomy demand an irruption or an articulation, this must be done in ways determined by the dominated. There does not appear to be a silence to break or a language to create. Perhaps we can speak of enabling a structured articulation.

Contextual Bible study work in South Africa has begun to recognize that something like Scott's analysis is a more adequate and accurate understanding of our experience. Resisting and potentially liberating and transforming readings (and theologies) are already present in some form in communities of the poor and marginalized, but they are often incipient (see Cochrane, 1995). Several points must be kept in view by way of explanation.

> First, the hidden transcript is a social product and hence a result of power relations among subordinates. Second, like folk culture, the hidden transcript has no reality as pure thought; it exists only to the extent it is practiced, articulated, enacted, and disseminated within these offstage social sites. Third, the social spaces where the hidden transcript grows are themselves an achievement of resistance; they are won and defended in the teeth of power. (119)

It would seem that contextual Bible study provides processes, critical resources, and a safe social site in which the unarticulated (and primarily religious) responses to domination of individuals are given expression in language, symbol, and ritual, and, if they carry effective meaning for the group, become the social property of the group.

There are a number of elements which can be identified here. Contextual Bible study seems to provide a *sequestered site* in which an offstage subculture can articulate a counterideology. For each subaltern, to use Spivak's term, who knows more or less what attitudes and values lie behind her "working" readings and theology and, if less reliably, what lies behind those of other subalterns in her group (Scott: 67), contextual Bible study provides both a place and the democratic group processes for discerning whether her "working" readings and theology resonate with and are representative of the group.

Contextual Bible study also offers additional critical resources for a structured articulation. Our research has shown that while poor and marginalized ordinary readers do have critical resources for interpreting their texts and contexts, they do not have the historical, sociological, literary, or symbolic tools to be critical of the biblical text in the same way as biblical scholars (West, 1995: 198–200; Scott: 116; Wimbush). These modes of reading provide systematic and structured sets of questions which can be brought to the biblical text, and which might enable what is incipient to become the social property of the group.

Finally, the presence of socially engaged biblical scholars is a further resource. There is, it would seem, a role for Gramsci's organic intellectual or Max Weber's "pariah-intelligentsia." Not only are they the bearers of additional useful critical resources which give shape to the readings and theologies of the poor and marginalized, but they usually inhabit the boundary regions between hidden and public transcripts, and as Scott notes, "The unremitting struggle over such boundaries is perhaps the most vital arena for ordinary conflict" (14). Boundaries are dangerous, precisely because of their ambiguity (Schreiter: 66), and so are those who cross boundaries. So it is only the "called" and "converted" biblical scholar who may be of service to poor and marginalized communities, those who have betrayed the hidden transcript of the dominant and who have chosen to be partially constituted by the hidden transcript of the dominated.[6] The experience of boundary crossing is a vital contribution, precisely because the boundary crosser is able to chart more clearly where the boundaries are. Also, in crossing the boundaries between communities of the poor and marginalized through time, the socially engaged biblical scholar is able to relate the experience of a particular community to the experience of other communities, both present and past (Schreiter: 18).

The contextual Bible study process, then, is a locale where subjugated and incipient readings and theologies can be openly declared, where we can recognize whether our "working" readings and theologies resonate with those of others we live and work with, and where we together give shape to counterideologies, resisting readings, and theologies that bring liberation and life. There is a place here for the socially engaged biblical scholar, although it is not perhaps the prominent place we expected.

Rooted as it is in both a community consciousness and a critical consciousness, contextual Bible study provides resources for "a theoretically well-grounded and culturally autonomous" discourse (see Mosala: 2–3). Resisting, liberating, and life-giving resources are found in our "belonging in difference."

Articulating and Owning What Is Hidden

What Scott's analysis helps us to understand, then, is the remarkable readiness of ordinary readers in poor and marginalized communities to use the critical resources of biblical studies in addition to their own critical resources. Some specific examples may be useful.

Typically, the Institute for the Study of the Bible (ISB) in KwaZulu-Natal, an interface between socially committed biblical scholars and ordinary readers of the Bible from poor and marginalized communities, is invited to work with particular Bible reading communities. The "generative theme" (Freire) of the workshops is always determined by the community, and they usually choose the biblical texts. For example, in a workshop with the Umtata Women's Group the theme of the workshop was determined by the group, as well as the programme, and some texts. But the ISB was asked to suggest additional texts for Bible study. Mark 5:21–6:1 was one of the texts used. The text was chosen because two of the

---

[6] Living "in between" would be impossible were it not for the sense of "belonging in difference" that constitutes the contextual Bible study process.

main characters are women, and so fitted the theme liberating ways of reading the Bible as women.

The ISB is committed to working with organized communities, groups who can "talk back" and who have the identity, structures, and resources to "own" the workshop process. In other words, the ISB deliberately chooses to work in those contexts in which it is possible for the subject positions of both the ISB staff and the community participants to be vigilantly foregrounded. The relationship between trained and ordinary reader is subject to subject and not subject to object. The trained reader reads the Bible "with" and not "for" ordinary readers.

Within such a framework of accountability to Bible study groups of ordinary readers, trained readers can participate fully in the Bible study process. Our role as facilitators in the workshop is to provide what Cornel West calls "enabling forms of criticism" (210). In this case, the process of reading Mark 5 entailed first, encouraging participants to read the text fully, carefully, and closely, and then, when asked, providing some historical and sociological resources for reflection on the type of society that produced the text.

So, more specifically, in this workshop we as trained readers suggested that this text, along with a number of other texts identified by the group, might be relevant to the chosen theme women. The advantage of a text like Mark 5:21–6:1 is that it is not usually perceived as a text primarily about women. Consequently, reading this unexpected text "surprises" the readers and facilitates a more critical reading of the text. The danger with well-known texts is that we think we already know what they mean; we domesticate and tame them. So it would seem that trained readers can enable the disclosive power of the "untamed" and "undomesticated" text both by encouraging readers to bring their questions to familiar texts and by drawing forgotten and neglected texts into the reading process. And this was the effect in this case. On an initial reading most readers did not recognize that the text was primarily about women. Healing, compassion, faith, love, hope, despair, suffering, power, and other similar themes were what the text was about. But once it was suggested, either from within the group or by a facilitator, that the text might be about women, there was great excitement and expectation as participants returned to reread the text more carefully and closely, finding in the process their subjugated and incipient readings being articulated and given shape.

In any reading of the Bible in the interface between trained and ordinary readers there is a great deal that ordinary readers can discover and recover in texts using their own resources, provided there is some facilitation of this process. In this workshop the Bible was read communally, in small groups. Instead of ISB staff providing evidence from the text to support the suggestion that text was about women, it was usually sufficient to give one or two examples from the text and then to ask the groups to find additional examples. Our task was then to help summarize and systematize the emerging reading. Contextual Bible study, then, is committed to corporate and communal reading of the Bible in which the trained reader is just another reader with different resources and skills, not better resources and skills.

As already indicated, the contextual reading process is also committed to critical readings of the Bible. While these ordinary readers did have critical resources, these were not the specific critical resources of biblical studies. Once again, creative facilitation can enable ordinary readers to read more critically than is their usual practice. In the reading of Mark 5:21–6:1 we concentrated on providing resources for two critical modes of reading.

A close and careful (literary) mode of reading was used in order to substantiate the suggestion that the text was primarily about women. The use of narrative transitions to delimit the literary unit, the reading of the whole text to discern its structure, the careful and close reading of the component parts, the return to reread the text as a whole in the light of the reading of the parts, and the continual attention to the internal relationships within the text, including reference to plot, character, theme, repetition, and other literary devices, are elements of this mode of reading. While ordinary readers are not familiar with these literary resources for reading in any structured or systematic way, they recognize and appreciate their usefulness and integrate these resources into their own modes of reading.

When questions from the group required it, a historical and sociological mode of reading was also used to situate this text in its first century context. The implicit use of historical-critical tools to delimit the text, and to locate it historically, and the reconstruction of aspects of the sociological setting and production of the text, including specific reference to the patriarchal and purity systems, are elements of this mode of reading. Once again, while ordinary readers are not familiar with these historical and sociological resources, they appreciate their usefulness and integrate these resources into their own modes of reading.

These critical resources were not used as the way into the text. The Bible study began with a life interest of the participants. The generative theme determined by the group provided an initial entry into the reading process. While not usually a critical mode of reading, a thematic approach does provide a useful way into the text, particularly as it draws on the needs and questions of the participants. The other modes of reading then develop and elaborate what is initiated through this thematic approach to the text.

The range of experience and resources that groups of ordinary readers bring to their reading of the Bible is various and vast. Creative facilitation, including asking questions instead of simply providing information, can draw on the resources of ordinary readers and in so doing empower them to construct their own critical and contextual readings. Once again, it must be stressed that our task as trained readers in such a workshop is not to do the reading for ordinary readers, nor to accept simply or uncritically their readings. Rather, our task is to read the Bible *with* ordinary readers. This requires that we constantly and vigilantly foreground our respective subject positions, and that we become explicit concerning the power relations implicit in the reading process.

The key contribution of the critical resources of biblical studies to the contextual Bible study process seems to be that they enable ordinary readers themselves to give shape to and so own what is subjugated, hidden, and incipient. While the first response in many Bible study groups is often the "missionary response" or the dogmatically "correct" response—the public transcript—critical modes of reading enable ordinary people from poor and marginalized communities to begin to articulate their "working" readings and theologies, what is incipient and usually deliberately hidden from public view. The latter is clearly dangerous; what is hidden from the dominant is hidden for good reason, and can and should only be openly owned in a context of trust and accountability. But within such a context, the intersection of community and critical resources enables the recognizing, recovering, and arousing of dangerous memories (Metz), subjugated knowledges (Foucault), and hidden transcripts.

The hidden transcript, as Scott reminds, is never a language apart. In constant argument with dominant discourses (135), it continually demands some response to material exploitation, colonialism, sexism, and racism, even if this response must take a disguised form. Because the argument demands a presence in the public transcript, it must of necessity "borrow heavily from the terms of the dominant ideology prevailing in the public transcript"; however, in the artful hands of the dominanted, the dominant discourse "is capable of carrying an enormous variety of meanings, including those that are subversive of their use as intended by the dominant" (Scott: 102–3). This explains why in contextual Bible study initial responses of participants to texts and themes may appear to conform to the public transcript. The contextual Bible study group is, after all, not initially a secure site, bringing together as it does people who may not already have close relationships. A more nuanced listening usually discloses a more ambiguous and polysemic expression that is capable of two readings, one which is innocuous, so providing an avenue of retreat if challenged, and one which is subversive, "smuggling...portions of the hidden transcript, suitably veiled, onto the public stage" (Scott: 157). Community consciousness, democratic group process, and the critical resources of contextual Bible study enable the articulation and "owning" of the latter.

In KwaZulu-Natal, as elsewhere among the poor and marginalized (see Scott: 164), "there is a tremendous desire and will to express publicly what is in the hidden transcript, even if that form of expression must use metaphors and allusions in the interest of safety." In other words, the hidden transcript constantly "presses against and tests the limits of what may be safely ventured in terms of a reply to the public transcript of deference and conformity." When the conditions that constrain the readings and theologies of the poor and marginalized are relaxed, as recently they have been in South Africa, "we may expect to see [as indeed we are] the disguises become less opaque as more of the hidden transcript shoulders its way onto the stage and into action" (Scott: 172). So as the hegemony of the apartheid state and its religious ideology, "Church theology"(see *The Kairos Document*), were beginning to weaken and have now been broken, there has been a growing eagerness and boldness not only to speak what has been hidden and disguised—to shout "what has historically been whispered, controlled, choked back, stifled, and suppressed" (Scott: 227),[7] but also to "own" what is liberating and life giving.

Contextual Bible study provides processes, resources, and a place for the making and shaping that it is a part of owning. It facilitates a more systematic and structured articulation.

Belonging in Difference

What is particularly exciting and challenging about reading the Bible with ordinary readers is that it is quite legitimate for ordinary readers and trained readers to emerge from the reading process with different elements of interest. The readings produced in this interface affect ordinary and trained readers differently, and this is not surprising because we come to the text from different places and after the reading encounter return to our different places. Our subjectivities as trained and ordinary readers are differently constituted, so the effect that the corporate reading has on our subjectivities will be different. However, and this is extremely

---

[7] If the results of the declaration of the hidden transcript "seem like moments of madness, if the politics they engender is tumultuous, frenetic, delirious, and occasionally violent, that is perhaps because the powerless are so rarely on the public stage and have so much to say and do when they finally arrive" (227).

important, we will have been partially constituted by each other's subjectivities. And this should always be a constituent element of the contextual Bible study process: a desire to be partially constituted by those from other communities. For me, this means choosing to be partially constituted by working with poor and marginalized communities.

Elsewhere I have published a reading of Mark 5:21–6:1 (West, 1996). The finished product which is that reading was not produced by ordinary readers. In its final form it is my reading. But it is a reading that had its birth among mainly ordinary black women who were struggling to hear God speak to their needs and questions. What they have taken away from the Umtata Women's Bible study workshop and how they will use it I do not fully know. For example, one of the women in the Umtata women's group summed up her group's discussion with the words: "The problem is that men don't bleed; men must bleed!" What this means for that group of women and what they will do with this reading is theirs; it belongs to them and to their context. And they must speak for themselves.

That is the challenge of reading the Bible with ordinary readers: allowing, even facilitating a reading process in which ordinary readers take and use what is empowering for their particular subjectivities and communities, and allowing, even facilitating, a reading process in which we as biblical scholars are partially constituted by the experiences, questions, interests, resources, and readings of those on the margins. And not only does such a reading process enable us to be partially constituted by the other, "the other" who is usually absent from Biblical Studies, but our readings now bring to the academic stage glimpses of readings that are to be found offstage among the poor and marginalized and which call us to share their struggle with the God of life against the forces of death.

WORKS CONSULTED

Arnott, Jill
1991 "French feminism in a South African frame?: Gayatri Spivak and the problem of 'representation' in South African feminism." *Pretexts* 3:118–28.

Bal, Mieke
1988 *Death and Dissymmetry: The Politics of Coherence in Book of Judges*. Chicago: University of Chicago Press.

Cochrane, James R.
- 1991 "Already, but not yet: Programmatic Notes for a Theology of Work." Pp. 177–89 in *The Threefold Cord: Theology, Work and Labour*. Ed. James R. Cochrane and Gerald O. West. Pietermaritzburg: Cluster.
- 1996 "Conversation or Collaboration? Base Christian Communities and the Dialogue of Faith." *Scriptura* 57:103–24.

Croatto, J. Severino
- 1987 *Biblical Hermeneutics: Toward a Theory of Reading as the Production of Meaning*. Maryknoll, NY: Orbis.

Ellsworth, Elizabeth
- 1989 "Why doesn't this feel empowering? Working through the repressive myths of critical pedagogy." *Harvard Educational Review* 59:297–324.

Fiorenza, Elisabeth Schüssler
- 1983 *In Memory of Her: A Feminist Theological Reconstruction of Christian Origins*. London: SCM.
- 1984 *Bread Not Stone: The Challenge of Feminist Biblical Interpretation*. Boston: Beacon.

Foucault, Michel
- 1980 *Power/Knowledge: Selected Writings and Other Interviews, 1972–1977*. Ed. Colin Gordon. Trans. Colin Gordon, Leo Marshal, John Mepham, and Kate Soper. New York: Pantheon.

Freire, Paulo
- 1970 *Pedagogy of the Oppressed*. Trans. Myra Bergman Ramos. New York: Seabury Press and Continuum.

Frostin, Per
- 1988 *Liberation Theology in Tanzania and South Africa: A First World Interpretation*. Lund: Lund University Press.

Giroux, H. A.
- 1985 Introduction. Pp. xi–xxv in *The Politics of Education*. Ed. P. Freire. London: Macmillan.

Gottwald, Norman K.
- 1979 *The Tribes of Yahweh: A Sociology of the Religion of Liberated Israel, 1250–1050 B.C.* Maryknoll, NY: Orbis.

Gramsci, Antonio
- 1971 *Selections From the Prison Notebooks*. Ed. and Trans. Quintin Hoare and Geoffrey Nowel Smith. London: Lawrence and Wishart.

ICT Church and Labour Project Research Group
- 1991 "Workers, the Church and the Alienation of Religious Life." Pp. 253–75 in *The Threefold Cord: Theology, Work and Labour*. Ed. James R. Cochrane and Gerald O. West. Pietermaritzburg: Cluster.

The Kairos Theologians
- 1986 *The Kairos Document: Challenge to the Church*. Braamfontein: Skotaville.

Lategan, Bernard C.
　1984　"Current Issues in the Hermeneutic Debate." *Neotestamentica* 18:1–17.

Lorde, Audre
　1984　*Sister Outsider.* New York: Crossing Press.

Memmi, A.
　1965　*The Colonizer and the Colonized.* London: Souvenir.

Metz, Johann Baptist
　1980　*Faith in History and Society: Toward a Practical Fundamental Theology.* Trans. David Smith. New York: Seabury Press and Crossroads.

Moore, Stephen D.
　1989　*Literary Criticism and the Gospels: The Theoretical Challenge.* New Haven: Yale University Press.

Mosala, Itumeleng J.
　1989　*Biblical Hermeneutics and Black Theology in South Africa.* Grand Rapids: Eerdmans.

Philpott, Graham
　1993　*Jesus Is Tricky and God Is Undemocratic: The Kin-dom of God in Amawoti.* Pietermaritzburg: Cluster.

The Road to Damascus Theologians
　1989　*The Road to Damascus: Kairos and Conversion.* Johannesburg: Skotaville.

Schneiders, Sandra M.
　1989　"Feminist Ideology Criticism and Biblical Hermeneutics." *BTB* 19:3–10.

Schreiter, Robert J.
　1985　*Constructing Local Theologies.* Maryknoll, NY: Orbis.

Scott, James C.
　1990　*Domination and the Arts of Resistance: Hidden Transcripts.* New Haven and London: Yale University Press.

Segundo, Juan Luis
　1985　"The Shift within Latin American Theology." *Journal of Theology for Southern Africa* 52:17–29.

Spivak, Gayatri C.
　1988　"Can the Subaltern Speak?" Pp. 271–313 in *Marxism and the Interpretation of Culture.* Ed. Gary Nelson and L. Grossberg. London: Macmillan.

Trible, Phyllis
　1984　*Texts of Terror: Literary-Feminist Readings of Biblical Narratives.* Philadelphia: Fortress.

Truluck, Ann
　1993　*No Blood On Our Hands.* Pietermaritzburg: Black Sash.

Weber, Max
    1964   *The Sociology of Religion*. Trans. Ephraim Rischoff. Introd. Talcott Parsons. Boston: Beacon.

Welch, Sharon D.
    1985   *Communities of Resistance and Solidarity: A Feminist Theology of Liberation*. Maryknoll, NY: Orbis.
    1990   *A Feminist Ethic of Risk*. Minneapolis: Fortress.

West, Cornel
    1988   *Prophetic Fragments*. Grand Rapids: Eerdmans.

West, Gerald O.
    1993   "No Integrity without Contextuality: The Presence of Particularity in Biblical Hermeneutics and Pedagogy." *Scriptura* 11:131–46.
    1994   "Difference and Dialogue: Reading the Joseph Story *with* Poor and Marginalized Communities in South Africa." *Biblical Interpretation* 2:152–70.
    1995   *Biblical Hermeneutics of Liberation: Modes of Reading the Bible in the South African Context*. Pietermaritzburg: Cluster and Maryknoll, NY: Orbis <1991>.
    1996   "The Dumb Do Speak: Articulating Incipient Readings of the Bible in Marginalized Communities." Pp. 174–92 in *The Bible and Ethics*. Ed. John W. Rogerson, Margaret Davies, and M. Daniel Carroll. Sheffield: Sheffield Academic Press.

Wimbush, Vincent L.
    1991   "The Bible and African Americans: An Outline of an Interpretative History." Pp. 81–97 in *Stony the Road We Trod: African American Biblical Interpretation*. Ed. Cain Hope Felder. Minneapolis: Fortress.

Race, Class, and Gender as Hermeneutical Factors in the African Independent Churches' Appropriation of the Bible

Itumeleng J. Mosala
University of Cape Town
South Africa

ABSTRACT

Recognising the prominent place of the Bible in the lives of the African Independent Churches, this essay examines the biblical heremeneutics operative in this particular sub-culture of black working class culture. More specifically, this investigation offers a preliminary analysis of race, class, and gender as hermeneutical factors in an African Independent Church in South Africa.

Introduction

The Bible plays a crucial role in the lives of black working class people in South Africa. It has such a grip on the minds and hearts of the majority of them that often they do not have the luxury, as do members of other classes and races, of choosing to be or not to be Christian. For many of them, to believe in the Bible and thus to be Christian is natural. This situation obtains with even greater force among members of the African Independent Churches. It may be somewhat natural that it should be so with these churches as they are made up of predominantly the underclasses of the black working class people.

Recognising the prominent place of the Bible in the lives of African Independent Church members, the research on which this essay is based examines the nature of the biblical hermeneutics operative among them. In particular, the research sought to determine how questions of class, race, and gender combined to produce what was hypothesised to be a working class biblical hermeneutics.

Some Definitions

Any treatment of these churches must begin with the problems already indicated by the names applied to them. Some people refer to them as Zionist churches, others as Apostolics or African Independent churches, and still others as Churches of the Spirit.

In one sense what these churches have been called indicates some aspect of their life and activity. Yet in another sense what they are called reflects something of the interests, the class position, the gender, and even the racial position of the one who is studying or describing them. This is to say that there is no politically, culturally, or even theologically neutral treatment of these churches.

Some people shy away from the term "African Independent Churches"; in their opinion this name defines these churches negatively. It is argued that the name makes the white mission churches the point of reference. It is then preferred to call them by what they do rather than from where they come. This argument is valid as far as it goes. The error of this line of thinking is that it confuses what the churches are called with what they are. Admittedly, there is a somewhat thin line of demarcation between what they are called and what they are. It is nevertheless crucial to separate these two things for the purpose of a more fruitful understanding.

For the present writer, then, the designation "African Independent Churches" is the most appropriate. This must be so for one who looks at the phenomenon from the point of view of being black in South Africa under apartheid, capitalism, and white western cultural imperialism. The term "African Independent Churches" connotes a specifically religious version of the wider African struggle for liberation from colonialism, capitalism, racism, and cultural chauvinism. This is so irrespective of the form that each one of these churches takes, whether it invokes the symbols of the biblical ideology of Zion, or whether it lays emphasis on the more messianic powers of healing and restoration drawn both from the Jesus models of the New Testament and from the diviners and medicine men/women models of African society, or whether they are more of a mass cultural working class movement with a feudal control structure such as the Zion Christian Church. However distorted a version, they all represent a particular articulation of a resistance struggle. This of course does not make them *a fortiori* politically progressive movements. They are a class in themselves but not necessarily a class for themselves.

I will return to this discussion more fully below, but first it is important to consider some of the theoretical approaches that have been used to analyze the African Independent Churches (AICs).

Theoretical Perspectives

Different theoretical approaches, from structural functionalist to historical materialist, have been brought to bear on the study of AICs. Keeping especially the historical materialist perspective in mind, this research has tried to locate the study of the biblical hermeneutics of the AICs within the cultural studies paradigm.

The cultural studies paradigm used in this study is drawn from the work of the Centre for Contemporary Cultural Studies at Birmingham University in England. One of the Centre's projects was a study of youth subcultures in post-war Britain. In a seminal essay entitled "Subcultures, Cultures and Class: A Theoretical Overview," John Clarke, Stuart Hall, Tony Jefferson, and Brian Roberts delineate the theoretical contours of an appropriate cultural studies paradigm. In addition to cogent explanatory concepts, the further attraction of their theoretical approach lies in the task it sets itself.

> The subject, of course, has been massively treated, ... Yet many of these surveys and analyses seem mainly to have multiplied the confusions and extended the mythologies surrounding the topic. By treating it in terms of its spectacular features only, these surveys have become part of the very phenomenon we want to explain. (9)

To posit African Independent Churches as a cultural configuration in articulation with other wider social configurations is to seek to go beyond a treatment of these churches in terms only of their spectacular features. It is rather to search for adequate theoretical concepts that can begin to explain rather than tautologically redescribe the phenomenon.

There are three main concepts in a cultural studies paradigm. These are class, culture, and sub-culture. The manner in which culture is defined indicates the interrelatedness of the concepts in this framework. In particular, a historically based and theoretically telling definition is provided:

> Culture is the way, the forms, in which groups 'handle' the raw materials of their social and material existence....'Culture' is the practice which realises or *objectivates* group-life in meaningful shape and form. As individuals express their life, so they are. What they are, therefore, coincides with their production, both with *what* they produce and with how they produce....Culture is the way the social relations of a group are structured and shaped; but it is also the way those shapes are experienced, understood and interpreted. (10)

The connection between culture and material existence makes culture in class structured societies necessarily *class* culture. In looking at African Independent Churches as cultural configurations, not only are there classes and corresponding cultural practices, but also sub-cultures that need to be theorized and explained. Studies of African Independent

Churches, however atheoretical, have long been aware of the class location and culturalism of the AICs. What they have failed to explain is why neither the totality of African people nor of the black working class are members.

In heuristic terms, the AICs can be understood as a sub-culture. As such, the AICs are related to, and distinct from, both black working class culture and the dominant culture. Black working class culture can be considered the parent culture of the AICs, but it is nonetheless subordinate to the dominant culture, which subjugates both black working class culture and its daughter sub-cultures.

The question which this study seeks to answer is: how does this sub-culture's relation to black working class parent culture affect the adherents' appropriation of the Bible? Is there, in other words, a distinctively sub-cultural appropriation of the Bible? Clarke et al. provide a particularly powerful description. (It is necessary to quote at length.)

> Members of a sub-culture may walk, talk, act, look "different" from their parents and from some of their peers; but they belong to the same families, go to the same schools, work at much the same jobs, live down the same "mean streets" as their peers and parents. In certain crucial respects, they share the same position (vis-a-vis the dominant culture), the same fundamental and determining life experiences, as the "parent" culture from which they derive. Through dress, activities, leisure pursuits and life-style, they may project a different cultural response or "solution" to the problems posed for them by their material and social class position and experience. But the membership of a sub-culture cannot protect them from the determining matrix of experiences and conditions which shape the life of their class as a whole. They experience and respond to the *same basic problematic* as other members of their class who are not so differentiated and distinctive in a "sub-cultural" sense. Especially in relation to the *dominant* culture, their sub-culture remains like other elements in their class culture—subordinate and subordinated. (15)

Many studies of the AICs have concentrated on the relation of this subculture to its dominant culture. This, of course, has not been done in a theoretically satisfactory manner. Nevertheless, there has been a general awareness of this phenomenon as some kind of deviation from mainstream Christianity. Explanations given have been predicated on anthropological dualisms of one sort or another. One example of this has been the claim that the phenomenon can be accounted for on the basis of the "Africanness" of the bearers of the sub-culture and the "Europeanness" of the bearers of the dominant culture.

What has not been done is to relate the AIC religious sub-culture to the parent class-culture with which it shares a response to the same *basic problematic*. How does it articulate with other elements of the subordinate and subordinated culture; what are the mechanisms through which the sub-culture is actually lived by those who are its bearers? To answer these questions one must enquire what the specific forms of "handling" the raw materials of its existence are. Is there a particular form of appropriation of the Bible which reflects this sub-culturally distinctive way of "handling" the raw material of its existence? In particular, how does this response contribute to the solution of the problematic faced by the parent culture?

The need to probe these questions is underscored by John Clarke et al. when they conclude:

> Negotiation, resistance, struggle: the relations between a subordinate and a dominant culture, wherever they fall within this spectrum, are always intensely active, always oppositional, in a structural sense....Their outcome is not given but *made*. The subordinate class brings to this "theatre of struggle" a repertoire of strategies and responses—ways of coping as well as of resisting. Each strategy in the repertoire mobilises certain real material and social elements: it constructs these into the supports for the different ways the class lives and resists its continuing subordination. (44)

Method

This research was undertaken in the African township of Mangaung in Bloemfontein. This area was chosen partly because my familiarity with the social and material topograpy of the place would facilitate research and save time for effective field work. More importantly, there is insufficient research on African Independent Churches in that region. It was hypothesised that there might just be important differences in this region that could add to our knowledge of these churches.

The method of research employed interviews using questionnaires and participant observation. It was originally intended to conduct surveys on a wide variety of churches throughout the township of Mangaung. Field experience in the first round of interviews soon indicated the projected scope was too large. In the second major round of interviews, I confined the research to an in-depth study of a smaller sample from one or two churches.

Two congregations of the same African Independent Church were studied. In one congregation interviews with individual members were conducted. These took place either when the members attended their individual healing sessions with the Healer or at a time and place mutually agreed on. In the other congregation services were attended with the permission of the minister. The object was to listen to sermons, hymns, and any other use of the Bible or biblical texts. In this second congregation Sartre's research strategy of regressive-progressive research was particularly pertinent. This strategy argues that a definite theoretical framework is necessary at the outset of the research, and yet once the actual practice of research has commenced, the data needs to be looked at in terms of historical/cultural mediations in order to make possible the production of new theory emanating out of the examined causal and structural connections. According to Steve Butters, "Sartre's strategy attempts a round-trip passage from a presumptive theory of the whole social order, to the level of the negotiated cultural nexus in which individuals make and live their experience, and back to the totality, carrying now some means to criticise the original account" (cited 270).

Analyzing the African Independent Churches

Having briefly outlined my theoretical perspectives and my research methodology, I will delineate more fully what these churches are. This is necessary as background for understanding the churches' use of the Bible as a strategy for responding to the basic problematic of the working class parent culture of the African Independent Churches.

The African Independent Churches are religious formations characterised by a number of sociological and theological factors. The concentration of these factors varies in any particular church. A key feature of the AICs is their indigenous African leadership. They make no effort to recruit whites; neither are whites naturally attracted to these churches (except as exotic objects of anthropological enquiry). In recent times some whites have deemed it necessary to take up honorary membership of the AICs. Apart from this no ideological commitment to them has arisen from non-indigenous Africans.

Positions of leadership in these churches are not attained by following a formal route of either educational study or birth. Leadership is a product of the work of the holy spirit, and is rooted in a spiritual democracy crucial to the life of these formations. This is as it should be, given the resistance basis of the African Independent Churches. In this aspect of their life they reflect their character as *anti-colonial cultural* movements. They represent a cultural subversion of official and "normal" Christianity and its structures and procedures.

African Independent Churches are religious solidarity networks. They arise initially out of the industrial urban gutters of capitalist civilisation and naturally extend into the rural hinterlands through the agency of migrant workers. I say naturally, because in the rural "homelands" they serve to fill the gap *ideologically* that has been created *materially* by the absence of a significant labour component of the rural household economy, the migrant worker himself. The prominent role played by women bishops in these churches must be correlated with the key role they play as heads of households in the rural economy from which their men have been dislodged, at least while they are physically strong. Of course later their men will be dumped back in these areas to become welfare burdens of, among others, religious organisations such as the AICs.

In trying to determine what the African Independent Churches are, it is essential to make some distinctions. One such distinction concerns the types of these churches. A huddling together of these formations under one rubric breeds confusion and obscures understanding. Another important differentiation is of a historical character. The AICs arose out of different historical periods and mostly draw their character from the historical circumstances to which they are a response. Thus a historically relativising perspective is necessary in understanding these churches.

The Ethiopian type

African Independent Churches are not oblivious to their character as resistance communities. The following statement exemplifies this: "The first 'Native Separatist Church' in South Africa, the Tembu Church, was founded by Nehemiah Tile, '...a fine specimen of a Tembu...' *who had grown impatient of European control*, and taking advantage of his position, he began to disseminate the ideas of a Separated Church *free from white control*" (Kruss: 6, emphasis mine).

This was a national church, irrespective of how narrowly the concept "national" was defined here, and as such it heralded the beginnings of the national liberation movement of black people in South Africa. It is noteworthy that this movement has never lived down its religious roots—this may be its blessing or its curse, only history will tell.

The Tembu national church, founded in 1883, was soon followed by others. The Ethiopian church was founded in 1892 under the leadership of Mangena Mokone and Brander. In 1895 the African Methodist Episcopal church was established under the combined leadership of Mokone, Brander, Dwane, and Khanyane. Mzimba led a breakaway from the Scottish Presbyterian church to form the African Presbyterian Church. In Natal the movement from white control was initiated by Samunqu Shibe to form the Zulu Congregational church. Meanwhile chief Kgantlapane of Botswana and a man called Matolo led the breakaway from the London Missionary Society to spawn the Native Independent Congregational church.

These churches and others like them are of a type. They originate in the same historical era, the late nineteenth century. By this time African communities had lost the wars of resistance against colonialism. They had been dispossessed of their land and cattle. Their social and political structures had been destabilised to the point of being totally in disarray. Also in this period the forces of proletarianisation, following the discoveries of gold in the Witwatersrand and diamonds in Kimberley, had begun to impose their own reorganisation of African society in the interests of the relentless logic of capital accumulation.

In this period the resistance struggle of the African peoples changed from a military form to a politico-cultural form. The sons of the erstwhile African ruling classes had been to mission schools and had adopted new weapons of struggle in the form of the values of liberal democratic ideology and of western Christianity. They provided the impetus and the leadership of this cultural form of resistance and struggle which the Ethiopian type of African Independent Church was to represent.

Thus both the form and the ideological content of this type of church reflect who its agents were and what kind of cultural socialisation they had received. The values of liberal democratic ideology and western Christianity were employed to wage a struggle to restore ideologically what had been lost materially. The Ethiopian manifesto of September 1896 remains the best articulation of its intent and character, as indeed of the intent and character of its political progeny—African nationalism.

> To unite together Christians of the African race and of various denominations in the name of Jesus Christ to solemnly work towards and pray for the day when the African people shall become an African Christian nation.
>
> To provide capital to equip industrial mission stations.
>
> To demand...by Christian and lawful methods the equal recognition of the African and allied peoples the rights and privileges accorded to Europeans.
>
> To solicit funds to restore Africans to their fatherland.
>
> To place on record...the great wrongs inflicted upon the African by the people of Europe and America and to urge upon Christians who wish to be clear of African blood on the day of God's judgement, to make restitution.
>
> ...Finally, to pursue steadily and unswervingly the policy AFRICA FOR THE AFRICANS and look for and hasten by prayer and united effort the forming of the AFRICAN CHRISTIAN NATION by God's power and in his own time and way. (Kruss: 81)

The concept of "African Christian Nation" represents both defeat and relentless struggle. Defeat, because Christianity (the Protestant version in particular) is the religious ideology of the Western capitalist society. As such its success presupposes that the erstwhile material social relations of African society had been dethroned and replaced by a different set of relations. Relentless struggle, because although the African people had lost militarily and had been disorganised materially by colonialism, they had retreated into the cultural terrains in order to continue the resistance.

The Zion City type

In a monumental study of the African Independent Churches, Glenda Kruss has isolated the Zion City churches as a distinct and significant type. Crucial among these differences, it seems to me, are the ideological content and style of the religious response of these churches. While the Ethiopian-type churches represented an anti-colonial African nationalist religious movement inspired by Western Christian liberal ideology, the Zion City churches were the Ethiopian churches of the *uneducated Africans*. As a consequence, their land demands, for example, were crudely unambiguous. Also, their style of religious response took the form of a millenarian and apocalyptic movement.

An indication of their apocalyptic and millenarian style is their use of the Zion city symbolism of the Old Testament. According to the Zion City ideology, God will intervene dramatically in history, at a time and place revealed to the leader, essentially in order to reverse the adverse conditions of the members and their community. The leader of the Zion City church is a messianic figure who has access to special religious knowledge primarily through dreams and visions. In this sense these churches prefigure the Zion Apostolics of the post-Second World War period, while they are at the same time a particular *historical mutation* of the Ethiopian churches of the late nineteenth century. I make this point in order to underline my contention that one could read off the history of the oppression and struggle of the African peoples of Azania from the story of these churches.[1]

While the Zion City adherents themselves were capable of heroic acts of resistance, their ideology and the discourse they represented were of a people a great deal more defeated than the Ethiopians three decades before. Their religious ideology projected a situation in which only a divine intervention could alter the scheme of things. This is so despite the contradiction that these movements often established land colonies in which they attempted autonomous economic and social structures. Describing the resistance in May, 1921, of Mgijima's group, the Israelites, Kruss quotes the telegram from the Commissioner of the South African Police: "The rushes by the natives were so determined that even the wounded after falling were observed to get up and rush forward again, many of them being killed by the bayonet and revolvers" (142).

The Zion City Churches are products of the first three decades of this century. They originate from a historical conjuncture in which the process of proletarianisation of the African masses in South Africa had intensified significantly. In particular, they were spawned by conditions in which

---

[1] "Azania" has been proposed as an alternative to the name "South Africa."

capitalist relations of production were inexorably penetrating the rural hinterland, capitalising agriculture. As if to make matters worse, this process of capitalisation of agriculture took root in the immediate aftermath of the infamous 1913 Land Act. The result was the isolated existence of migrant labourers in mine compounds and overcrowding in locations and shack communities. In the rural areas blacks had only limited access to land either as sharecroppers or as rural wage labourers (Kruss: 124).

These churches are, therefore, churches of the dispossessed peasants and dislocated working class Africans. They are nevertheless rooted in the feudal ideology of pre-colonial African societies as well as in the ruling class zionist consciousness of the Old Testament. Thus although these churches are, like the Ethiopian churches, religio-cultural resistance movements, they seem to have been ideologically even less liberatory than the Ethiopians.

The best examples of this type of the African Independent Churches are the Israelites of Mgijima, who are known through the Bulhoek massacre in 1921, and the Zion Christian Church (ZCC) of Lekganyane, perhaps the most well-known church in modern times, headquartered in Moria in Pietersburg. The ZCC is a black working class religious movement with an hierachichal feudal/tributary control and leadership structure. While its membership consists of the poorest of the poor, its leadership is made up of the richest of the rich. And, of course, the wealth of the leadership is not unlinked to the poverty and desperation of the membership.

The spirituality of this type provides liberation from the brutalities of late capitalism. Monopoly or late capitalism enters the sphere of culture and rules it through the dictatorship of the commodity. It "overcomes the sheer separation of the symbolic from the economic, but does so by bringing the symbolic under the dominance of the economic. The processes of this subsumption are precisely designed to block the overcoming of the subjective divisions inaugurated by capital" (Brenkman: 95). While ZCC discourse provides a form of liberation for its adherents, it is possible only through an ideological enslavement to the authoritarian structures of a feudal leadership with capitalist aspirations and activities.

It is important, however, not to lose sight of the contradictory character of ZCC discourse, which, for example, enables it to be at the same time the most powerful black working class religious movement in the country and to have the chief of the apartheid state [the then State President, P. W. Botha] as its honoured guest. Kruss succinctly articulates this contradiction. She notes that while the leadership and hierarchy of the ZCC identify with and act to legitimate apartheid structures, "it cannot be assumed that 764,300 members do the same in any meaningful way" (197).

Briefly, then, the Zion City church type, exemplified in modern times by the ZCC, is essentially an *African* peasant form of resistance against the capitalist threat of proletarianisation.

The Zion Apostolic type

This type, the focus of my research, is made up of small healing bands with a colourful unstructured liturgy and leadership. They are the product of a completely eradicated material base in African society and a hostile white Western capitalist culture and economy. The Zion Apostolics are neither classically African nor Western. No form of dualist explanation will help to illuminate them. They are a new phenomenon made of the conflictual convergence of two histories. They are an autonomous cultural discourse under conditions of a monopoly capitalist system which is overdetermined by a racist political and social structure. Members of the Zion Apostolic churches are Africans whose societal material base and its cultures have been eradicated by colonialism and capitalism, on the one hand, and whose presence in capitalist society and culture is unwanted excepted as superexploitable wage-slaves, on the other hand. They are an integral part of the black working class people in South Africa. Instead of being simply an anti-colonial discourse, they are a socio-religious sub-culture that lives its relation to the contradictions of monopoly capitalism in distinctive ways.

In the era where the commodity form reigns supreme they have carved out a control base in which they manipulate the most important commodity in the lives of the commodity-less, the landless, the capital-less masses of African descent, namely the Spirit—*Moya*. If they cannot control the means of *material* production, they can at least control the means of *spiritual* production. This indeed underscores a crucial feature of this sub-cultural movement—the ideological dimension that is so central to it. Clarke et al. make the point cogently.

> Though not "ideological," sub-cultures have an ideological dimension....In addressing the "class problematic" of the particular strata from which they were drawn, the different sub-cultures provided for a section of working class...*one* strategy for negotiating their collective existence. But their highly ritualised and stylised form suggests that they were also *attempts at a solution* to that problematic experience: a resolution which, because pitched largely at the symbolic level, was fated to fail. The problematic of a subordinate class experience can be "lived through," negotiated or resisted; but it cannot be resolved at that level or by those means. (47)

Among these churches the Bible plays a crucial role even though many of the members are illiterate. My research examines whether any specifically sub-cultural biblical hermeneutics exist in it. What follows represents some of the preliminary findings.

Race and Class in the Biblical Hermeneutics of an African Independent Church

The question of the social class composition of AIC members is painfully unproblematic. As has been attested to by almost all previous studies on these churches, our study confirmed that these are black working class churches *par excellence*. The specific church studied is the St. John's Apostolic Mission, Rockland, Bloemfontein. An Zion Apostolic type, it falls unproblematically into the sub-cultural category discussed above.

The average age of the individuals interviewed was forty-one years old; people in the prime of their life. The church does not comprise an inordinate number of children, nor is its membership largely old people and pensioners. The majority of the members interviewed were people who could have had a good education; who could have had a good job; who could have had good health, a good house, and good investments, if their class position had been different. With the sole exception of the leader of the congregation, these people were the proletarians of the proletarians. In fact, many of them were members of the "reserve army of labour," the unemployed. Most members of the church had originated from the towns and farms neighbouring Bloemfontein. Occassionally, a member would come from as far away as Bloemhof to the north-west of Bloemfontein. The search for employment is the universal reason why members or their parents moved to Bloemfontein. Many of them are second and third generation former new urbanites.

Their leader was 36 years old, a professional nurse, a woman, earning about R700 per month. It was not clear how significant it is that she had a nursing specialisation in psychiatry. It is certainly not unimportant, and may even qualify her presence in a predominantly working class movement. This, plus the fact that she is herself of thoroughgoing working class origins, may necessitate invoking Antonio Gramsci's notion of the 'organic intellectual' and applying it to her.

The fundamental class issue that affects Bible reading in the AICs is education. Most members are of very low educational standard. Many have only a primary school education. Illiteracy is a key problem. This reflects itself in many members' knowledge of the Bible in the first place. The assumption of this study and the way in which its hypotheses were constructed presupposed a literate community. The error in this manner of approaching the question of the biblical hermeneutics of the AICs was exposed by the difficulty encountered in trying to elicit favourite passages from the members. They simply do not have a literate knowledge of the Bible. Further, the source of knowledge is not the biblical texts themselves. Members have an oral knowlege of the Bible. Most of their information about the Bible comes from socialisation in the churches themselves as they listen to prayers and sermons. It is not appropriated in terms of what it says, but in terms of what it stands for—a canonical authority.

Most other black working class people in non-sub-cultural religious contexts appropriate the Bible in terms of its contents. Many *Madodana* (men's guilds) or *Manyano* (women's guilds), while not having significantly more education, have been assimilated into a reading culture of the Bible. Thus for them the authority of the Bible derives from its contents. Consequently a specifically black working class hermeneutics, drawing its weapons largely from the work place experiences, is discernible in these groups. This hermeneutics addresses the contradiction of class relatively less ideologically. As such it represents a better chance of enabling its bearers to find a resolution to the problematic of the entire class of which they are members.

It is not so with the sub-cultural members of the AICs who form a part of this same class. Theirs is a more symbolically pitched attempt to resolve the problem. While it does enable them to negotiate their reality and even to resist the forces of brutalisation with which the whole class is faced, their hermeneutical weapons are not drawn from the concrete experiences of the work place and social life of its members. Instead, they are derived from the mystifications generated by the authoritative status of an unread Bible.

My preliminary research demonstrates, I would argue, that in themselves the AICs sub-cultures cannot provide the tools of historical intervention required to tranform the material conditions of its members. Interventionist structures located externally in the parent culture of the black working class would need to be invoked before such a transformation can be hoped for. These may be of a theological or non-theological kind.

In short, working class members of the AICs do not search their contemporary historical experience to find tools with which to unlock the mysteries of the Bible. Rather, they appropriate the mysteries of the Bible and indeed of traditional African society in order to "live through" their problematic as members of a subordinate class.

The African symbols and discourses that exist in the AICs faith and practice are the only thing *black* in their hermeneutics. As such they articulate with the class character of the movement only in specifically sub-cultural ways. There is neither social nor theological deliberateness in the movement's manner of appropriating the Bible from the perspective of a dominated race. This once again underscores the earlier observation that the AICs are a class in themselves and not a class for themselves.

Gender in the Biblical Hermeneutics of an AIC

There are two reasons why this research included gender as a factor in biblical hermeneutics. Not to do so would be grossly unjust and prejudicial, since AICs have a predominantly female membership. Omitting gender would result in a truncated treatment of a sub-culture in which class and gender are inseparable. In the monopoly stage of capitalist development, the service industry has drawn millions of women into the labour market under conditions of extraordinary exploitation. Gender is also an important factor in the process of developing a biblical hermeneutics of liberation.

On the question of gender as on the issues of race and class, my research revealed that a hermeneutics of mystification existed that is based on a patriarchal consciousness, which, ironically, is foreign to the religious practice of at least the Zion Apostolic version of the AICs.

It is common knowledge that in the AICs there are fewer barriers against women than in other churches, particularly in the area of leadership. In addition, when encouraged to speak about women in the church and in the Bible, members of the AICs exhibited an underlying awareness of the usefulness of certain parts of the Bible for addressing specifically women-related issues. There is, however, no doubt that the class base of these members circumscribe their ability to read the Bible within the sub-culture in ways that are historically transformative. The question here again is not that the AICs do not represent a form of struggle that is recognisably gender specific. The issue is simply that the gender realities of the members are negotiated in an overly ideological way.

This particular problem becomes clear when the central activity of the faith practice of the AICs—healing—is looked at in terms of its political economy. Members draw heavily from the Bible to make sense of the problems of illness that bring so many of them to these churches; but no connections are made between gender, illness, and social condition.

Nonetheless, there is an acute awareness of the problems faced by members as women. The inability to translate awareness into a weapon for appropriating the Bible is a function of the sub-cultural character of the movement.

Conclusion

This preliminary study has led to one major conclusion, namely, that there is no distinctive sub-cultural biblical hermeneutics among the AICs. The search for such a distinctive biblical hermeneutics will need to situate itself within the wider black working class parent culture of which the AICs are an integral part. A consideration of the issues of class, race, and gender has shown that they play no distinctively sub-cultural role among the AICs. What role they play is identifiable with the role they play in the wider class response to the problematic of black underclass Christians.

Thus the only identifiable hermeneutics is one that for lack of a better word has been referred to here as *the hermeneutics of mystification*. The precise nature of this hermeneutics of mystification requires a fuller and more detailed study.

Future study must reconsider the appropriateness of the central question behind this project. Given the nature of the movement under study, the notion of "text" as used in our concept of the Bible is not an adequate one. It became clear in the responses of the AIC members that the text in a narrow sense of the biblical text is an extra-class problem for them. Should we not, when looking at the biblical hermeneutics of the AICs, broaden our concept of text to include the historical text of the lives of the members themselves? The implications of this are not clear yet, but it is certainly a question that arises out of this study.

Works Consulted

Brenkman, J.
    1987   *Culture and Domination*. Ithaca, NY: Cornell University Press.

Clarke, John, Stuart Hall, Tony Jefferson, and Brian Roberts
    1976   "Subcultures, Cultures and Class: A Theoretical Overview." Centre for Contemporary Cultural Studies, Birmingham University.

Kruss, Glenda
    1985   *Religion, Class and Culture: Indigenous Churches in South Africa, with Special Reference to Zionist-Apostolics*. Cape Town: University of Cape Town Press.

II
"READING WITH" SOUTH AFRICAN READERS

CONFESSIONAL WESTERN TEXT-CENTERED BIBLICAL INTERPRETATION AND AN ORAL OR RESIDUAL-ORAL CONTEXT

Jonathan A. Draper
University of Natal
Pietermaritzburg
South Africa

ABSTRACT

This paper presents the findings of sustained field-work into the relationship between literary study of the Bible and its actual use among grassroots groups of black Christians in South Africa. It concludes that the perception of the Bible is not literary at all, but mediated by oral performance. The paper also highlights the richness of oral responses to the Bible. The centrality of orality has important consequences for reader response theory in the Two-Thirds World context. It also poses problems for teaching biblical studies in the universities and seminaries. *Sola scriptura* in Two-Thirds World contexts has a hegemonic aspect.

INTRODUCTION

In 1988 I was asked to produce an article on Anglicans and Scripture for a *Festschrift* for Dean Ted King of Cape Town. My attempt to find out what Anglicans really were doing in Bible study groups across the various socio-economic divides of Southern Africa has led me on a long and yet unresolved search. Initial results (Draper and West, 1989) indicated that the Bible remained authoritative for most Anglicans in the wider Pietermaritzburg region. Attempts to broaden the base of the study in black congregations (Draper and West, 1991) have proved curiously frustrating. This paper is really a long steady look at the cause of that frustration.

At the time I began my research I had read nothing about reader response theory. It was a case of fools rushing in where angels fear to tread! Having now read the theoretical material (e.g. the authors represented in Tompkins), I am convinced that they leave out of account something of vital importance in our Southern African situation. They assume a printed text and readers who have internalized textuality and whose consciousness has been restructured by textuality. In Southern Africa, by way of contrast, the vast majority of our people are living in a context of either primary orality or, for most, of residual orality. This does not mean that they do not read or write, although many do not. It certainly has nothing to do with intellectual ability (Ong, 1982:55), a fact our own educational processes are slow to recognize. Rather they function in an oral culture in which text plays a minimal role.

Extensive research by A. R. Luria in the Soviet Union in the 1930s (1976; cf. Ong, 1982:48–57) has shown that literacy restructures consciousness, and that even minimal literacy can make a change, but nevertheless it shows that those with only a passing exposure to literacy remain firmly within an oral culture: "Passing acquaintanceship with literate organization of knowledge has, at least so far as his cases show, no discernible effect on illiterates. Writing has to be personally interiorized to affect thinking processes" (Ong, 1982:56). Or to use Werner Kelber's words, "If one takes the long view, print technology, the scribal arts, and orality appear less as neutral containers and more as active contributors to thought and ideas" (1989:11).

Since Kelber's challenging book *The Oral and the Written Gospel* (1983) was published, there have been many attempts to refute it (e.g. Hurtado). In particular, it has been argued that the interrelationship between literacy and orality is more complex and complementary than he allows (e.g. Halverson). This is no doubt true, and Kelber has taken a more cautious line in recent articles. However, attempts to blur the distinction between primary and secondary oral and literate communities are not particularly helpful.[1] There are distinctively different perceptions of reality which it would be ethnocentric or anachronistic to deny. Galilean peasant society, out of which the Jesus movement emerged, would have had scarce contact with actual texts. Scrolls were expensive and unwieldy. They were controlled by ritual experts: that is the function of the scribes. There is much evidence that Jesus' replies to these officials (attempting to extend the influence of Jerusalem to independent Galilee) draw on popular and oral traditions of the old Northern Kingdom. This is not to argue that Jesus was illiterate or that there was no influence of the written Torah on his teaching. Likewise, the kind of orality envisaged in this article, in which many if not most South Africans live, is not a matter of illiteracy but of world view.

---

[1] The argument of Halverson, that the skill of the speaker creates the responsive, community oriented environment characteristic of orality, is not persuasive. The academic lectures and sermons to which he refers are creations of literacy. There may be good or bad examples of these, but it is precisely because they are written and read that they are what they are. Literary productions read by oneself produce a response different in kind from the experience of an oral recital.

The question posed by orality is a fundamental one: most of the lecturers, writers, and critical readers in our theological institutions and academies assume a textually constructed universe. It is so natural to us that we assume it is universal. But we should heed the warning of Walter Ong:

> Many of the features we have taken for granted in thought and expression in literature, philosophy and science, and even in oral discourse among literates, are not directly native to human existence as such but have come into being because of the resources which the technology of writing makes available to human consciousness. We have had to revise our understanding of human identity. (1982:1)

The consequences of residual orality on reader response theory have nowhere been explored, as far as I know. It must raise the question: Is the text the same text (if we may use a word so defined by cheirographic culture) for those whose thought processes are shaped by literacy as for those still living in a residually oral culture? Further, if they do read or use the text of the Bible, do they read or interpret in the same way? Beyond both of these questions is the question: How do those who are still living in primary orality appropriate the Bible (because they do in fact use it)? Finally, there is the question: what is the power dynamic at work in the use of a sacred text in a residually oral society, since "ritualization is a strategic arena for the embodiment of power relations" (Bell: 170)?

THE REFORMATION AND *SOLA SCRIPTURA*

In our first research into Anglicans and Scripture, we set out to explore to what extent the famous definition of the Thirty-Nine Articles, "Holy Scripture containeth all things necessary to salvation," was still operative in Anglican congregations. This definition reflects, of course, Luther's famous dictum, *sola scriptura*, with its concommitant assertion that what is written interprets itself and not extraneous tradition (*scriptura sui ipsius interpres*). It was no accident that this new emphasis on text coincided with the discovery of the printing press (Kelber, 1989). Luther and other reformers used the printing press and the possibility of mass-produced propaganda and mass-produced Bibles with devastating effect. Luther himself distinguished between the printed text and the Word of God, which is contained in preaching. However, in the popular mind, the printed text of Scripture and the Word of God have become totally identified.

The missionaries came to South Africa with a printed sacred text. They confronted a primary oral society with a printed text as the Word of God. This had the effect of privileging literacy and conferring on it the mantle of the Holy. Along with mission must go education to enable converts to read the Bible. The ritual experts the missionary churches trained to lead indigenous congregations were required to be above all literate, experts in the interpretation and use of the printed text. In the process, the missionaries of textuality all but destroyed the primary oral traditions and skills of the indigenous people of Southern Africa. We New Testament academics stand at the end of this process, paid to induct our students into the mysteries of textuality.

The grassroots culture of black South Africans has remained a residually oral culture. This is one of the immediate clashes faced by black students beginning their theological studies at university. We held a full public meeting with our students some years ago, at their request, to try and work out what exactly they found problematic. The meeting was indecisive. There is a sense of unease and betrayal among many of our Biblical Studies students at what they are taught, a disquiet which they find hard to put into words. But at the heart of it is the overwhelming textuality of our approach. The New Testament is a thing which can be dissected, analyzed, projected on screen. It is no longer Word in any sense, but only text.

The Mark Project in Sobantu

Our initial project had used Mark's Gospel, on the assumption that its more direct style and its origin in all probability in peasant Galilean communities might make it more suitable for use in the peri-urban congregations we had in mind. One of the weaknesses of the study was the inadequate empirical base in black communities in the Pietermaritzburg area. Data was only collected from one black congregation, St. Mark's in Imbali. We therefore decided to broaden the research by working with other black congregations. Most of the work was, nonetheless, conducted in the Anglican congregation of St. Christophers's in Sobantu, where the priest was keen to develop Bible studies in his congregation and asked us to assist. Further work was done with the youth group at another Anglican congregation of St. Martin's in Edendale.

An assumption underlying the initial research was the centrality of the printed text of the Bible. Our subsequent studies in Sobantu were attempts to explore in what way the findings of the academy could be mediated to grassroots black communities. They were also premised on the assumption that what was operative in the black community was the printed text of the Bible.

A further dimension of the extended research was that of testing what happened when Bible study facilitators did not merely stimulate a close reading of the text, as in the initial research, but made direct input into the group. In the first study, we had deliberately avoided giving any explicit form of information to the groups we studied. We only enabled the groups to pay close attention to the text by asking leading questions. Historical, geographical, socio-economic, and other background information was left to the groups to raise. In the second study we were interested to explore the dynamics of introducing such information into the study groups.

What had proved an effective method in other studies of the Institute for the Study of the Bible (ISB) was the production of study material by means of small groups of students and sympathetic associates. Material was workshopped and shaped in small groups before being tested in more grassroots settings. Since most of the students were black and from grassroots communities it was felt that this was a good route to approach the wider community.

We used a (mostly black) post-graduate group to study the text itself and then presented their findings to the ISB group to workshop. This method proved to be unsuitable for the following reasons. The postgraduate students could not agree on a common approach to Mark. The student groups also picked up the critical problems associated with the study of Mark and found little common ground. They had also by this time become rather sophisticated in their expectation of study material and critiqued the structure of the groups. In other words, the groups of students showed quite clearly that they were not grassroots groups or "ordinary readers" at all, even if they considered themselves that.

This beginning did produce some material, but it was clearly flawed as a way of approaching ordinary Anglican parishes. This led us to seek a new way of both material production and also of approaching the grassroots.

Stage One: Participatory Research

This experience raised the question of who is the ordinary reader and how could university academics mediate their findings to the community. Clearly groups of students were trapped in the same place as their lecturers! We decided on a new approach.

Our university has a system of internships for black students, which enables them to earn money to support their studies while developing a mentor relationship with a member of staff. We decided to work indirectly with black congregations through the student interns, using a participatory research method, which brought all parties in the study into conscious reflection on what they were doing. At each stage of research, the interns and their groups would discuss the process and the conclusions. The contribution of the fieldworkers, Shepherd Khosi, George Hlungwane, Elijah Mkhatshwa, Alfred Ramphele, and Derek Siyothula, to this paper is freely and gratefully acknowledged.

The first stage involved a two-fold training of the interns in participatory research in the community: firstly, they were trained in facilitating group study, so that they would not dominate the groups but enable participants to explore the material and come to their own conclusions; and secondly, they were trained in critical approaches towards the text to help them to achieve a critical distance. This built on the students' training in Biblical Studies. Half the students were first-year Biblical Studies students, the other half were senior students. Nevertheless, the experience of the training already produced surprises, with students saying that they had never looked at things in this way before; some maintained that if they said this kind of thing—e.g. that the talking trees of the book of Judges were not to be taken literally but as political satire—in their home congregations they would be regarded as unbelievers.

The second stage involved workshopping material with the students. This consisted of an examination of the literary context (the deliberate move to Jerusalem from Galilee; the healing of the Blind Man who cried out to the Son of David) and geographical and socio-historical information on the background of Mark 10 (the Triumphal Entry and the Cleansing of the Temple). Resources drawn from the sociology of peasantry and the sub-Asiatic mode of production were also used, in which Jesus was viewed as the leader of a Galilean peasant reform movement (Horsely, Waetjen, et al.). Elements stressed were the dominance of the Temple mount by the Antoniad, the careful preparations of Jesus, the passwords, the background to his action in the similar entry of the Maccabeans a century or so earlier, his swift withdrawal back to the safety of peasant families after the symbolic action.

In the third stage, the student interns were divided into groups of two and asked to formulate what they had learned into Bible study outlines, which were then brought back and discussed by the whole group.

Meanwhile each group was asked to build links and investigate the possibility of study groups in targeted black Anglican congregations. The cooperation and understanding of the congregations was required before anything was attempted. When congregations and priests concerned understood what was being asked and proved willing to participate, then the interns would use the material they had prepared, while recording the studies on tape for transcription and study. Negotiation and consultation with congregations was difficult. The priest in one congregation was suspicious and threatened, and refused to have anything to do with them. In another, the priest was eager to work with us, but his congregation had never had Bible studies before and did not want to start now. Their custom was for house meetings to involve healing and fervent prayer, which would go on through the night. People did not feel that Bible study was a legitimate substitute. The interns had to spend much time attending these prayer meetings before the groups would allow them to do anything. The third congregation had a priest who wanted to cooperate, but had a huge parish, never stopped moving, and was not easy to contact. His youth group was keen to do the studies, but time was needed first to gain their trust.

Stage Two: Preliminary Findings

The attempt, therefore, to broaden our first study took much longer and was much less successful than anticipated. The black community in Pietermaritzburg has been severely damaged by three years of bloody fighting and police harassment. Suspicion and disorganization are consequent factors in everything one tries, which is hardly surprising. The unfamiliarity of the communities with Bible study, as a focus on the text, rather than as something presented from the pulpit in an authoritative fashion by the priest, also led to hesitation or even resistance to embarking on the project by either the priest or the people.

Nevertheless, the project did finally result in four Bible studies, and our preliminary findings include the following. In the first place, the communities had a reverential attitude to the Bible, which they uniformly regarded as "the Word of God." This did not mean that they wished to read it. The holy status of the Bible was symbolic and not literary. In fact, there was a certain resistance to beginning to read, since a sermon-orientated Christian culture had resulted in a feeling that interpretation was for religious experts. This attitude is most prevalent with the older people, who expressed the opinion several times that "the youth" would benefit, even if they wouldn't! The youth were indeed more open to Bible reading and less inhibited in seeing contextual relevance there.

Secondly, what emerged was an unresolved tension between oral and textual cultures. These black communities had a predominantly oral culture, rich in traditions, and the introduction of a technique which demanded a close reading of the text, standing by itself, was an alien and suspicious idiom. Weli Mazamisa has pointed to the same factor:

> In my opinion it is necessary to speak about the participating reader, who is the one who participates fully in the reading act, and the "listening" reader. This reader has no access to the written text, but participates through his/her ears. Incidentally, this is the biggest constituency of "readers" in South Africa, due to the fact that between 50% and 60% of the black population is not able to read and write. This is a community that has been socialised in the oral tradition. (69)

Thirdly, there was a considerable lack of basic historical information concerning the Bible. For example, people wanted to know whether Mary was married to David, since Jesus is called David's son. Providing background information was essential to get the process moving in a Bible study, and even then it was only when the fieldworkers raised the question of the relevance of the passage "to us" that the group started getting interested.

Fourthly, it seems clear that most of the people in the study had not ever related the Bible to their socio-economic situation. Indeed, when this suggestion was made to a group in Sobantu, the accusation was levelled that there was nothing "spiritual" in this.

Fifthly, the groups uniformly expected to find so-called "spiritual meaning" in the text. At the end of one session, after extensive discussion of the role of the Temple, "son of David" and Roman soldiers, a woman asked: "When are you going to give us the spiritual meaning?" Earlier her husband had drawn political meaning from the text relevant to South Africa. Despite their training, the facilitators immediately re-assured her by providing a ready made "spiritual meaning." This seemed to be an irresistible pull for the facilitators. The group of fieldworkers had agreed beforehand that they would try to explore with the Bible study group the act of Jesus in his triumphal entry of Jerusalem as a deliberate challenge to the authority of the Temple and of Rome. We had agreed that we would use the framework of a peasant society confronting the injustice of a sub-Asiatic mode of production modified by Roman occupation. However, when faced by the challenge of a "spiritual" meaning, the fieldworkers fell back on the theme of humility: "The main lesson we can gather is that we should be humble, lowly, and peaceful as Jesus was. Secondly, we should not look down upon certain people, we should treat all the people equally." In this way, they returned to the tradition of the interpretive community from which they had originally come. (This is a microcosm of what happens when theologically trained pastors make their re-entry into the community!)

Clearly, a participatory mode of research is going to take time and patience. At the same time the project has generated great enthusiasm in both the student facilitators and the congregations.

Stage Three: Finding Where the People Are

As indicated, our attempts to establish Bible Study groups in Sobantu were fraught with difficulties. Often fieldworkers would arrive and find no one there, or the venue had changed, or some other problem. However, a shift took place when we discovered that the members of the congregation already attended a Revival service every week, and that the Bible studies were more of a programmatic desire of the Rector than of the congregation. After considerable discussion, the people agreed that they would attend the Bible studies if the fieldworkers would attend the Revival! This Revival was a weekly meeting of members of the congregation, where prayer, testimony, Bible sharing, and singing all merge freely. As a result, we extended our study to include an examination of how the Bible was used in the Revival service.

Inviting the students to the Revival proved to be the real breakthrough. They not only participated in the weekly meetings, but also recorded and transcribed them. The Revival demonstrated far more effectively the way the Bible is being used than did our various attempts at recording Bible studies. This is not to say that there is no space for Bible studies in the black communities. Indeed the ISB has shown that there can be a very enthusiastic response. But the dynamics are complex and are affected by the residual oral culture of the people. In a recent paper Werner Kelber has argued that the idea of a pure oral society suddenly becoming a literate society is wrong. Texts do not, as he had earlier argued, present quite such a total breach of a purely oral tradition. Rather, as Brian Stock says, "Oral and written traditions normally function in relation to each other":

> Writing was linked to speech in so many ways that the term textuality itself may be a misnomer for the products of scribal labors. And orality could both originate from writing and in turn generate writing in ways which compel us to focus on one without losing sight of the other. But once we perceive *Scripture and Logos* as *interactive forces,* we must admit the presence of another dynamic, something other than just orality and literacy, something for which we have no name and about which we have very little knowledge. (1989:14)

The Revival as a Residual Oral Hermeneutic

In order to further our discussion of the Revival, it is necessary to grasp something of the dynamic of primary orality, bearing in mind that most South Africans are no longer in a primary oral culture. Drawing on the work of Walter Ong, I will set out the main traits of orality.

In oral cultures, the sounded word is closely related to power and action. It is dynamic, not static, in the sense that once spoken it is gone without possibility of representation. Thus an oral recitation is an unrepeatable event in time, unlike text which can be repeatedly read and referred to. Further, "in an oral culture, restriction of words to sound determines not only modes of expression but also thought processes. You know what you can recall" (Ong, 1982:33). Memory, and the forms of speech that facilitate remembering, mnemonic patterns, rhythmic expression, balancing and formulaic composition (Ong, 1982:33–36), are the primary concern of an oral culture. Dialogue and open communication are key to the development of an argument, which is always rooted in the specifics of a concrete context.

Ong provides nine characteristics of orally based thought, many of which are present in the Revival meetings.

- It is additive rather than subordinative.
- It is aggregative rather than analytic. Clichés serve an important function in stabilizing the recitation in memory.
- It is redundant or "copious." Since there is no possibility of backward reference as there is in a text, effectiveness in oral communication depends on constant repetition, summary, reduplication.
- It is conservative or traditionalist. Knowledge is hard-won and preserved by repetition. Experimentation is not encouraged and age becomes a form of status, since the old are the guardians of tradition.
- It is close to the human lifeworld. In the absence of analytic categories, oral peoples assimilate the objective world to the human lifeworld. Knowledge is stored in narrative.
- It is agonistically toned. There is no separation of the knower from the known, and knowledge is located in the everyday struggle of human beings with each other. Struggle or exterior crisis is privileged over interior crisis: "When all verbal communication must be by direct word of mouth, involved in the give-and-take dynamics of sound, interpersonal relations are kept high—both attractions and, even more, antagonisms" (Ong, 1982:45). Neutrality is not a characteristic: either struggle or fulsome praise are preferred.
- It is empathetic and participatory rather than objectively distanced. Writing alienates and separates people in the process of reading. Oral culture is relational and communal.
- It is homeostatic. Since what is not constantly repeated aloud is lost, oral cultures are constantly updating their tradition, even when they see themselves as preserving it intact. "Oral societies live very much in a present which keeps itself in equilibrium or homeostasis by sloughing off memories which no longer have present relevance" (Ong, 1982:46). Words change their meaning or are discarded with no dictionaries to keep them artificially alive. Stories change their shape and reference or simply disappear: "...the part of the past with no immediately discernible relevance to the present had simply fallen away. The present imposed its own

economy on past remembrances" (Ong, 1982:48). Only the winners are remembered and recited.
- It is situational rather than abstract. "Oral cultures tend to use concepts in situational, operational frames of reference that are minmally abstract in the sense that they remain close to the living human lifeworld" (Ong, 1982:49).

With this brief outline of the major characteristics of orality, we can return to an analysis of the Revival. Transcriptions of the Revivals present more interesting data than do the textual studies. They seem to confirm my suspicion that the black communities we were working with in our research are still operating with a residual oral culture.

After a period of singing and prayer, a leader chosen for the week reads a passage of the Bible which s/he has selected. This person then repeats the story in her/his own words, adding a pointed, situational application. After this, various people in the meeting add their interpretations, repeating the original message with minor variations and different applications, interspersed with song. Below are two examples.

"Reading" Matthew 18:12–17

A leader read Matthew 18:12–17 on the Lost Sheep and the right procedure to discipline an offender. This was applied directly in a challenge to teachers who do not care properly for weaker pupils and nurses who lose interest in caring for terminal cases. More specifically, the leader chastened church leaders about the fall-off in attendances at the Revival, and challenged them to approach conflict in the community in the way Matthew suggests. The first interpretation is followed by a song. A second person then responds, repeating and affirming the message of the first speaker about concern for those who have stopped attending. She points to someone she has brought along that night straight from work. A third respondent then re-affirms the same message, but emphasizes the need to forgive genuinely and seek reconciliation with their enemies. A further song is sung before a fourth respondent testifies that she has come straight from work. A fifth repeats the story of the one hundred sheep and emphasizes the importance of the one over the ninety-nine, which means that not only blood relatives but outsiders must be cared for. A further song is sung.

Several aspects of this procedure highlight an oral world view. In the first place, no one uses a text except the person reading the passage at the beginning. Secondly, the story is repeated with slightly different interpretations. Redundancy drives home the story and creates a communal interpretation by the interaction of the participants. The interpretation is immediately applicable to the life world of the participants. In oral communities the message is always open to correction, responsive to the dynamics of the occasion, as people grunt and sigh and respond "Hawo!" The songs frequently interspersed keep the dynamic and excitement moving forward as the next respondent prepares to speak. Sometimes the songs relate to the theme, but more often they are simply punctuation marks, preserving the right atmosphere for the interpretive framework. Finally, challenge and parry seem to be a constant undertone of the response, which reflects in a toned-down way the agonistic world-view of oral culture.

"Reading" Isaiah 43

On another occasion, the leader read Isaiah 43, emphasizing the words "Have no fear, for I have redeemed you; I call you by name; you are mine." The meeting was held in a house of recent bereavement. The leader referred to his own experience of recent bereavement and argued that God is always with us in such situations. The first response was an accusation against the leaders who had not attended, but picked up the phrases "don't fear" and "called by name." No less than eleven respondents followed, interspersed with songs, each repeating in various forms the "do not fear" and "called by name" theme, but adding a minor variation or new slant. One woman picked up the idea of "bringing offspring from the east and west" to talk at length of birth and the blessing of parents. Another young woman used the same idea of "sons and daughters" to speak of her struggle to preserve her virginity. Running through all the responses was a reference to the ongoing violence of the Pietermaritzburg area in the conflict between Inkatha and the African National Congress (ANC). "Do not fear" and "called by name" were placed in opposition to the very real physical fear of murder and violence.

At this point in the Revival meeting the priest of the congregation introduced a story about Chaka and Ngcugcwe, where the latter stole cattle from the King to gain a name for himself but ended up being killed for it. He pointed to the difference between seeking a name for oneself and being given a special name by God as one who has been redeemed: "Names given to us by others can destroy us, but the one given by God can redeem us as we seek to live it out." The priest illustrated his response with several Biblical references (Acts 28:1–6; 1 Peter 5:8–11), indicating his assurance in the textual culture of his theological training, just as his introduction of stories from Chaka showed that he moved comfortably in the oral culture of his people.

The same characteristics of oral culture can be seen in this example. The agonistic tone of the meeting is found both in the violence of the group's context and their sense of opposition to it, and also in frequent challenges to other members of the group or those absent for failing in commitment or dedication. The redundancy of the repetition of the central text and message guarantees its memorability. There is wide participation by members of the group in the process of interpretation, both by gestures and noises and by the number of responses and by the songs. The interpretations are all immediately situational. They are "homeostatic" in the sense that there is no feeling of historical distance between the story and the Revival group. It is interpreted as contemporary and the words as having an immediate reference to their own world. Doctrine or abstract concepts are entirely absent from the interpretations, and the oral process of building an interpretive framework by dialogue and concensus is clearly present.

Some Provisional Reflections

The fieldworkers were black theology students with two or three or more years of study behind them. They had taken courses in historical criticism of the Bible, as well as received training in hermeneutics and group dynamics from us. Yet they proved in the end to be most comfortable with the world of the Revival and not of the Bible study groups. They found it diffucult to motivate the community to attend the Bible studies and lacked enthusiasm themselves. The Revival meetings proved very attractive. Many friends from campus went with the fieldworkers each time. The local community found their presence a major boost at the Revival. And when it came to key points in the Bible studies it was significant that the fieldworkers reverted to the interpretive mode of the Revival.

My own conclusion from the analysis of the data I have to hand so far is that the Revival and the Bible study, as we had conceived it, represent the cultural worlds of Orality and Literacy respectively. The world of oral culture won hands down, both with our black fieldworkers and with the people of the community. This highlighted for me certain important questions concerning biblical hermeneutics in South Africa. More pressingly, for me personally, it raised the question about what exactly we are doing teaching historical critical studies to theological students. It is clear that this textual approach in the classroom has produced alienation for our black students, whereas the Revival reinforces community, belonging, and solidarity with grassroots church members. Again, Mazamisa has put his finger on the centrality of this conflict for black students entering the world of Biblical Studies in the academy:

> Textuality for the black biblical scholar is a form of resocialisation process to the extent that it is in discontinuity with previous socialisation (oral tradition). Through the resocialisation process the trained reader negotiates a new identity in a new universe of discourse. The new universe of discourse is learned and internalised in the form of literacy. Textuality is a movement away from orality to literacy. (1991:72)

That movement is experienced as loss, and all too often it is not clear to students what gain is made in compensation.

The Role of the Biblical Text in "Illiterate" Communities

These intriguing indications from urban communities suggested that explorations of the Bible in "illiterate" rural communities would provide valuable insights into the role of orality in text-reception. In discussion with the fieldworkers, I was assured by one of those involved in the Sobantu project that the Bible did function in such communities. His own parents were "illiterates" from rural Kangwane, as were most of the people in his home community. In church meetings his parents would ask one of the few literate people in the community to "read John 6" or some other text, which they knew by heart. They would then expound on it. In this way all the people of the community were able to relate to the printed text of the Bible, although it was the story held in the memory and filled with meaning by constant repetition and functional interpretation.

Further field work was done in two Christian groups in Majaneng village among mostly "illiterate" Pedi women by Alphaeus Masoga, a graduate student at the School of Theology. Bible studies were recorded and transcribed by him, and the importance of his contribution to this paper is gratefully acknowledged. Meetings were always opened in song, followed by the reading aloud of a text by one of the literate people. This was usually followed by retelling of the story with significant variations and additions by several of the women, who related the story to their own situation.

"Reading" John 4:27–34

In one session John 4:27–34 was read aloud, and a respondent referred to the problems of travelling in the village, the importance of water, the scarcity of food, and the time of harvest. Another respondent told the following story:

> There was a woman who used to work in the field. She often resided in the field. One day a stranger came to her field. He was an old man. He appeared to be coming from far away. He asked food from the woman. The woman refused. The old man looked miserable. After some time he started to speak prophecies to the woman. He revealed many hidden things about the life of

this woman. The woman then ran to the village to tell her friends about this authentic friend.

This rephrased version of the story was then related to the prophetic gifts of Jesus and the important of prophetic gifts in the community itself. The free-flowing interaction of participants promoted memorization of the text in a new setting by repetition, redundancy, and additions of extra-textual details.

"Reading" Mark 5:21–43

In another group, entirely "illiterate," Masoga read aloud the text of Mark 5:21–43. The women at his request identified key words in the story: Jairus' daughter, sick daughter, blood, fear, faith (women are faithful), and child (a child is close to its mother). In a further session the women responded with their own poem, song and role-play as follows:[2]

---

[2] The translation is provided by Alphaeus Masoga. The Pedi text is included here.

A poem
Agaa Mosadi!!
Moadi segatlhamelamasisi
Mosadi mmangwana o tshwara thipa kamo bogaleng
O nyaditswe efela Modimo o go file bokgoni
Tsoga o eme lefatshe le go emetse
Se inyatse Mogaugedi o re, "Se boife"

Emelela o fete banna bao ba go gateletsego
Ba bontshe gore o na le bokgoni
Ke re "Ema Mosadi"
Ema byale ka mosadi o la wa go kgoma Jesu
O eme a sena le ge e le go tshaba

Mosadi ke eo a sa tshabego
Mosadi ke eo a rego, "Ke nna E"
Byale le wena o tshwanetse ke gore, "Ke nna E"
Ema byale ka mosadi wa Gerasini
Emang basadi nako e fitlhile!!
Tsogang barobadi!

A song
Re sa na le kgatelelo ya basadi le lehono
E gona mo malapeng a rena
E gona mo mebusong ya rena
E gona ka mo kerekeng
Ga ele kgatelelo yona ke seo re se phelelang
Mo gong bophelo botla ba kaone
Re tshwana le mosadi wa Gerasini.

A poem

Agaa Mosadi!!
A woman is brave and strong
A woman holds the knife by its cutting edge
You were despised but God gave you the ability
Stand up and move, the world awaits you
Do not despise yourself
The Gracious one says, "Do not be afraid."

Stand up and outrun men who oppress you
Show them that you have abilities
I say, "Woman stand up."
Stand up just like that woman who touched Jesus
She stood up without any fear.

A woman is she who is not afraid
A woman is she who says, "I AM."
The same should apply to you
Say, "I AM."
Stand up just like the woman of Gerasene.

Stand up women it is time
Wake up you sleepers.

A song

We still have women oppression even today
We have it in our families
We have it in our government structures
We have it in the church
We live for oppression.
Maybe life will be better
We are just like the Gerasene woman.

A Role Play

Husband (to his wife): You wife, stupid for that matter, where were you?

Wife: I am from my mother-in-law's home. She is very sick.

Husband: You speak lies. Don't you know that I bought you by magadi? You are mine. Forget about going in the village with nothing to do. You should stop this behaviour.

"Reading" Luke 1:46-49

In a group which is mostly "illiterate," but with several semi-literate women, part of the text of the Magnificat was read aloud. In this case the reading followed extensive singing and dancing, accompanied by drum beat, and spontaneous group prayer. The song chosen in the dance was "Yehla moya uyingcwele" ("Come down Holy Spirit"). The leader of the group on this occasion gave an address, focussing on the plight of women who are pregnant, the travel to distant clinics in the hope of a healthy baby, the drudgery of continuing to serve the family right up to the time of birth, the pain of birth. Mary becomes an example to the women of perseverence and hope.

FURTHER PROVISIONAL REFLECTIONS

This preliminary field work seems to confirm the patterns apparent also in the black urban setting. The Bible does not operate primarily as printed text, but as a starting point for oral performance in the Christian community. A Bible study in which participants sit round with the text on their laps and discuss it word-by-word does not seem to play a part in the life of the communities studied. The text is always read aloud in the context of community singing (sometimes with dancing) and praying. It is elaborated by repetition and addition, and related directly and unreflectively to the everyday life of the community.

CONCLUSION

Why then do we insist so strongly on the text and on *sola scriptura* in our theological education and doctrine? It is certainly our Western heritage from the Reformation and the Renaissance. We are heirs to the process of alienation from the oral world produced by writing and print. We have internalized it until it seems natural, and we do not recognize that there is another world view. But there is a power dynamic to it as well. There is always a power dynamic to text, since it freezes the Word and places it in the hands of interpretive experts. This was recognized by Max Weber, when he highlighted the process of conflict between (oral) prophet and (literate) priest. The oral words of the prophet are reduced to text and the priest re-establishes control by becoming guardian and interpreter of the text (Weber, 1968:457). Our university Biblical Studies courses and their implicit or explicit hermeneutics are not neutral. When Takatso Mofokeng talks of historical critical study of the Bible as the "hermeneutical yoke of the oppressor" (39), he has a point. It would apply even when the experts use their skills in the cause of the struggle for liberation, as for example Itumaleng Mosala (1989) does with his Marxist analysis of the struggle within the text.

It is also true that oral culture is conservative and traditionalist. It does not easily absorb new ideas or provide the kind of critical analysis required to recognize the dynamics of oppression which blacks have been forced to suffer by apartheid. The experience of suffering is present everywhere in oral performances of Bible reading, which we have described in this paper. Recognizing the danger of hegemony implicit in our Western interpretive methods, we need to recognize also a responsibility to contribute to the process of transformation which is inevitable and irreversible. The world of oral culture is slowly retreating, whether we like it or not. We should treasure its insights and preserve its sense of community. We should try to bring over as much as possible of its dynamic, participatory, and situational character. But we cannot condemn people to remain trapped in "illiteracy," and print will work its spell willy-nilly in transforming consciousness.

The possibility for such a contribution by New Testament scholars is there, but it requires humility and sensitivity. I would like to conclude by pointing people to the Bible studies recorded in the book by G. Philpott *Jesus is Tricky and God is Undemocratic*. It is possible to work in complementary fashion with residual oral culture in a way which respects and recovers its insights and yet contributes the analytical and transformative insights of textual culture also.

WORKS CONSULTED

Bell, C.
    1992   *Ritual Theory-Ritual Practice*. Oxford: Oxford University Press.

Botha, P. J. J.
    1989   "Ouk estin hode...Mark's Stories of Jesus' Tomb and History." *Neotestamentica* 23:195–218.
    1990   "Mute Manuscripts: Analysing a Neglected Aspect of Ancient Communication." *ThEv* 23:35–47.

Draper, J. A. and Gerald O. West
    1989   "Anglicans and Scripture in South Africa." Pp. 30–52 in *Bounty in Bondage: The Anglican Church in Southern Africa*. Ed. F. England and T. Paterson. Johannesburg: Ravan.
    1991   "The Bible and Social Transformation in South Africa: A Work-in-Progress Report on the Insitute for the Study of the Bible." Pp. 366–82 in

Seminar Papers of the Society of Biblical Literature: 127th Annual Meeting, 1991. Ed. Eugene H. Lovering, Jr. Atlanta: Scholars.

Foley, J. M.
1989 "A Response to Werner Kelber's 'Scripture and Logos' from Studies in Oral Tradition." Seminar Paper delivered at the 1989 Congress of the SBL in Los Angeles.

Halverson, J.
1994 "Oral and Written Gospel: A Critique of Werner Kelber." NTS 40:180–95.

Hurtado, L. W.
1990 "The Gospel of Mark: Evolutionary or Revolutionary Document?" JSNT 40:15–32.

Kelber, Werner H.
1983 *The Oral and the Written Gospel: The Hermeneutics of Speaking and Writing in the Synoptic Tradition, Mark, Paul, and Q.* Philadelphia: Fortress.
1989 "Scripture and Logos: The Hermeneutics of Communication." Seminar Paper delivered at the 1989 annual meeting of the SBL in Los Angeles.

Loubser, J. A.
1993 "Orality and Pauline 'Christology': Some Hermeneutical Implications." *Scriptura* 47:25–51.
1993b "The Oral Christ—Believing in Jesus in Oral and Literate Societies." Paper presented to the Theological Society Congress, University of Cape Town, 18–20 August 1993.

Mazamisa, W.
1991 "Reading from this Place: From Orality to Literacy/Textuality and Back." *Scriptura* 9:67–72.

Mofokeng, D.
1988 "Black Christians, the Bible and Liberation." *Journal of Black Theology in South Africa* 2:37–39.

Mosala, Itumela J.
1989 *Biblical Hermeneutics and Black Theology in South Africa.* Grand Rapids: Eerdmans.

Ong, Walter
1967 *The Presence of the Word: Some Prolegomena for Cultural and Religious History.* Minneapolis: University of Minnesota Press.
1982 *Orality and Literacy: The Technologizing of the Word.* London and New York: Methuen.

Philpott, Graham
1993 *Jesus is Tricky and God is Undemocratic: The Kin-dom of God in Amawoti.* Pietermaritzburg: Cluster.

Tompkins, Jane P., ed.
1980 *Reader-Response Criticism: From Formalism to Post-Structuralism.* Baltimore and London: The John Hopkins University Press.

A REAL READER READING REVELATION

Tim Long
Trinity Church
Pretoria
South Africa

ABSTRACT

This essay begins by using Gadamer, Derrida, and Ricoeur as three significant examples of the post-structuralist conviction that human subjectivity is formed through the interpretation of texts. This post-structuralist understanding of subjectivity, the paper argues, mandates a real-reader reader-response criticism, as distinct from the text-centred "reader-response" criticism which has been practised so far in biblical studies. The work of David Bleich on the interpretation provides a guide for real-reader reader-response criticism.

I analyse myself-as-reader, emphasising the ways in which I am a South African reader, and foregrounding the web of sometimes contradictory socio-structural systems in terms of which I read. I then undertake a reading of Revelation 2.1–7, demonstrating how the particularities of my presence-as-reader impact on my reading of this biblical text. I demonstrate that this method of reading makes contextual interpretation part of the meaning of the text, and argue that the idiosyncratic nature of my reading is, in fact, no more idiosyncratic than readings in conventional biblical criticism, and is equally committed to engaging with the text.

INTRODUCTION

Nearly a decade ago Lategan succinctly diagrammed three profound shifts in biblical interpretative strategy (3), the last two of which have occurred since World War II. First, there was the historical shift, which focused on questions of origin. This became the most widely accepted method of interpretation among scholars, though not in the Church. The first major "paradigm switch" occurred in the early post-war period with structuralism, which moved attention to the text itself. It was followed by another major shift which is still happening. I refer to the movement away from origins and text to the *reader*, though Lategan's diagram clearly shows that the three methodologies overlap and converge. "Reader-response" criticism is the result of this second major "paradigm shift" and the focus of my essay, whose central argument will take up Stephen Moore's critique that biblical studies has not, in fact, moved to a "*real-reader*-response criticism." My aim will be to provide a framework within which such a move might be possible and to suggest the significance of making such a move in the South African context.

I seek first to lay a philosophical and hermeneutical framework for a reader-response approach to the biblical text. I do this by using three seminal thinkers, namely Gadamer, Derrida, and Ricoeur. I then "complete" the framework with a summary of the work of David Bleich, whose "subjective criticism" is dependent on the thought-world I describe while taking its implications for reader-response criticism farther than anyone else has done.

A Philosophical and Hermeneutical Framework for Reader-Response Criticism

It is relatively easy to speak of Gadamer and Ricoeur in the same breath because they obviously share many positions, not least in their confidence that language communicates meaning. It is much harder to see Derrida sharing a position with either, not least because central to his work is the confidence that language does *not* communicate meaning. Nonetheless as the fascinating (non)dialogue between Gadamer and Derrida captured in the volume by Michelfelder and Palmer (1989) shows, there are many and strong links between these two thinkers. For my purposes here, I am interested in one such link, which informs the work of all three: each believes that subjectivity is made by interpretation—the all-knowing, all-controlling subject is a myth. It follows from this that for each *the reader is a maker of meaning* in the act of reading. Certainly, they use different language to present this belief, and they come at it with different presuppositions and interests. Only Ricoeur, for example, has any kind of direct interest in actual reading, and even then his interest is highly theoretical and generalized. However, the presence of active readers is assumed in most of their major discussions. To put it differently, a reader-response criticism is mandated by the need of readers to use texts in the formation of their subjectivity. My presentation of their work is selected to support this shared, post-Enlightenment view of subjectivity which, with its corollary, provides the theoretical basis for the approach to Revelation I undertake in the final part of this paper.

The concept of dialogue is central to Gadamer's thought about interpretation: "[Interpretation] is like a real conversation in that the common subject matter is what binds the two partners, the text and the interpreter, to each other" (1989:388). "Dialogue," however, is so common a word as to carry a danger that the complexity and richness of Gadamer's conception may be replaced with some vague, generalized notion of communication. "Dialogue," for Gadamer, has six essential components. First, it takes place always in relation to *tradition*, by which Gadamer refers not to some body of knowledge but to historical consciousness. In *Truth and Method* Gadamer uses a vivid metaphor to describe "tradition": he says that it is as water to a fish—that is, the element in which we live, invisible yet all-pervasive. Expressed differently, it is "not simply a process that experience teaches us to know and govern; it is *language*...a genuine partner in dialogue, and we belong to it, as does the I with a Thou" (1989:358). Historical existence is the "horizon" of human existence, and no interpretation can transcend it. Although for the purposes of my discussion I have subordinated "tradition" to "dialogue," in Gadamer's work "tradition" is the base upon which everything is built. Following from it is a necessary rejection of the Cartesian subject who, already wholly constituted, interprets from a position outside experience.

Second, "dialogue" "rehabilitates" prejudice as a fundamental dimension of interpretation. Acknowledgement of the legitimacy of "prejudice" guards against the constant temptation to objectify tradition (Gadamer, 1989:358–59). Third, "dialogue" is to the interpreter as a game is to sportswo(men): it is play. "The mode of being of play does not allow the player to behave toward play as if toward an object." Applied to texts, this means that "the work of art is not an object that stands over against a subject for itself. Instead the work of art has its true being in the fact that it becomes an experience that changes the person who experiences it" (Gadamer, 1989:102). Thus, understanding has the character of "event." Fourth, "dialogue" necessitates goodwill: genuine dialogue precludes dogmatism and subjectivism in two ways essentially: first, by virtue of the stance of "learned ignorance" (*docta ignorantia*) which the interpreter adopts and by which (s)he disclaims knowledge of the truth, and second, by attention to the *sache* or subject-matter of the text. "Dialogue," in other words, exists only where there is a real respect for the otherness of the other. Such respect, born of awareness, is intrinsic to an historical understanding of human existence (Gadamer, 1989:306). Goodwill, it is also important to note, does not deprive interpretation of criteria for judging between the good and the bad, as some critics have charged. Fifth, "dialogue" creates a fusion of horizons: "Understanding is always the fusion of these horizons supposedly existing by themselves...In a tradition this process of fusion is always going on, for there old and new are always combining into something of living value, without either being explicitly foregrounded from the other" (Gadamer, 1989:306).

The sixth and final aspect to "dialogue" is Gadamer's understanding of application as an integral part of the act of reading, rather than the third, separate stage assigned to it by an older hermeneutic. The significance of this insight for my topic is well expressed by Weinsheimer: "Gadamer's affirmation of human finitude implies that understanding is always tied to a concrete historical situation, a particular case: it is always applied understanding, even when application is not the interpreter's conscious purpose" (187). Because the reader is embedded in history, as is the text, interpretation involves the application of each to the other: "Understanding makes the traditions of which it is made; and since it is productive, understanding...adds itself to the whole that is to be understood. For this reason self-understanding is always to be achieved" (Weinsheimer: 195). The real reader, in short, cannot be excluded or even side-lined if one accepts Gadamer's notion of interpretation.

Gadamer appears not to be naively positivistic in presenting his hermeneutical theory, but seems fully aware of difficulties which hinder understanding. For example, he acknowledges "the barrier of alienness, that our understanding has to overcome" (1989:342), and directs his hermeneutics at providing an understanding of interpretation which will achieve precisely this victory over this "barrier of alienness": "To be in a conversation...means to be beyond oneself, to think with the other and to come back to oneself as if to another" (in Michelfelder and Palmer: 110). It seems clear—and Gadamer insists on this (Michelfelder and Palmer: 114–25)—that his "dialogue" is fully cognisant of differance. Conversation does not exclude differance, either in the process or in the result. "Difference exists within identity" (in Michelfelder and Palmer: 125). In fact, Gadamer's insistence on historical consciousness, which is one of the most clearly argued and impressive aspects of his work, is rooted precisely in this insight that "Difference exists within identity." Alienation remains in the false attempt to transcend historical conditionedness.

Gadamer has failed to see an important implication of his insight, which the political struggle in my country, South Africa, has made clear, namely, that "dialogue" can be, indeed usually is, hindered, and perhaps even entirely prevented, when the participants are situated unequally in the structures of their society. "Goodwill," in Gadamer's sense is by no means enough, in other words, to ensure dialogue. In my reading of Revelation I expose how the narrator uses the inequality structured into his relationship with his audiences to prevent dialogue with them. Thus with his fundamentally optimistic, even noble, hermeneutic, which is aware of, but hardly takes real account of, alienation in its various guises, Gadamer constantly underlines his faith in language as an effective "bridge": "The ability to understand is a fundamental endowment of man [sic], one that sustains his communal life with others and, above all, one that takes place by way of language and the partnership of conversation" (1989:21).

When we turn to Derrida, we find the subject-in-formation approached through *différance*. "There is no chance that the mandated subject 'exists' somewhere, that it is present or is 'itself', and still less chance that it will become conscious...This radical alterity, removed from every possible mode of presence, is characterized by...delayed effects" (1976:xliv). In a system characterised by *différance*, the being of the subject is also always deferred, never present. There is no "I" but only a system of signs. Everything is always "trace."

Tied to this ontological implication of différance is Derrida's notion of intertextuality: "A 'text'...is henceforth no longer a finished corpus of writing, some content enclosed in a book or its margins, but a differential network, a fabric of traces referring endlessly to something other than itself, to other differential traces" (1991:257). In other words, the reader is one text in "a field of forces" (1986:168), and thus an "effect" of interpretation, integrally part of the linguistic system which is characterized by différance.

Ricoeur's work has reached a climax in his three-volumed *Time and Narrative* (1984–1988), which synthesizes his life-long concern to construct a poetics of temporality, to understand what it means to live in time. The essence of Ricoeur's argument is that while poetic texts—which means all texts that arrange time in whatever way—mimic reality, they do not do so iconically. Rather, mimesis proceeds in three stages of redescription. The first stage Ricoeur calls "reduction to the same," by which he refers to the recovering of traces of the past in the present. The second stage refers to the opposite movement, "the recognition of otherness," by which present and past are distanced; and the third stage is the "analogizing of apprehension," by which the previous two categories are held in the correct dialectical relationship: "being-as is both to be and not to be" (1988:155). In short, texts mimic reality by the character of "Standing-for" as they disclose their "world" to the reader. Ricoeur defines "the world of the text" as "the ensemble of references opened up by the texts" (1975:25).

This "world of the text" is not, however, something present in the text in a Cartesian sense. Rather, it is discovered and its power to refigure reality disclosed only in the act of reading. Until the text has a reader, its "world" remains locked within its borders: "...considered apart from reading, the world of the text remains a transcendence in immanence. Its ontological status remains in suspension—an excess in relation to reading. It is only in reading that the dynamism of configuration completes its course" (1988:158).

Thus far, Ricoeur may be felt to be in strange company—after all, his work as I have described it seems to epitomize the Enlightenment view of subjectivity which Gadamer and Derrida abandon. Ricoeur seems to present us with a helpless text, full of an imprisoned "world," waiting for an all-powerful reader to set it free. Indeed, Ricoeur's standpoint in relation to the shift from an Enlightenment to a post-Enlightenment paradigm is considerably ambivalent. However, I believe I have put Ricoeur in the right company, for the "refiguring" of reality that occurs in interpretation is a refiguring of the reading subject and of the text. In Ricoeur's work, interpretation involves an interplay or "mediation" between the "worlds" of text and reader, both of which are refigured in the act of reading. Thus, his work does not present us with a Cartesian subject, but with a postmodern one: "It is the text, with its universal power of world disclosure, which gives a self to the ego" (1976:94).

Finally in this introductory survey, I come to the work of David Bleich (1975; 1976; 1988). In a number of senses it may seem odd to include Bleich in the company of Gadamer, Derrida, and Ricoeur. For one thing, he is far less well-known and influential; for another, he himself is strongly critical of aspects of the work of Gadamer and Derrida (1988:17–19). Nonetheless, I believe his work fits and strengthens the framework I have been erecting for a real-reader reading of the Bible in a number of ways. First, Bleich's "subjective criticism" is dependent on the thought-world shaped by Gadamer, Derrida, and Ricoeur in which human subjectivity is formed through interpretation. Second, unlike the other three, Bleich's work is directly concerned with the practicalities of reading texts, and this orientation provides insights lacking in the much more theoretical work I have already sketched. Third, Bleich is the only theorist who shows that actual-reader self-disclosure is the crucial hermeneutical move reader-response criticism has to make to release fully the active subject forming itself through interpretation and building community in the process.

If interpretation of texts (of whatever kind) is critical to the formation of human subjectivity, then it follows that interpretation is inseparable from concrete human experience. Bleich's work, rooted in analysis of actual readers reading specific texts, is helpful in illuminating this link between reading and human experience. Bleich's major thrust has been to critique the individualistic, technological understanding of knowledge, which he sees as a product of the "objective paradigm" we inherit from the Enlightenment. Some signs of these features, he argues, are the competitiveness of our educational system, its exclusion of the emotions from interpretation, its interest in ranking readings in terms of institutional definitions of "quality," its authoritarianism, and its tendency to paradox and abstraction.

Bleich describes the current educational system as "technological," to distinguish the current pursuit of knowledge from the "relational" approach he believes to derive from the fact that language is the instrument by which human beings live together in society. Being "relational," knowledge is necessarily "subjective," rather than technological and "objective": "Every linguistic act has cognitive, expressive, interpersonal, and ethical dimensions which render such acts subjective" (1976:326).[1] Thus Bleich's work has come to bear the label "subjective criticism."[2] Its insights are based on the way language functions. Of course, so are Derrida's; but where Derrida is interested in language as an autonomous system, Bleich is interested in its *social function*, which is to construct community. Therefore his insights have particular importance in the present South African context.

Bleich's work complements Gadamer's notion of "dialogue" with particular immediacy: "There is no way to separate the individual's capability for and use of language from the continuing situation of dialogue—the necessity to speak with someone else...Intersubjectivity is the framework for the intermingling of the cognitive and the affective, and it makes it possible to conceptualize language as dialogic or interactional" (1988:73). Further, however, Bleich's notion of "dialogue" is explicitly and intentionally egalitarian. Quoting Paulo Freire, Bleich affirms that

> Dialogue is thus an existential necessity...[which] cannot be reduced to the act of one person's "depositing" ideas in another, nor can it become a simple exchange of ideas to be "consumed" by the discussants...Because dialogue is an encounter among men [sic] who name the world, it must not be a situation where some men name on behalf of others. It is an act of creation. (1988:158–59)

If language and knowledge are interpersonal, then interpretation necessarily involves self-disclosure. Reader self-disclosure is therefore the move Bleich forces on interpretation-as-"dialogue." In addition, Bleich's work, as I have already suggested, is particularly appropriate to counter the individualism of Gadamer, Derrida, and Ricoeur, and to enable the essentially-communal nature of biblical interpretation.

I want to enlarge on why the move of explicit-reader self-disclosure is crucially important. First is a pragmatic reason: no reading ever occurs

---

[1] Bleich's intention to foreground the communal nature of language acquisition and usage does not deny the importance of the individual. Rather, one of Bleich's concerns is to recapture the dialectic between individual and social which, he argues, is intrinsic to language. The first part of the title of his latest book, *The Double Perspective* points to this dialectic as basic to all language: "To name oneself...is at the same time to know oneself *as distinct from and as implicated in* other people" (1988:92).

[2] Clearly, "subjective" for Bleich describes the interpersonal dimension at the heart of all language use, including the emotional dimension of interpretation which is currently excluded from "quality" interpretations, and is to be distinguished from "subjectivism" which might describe a belief that all meanings are equally valid.

without an explicit reader. Second, it is congruent with the claim reader-response criticism makes that the reader is part of the act of interpretation. Much more significant is the third, that explicit-reader self-disclosure creates an egalitarian reading context. The "expert" can no longer hide behind esoteric knowledge, behind the plural "we" (a wholly false declaration of community). (S)he must declare self and thus be open and vulnerable—in dialogue with—others. Especially, Bleich's insistence on the emotional dimension of interpretation forces the "expert" reader onto terrain where greater "expertise" may be shown by untrained readers.[3] Fourth, and following directly from the third, explicit-reader self-disclosure therefore creates and activates community in a true sense, that is, as a context in which everyone is accepted and is therefore freed to speak. However, lest it be thought that this raises the spectre of subjectivism, Bleich argues that critical reading *can* go hand-in-hand with every-member acceptance, provided different questions are asked. Instead of asking: Which is the better/best reading?, assuming some essentialist notion of correctness which, Bleich argues, in practice usually means 'the expert's' own reading, the more helpful question (to building community, that is) is: How and why does each reader see the text differently?

The real questions are *why* and *how*, questions, Bleich comments, that few are willing to look into. Bleich's emphasis on explicit-reader self-disclosure shifts the focus of critical activity from its normal hierarchicalism to something more democratic and potentially liberating.

READER-RESPONSE CRITICISM AND BIBLICAL STUDIES: A CRITIQUE[4]

It is evident that a wide range of contemporary thought reveals a subject-in-formation rather than a subject-constituted. If this is so, then interpretation can be thought of no longer as a matter of finding what is "there" in the text. However one conceives of what happens when an active reader engages with a text, meaning is a product of that engagement, transforming both partners in this dialogue. This recognition has given birth to "reader-response criticism," a glance at which reveals a plethora of "readers": we have Booth's *mock* reader, Fish's *informed* reader, Culler's *competent* reader, Iser's *implied* reader, Eco's *model* reader, Riffaterre's *av-*

---

[3] Bleich's work has important implications for work being undertaken with "ordinary" (i.e. untrained) readers. See West, 1991:142–83 and 1992.

[4] The critique offered here concentrates, as already mentioned, on the failure of reader-response criticism to disclose the real or explicit reader. However, it is fair to acknowledge that reader-response criticism has two other aspects to it which have contributed to new insights into and readings of the Bible. The first is its stress on the *reading process* (e.g. Staley, 1991); and the second is its ability to nuance reading by identifying implied readers and their responses.

erage and *super* readers, Bloom's *strong*, or *mistaking/mistaken* reader, Derrida's *deconstructing* reader, Barthes' *perverse* reader, Hartman's *feasting* reader, Bleich's *subjective* reader, Holland's *transactive* reader, Hirsch's *validating* reader, Rogers' *amazing/a-mazing* reader, Fetterley's *resisting* reader, etc.[5] However, these readers, while very different, all have one important feature in common: none *actually exists*. All are textual constructs, "fictive" readers.[6] During the past few years, a few scholars in literature and biblical studies have begun to express dissatisfaction with this fictive reader, on the ground that it brings us no closer to the actual experience of "real," flesh-and-blood readers.

In *Literary Criticism and the Gospels*, Stephen Moore makes just this criticism, among others. His all-embracing criticism of this "reader" is that it is an *unfeeling* reader, lacking the emotional responses real readers bring to stories (96).[7] Moore comments on an attempt by James Resseguie to explore a "real," contemporary reading of Mark, but judges it a failure, privileging the text and offering no new perspective. The reason he identifies is that biblical studies, as a discipline, has no place for real readers: "The factors inducing us to remain author-oriented critics in readers' clothing are powerful ones....Symptomatically, projects in secular literary criticism [that] vigorously affirm the rights of the reader have run counter to the organizing principles of the discipline and been duly relegated to the margins" (Moore: 105).

Moore suggests that this may reflect a fear of the "individualistic" (subjective) nature of the actual reader.[8] This leads him to conclude: "For

---

[5] See Rogers for explanations of some of the names so far; Fetterley for an extended treatment of her *resisting* reader; and Moore, chapter six, for more names and kinds of readers.

[6] Anderson (72) interprets Iser's implied reader as a combination of textual construct and actual reader: "...the implied reader is made up of the set of directions formed by the text and the stance that an actual reader takes as he or she creatively reads." Such an unproblematic marriage of fictive and actual reader, however, is unconvincing. This does not imply that they are not useful or that the whole concept of the implied reader is not useful. Gerhart (168) explicates her notion of the "genric reader" who is both a real reader and a textual construct in the sense of being acted upon by the text. Gerhart's discussion, however, is spoilt by her lack of clarity about explicit and implicit readers.

[7] Staley (especially 1992 and 1994), to my knowledge, is the only scholar who has taken this critique to heart and attempted a reading of a biblical text in terms of his own life. His work is of particular importance to biblical scholars interested in the real reader. In the field of Christian ethics, see Pellauer (1993) who incorporates into her discussion of sexual ethics an account of her own experience of orgasm.

[8] This is somewhat ironic! Bleich's argument is precisely the opposite: the ideological attachment to individualism in the Academy is responsible for the repression of the real reader. The typical fear, however, of the explicit reader is shown by Jauss (1978) who, writing to recommend an aesthetics of reception in fact continues to grant the text powerful rights when he asserts the primacy of the implicit over the explicit

biblical studies the moral is plain: criticism is an institution to which real readers need not apply" (106). Thus, Moore characterizes real readers of the Bible as repressed readers.

While Moore puts his finger on the problem, he offers no solution. There is a reason for this, I believe: I do not think Moore had any clearer an idea of what to do with the real reader than any of the scholars he critiques. This is where Bleich's contribution is most significant. However, Moore's analysis, which focusses on the institutional barriers to a shift to reader-response criticism in biblical studies, is developed by Temma Berg who, working from a deconstructionist perspective, argues that the prison of Christian dogmatism is primarily responsible for that failure. She then reads *Mark* as a "real" reader.[9]

Essentially, Berg's argument is that the "readers" reader-response critics identify with are really dishonest "blinds" for the real reader, the "author" of the reading (cf. Tolbert: 205). What scholarship is doing, in other words, is pretending that readings have an authority which is supra-individual, hence the "cultural imperialism" of the "we" scholars use to pretend that they have escaped the limitations of "I". Paradoxically, though, the effect of this is to "disempower" the actual reader, by continuing to privilege the text, as well as by denying the real presence of the actual reader.[10]

Berg develops her poststructuralist notion of subjectivity in terms of the problematic of borders: in a world of ceaseless deferral in which everything is trace, the boundaries we have assumed are found to be absent

---

reader. His reason: "The implied reader's role may be discerned from the text's objective structures. For this reason, it is easier to grasp the implied rather than the explicit reader's role, with its often concealed social dependencies and subjective conditions. Therefore, the role of the implied reader deserves methodological preference" (142). Apart from an underlying fear of the "uncontrollable" explicit reader, his methodological preference is the product of his historical interest in exposing "the ideological projections of different strata of readers" (142).

[9] Moore comments patronizingly on Berg's article: "The many faux pas that ensue [from her "nonspecialist" reading of *Mark*] bespeak the gulf separating even radical biblical critics such as Phillips (1985) from nonspecialist Bible readers such as Berg" (104). In his attitude to Berg's reading, Moore shows himself to be typical of the institutional reader Bleich criticizes, whose notion of critical reading is to discover which readings to exclude and which to include. Moore's typical approach should be set alongside Bleich's book, *Readings and Feelings*, in which Bleich shows an approach which accepts all readers in the reading community and their readings, without sacrificing critical judgments about accuracy, insight, etc. It is also interesting to see how closely Berg's reading of *Mark* follows Bleich's "subjective criticism," even though Berg shows no familiarity with Bleich's work.

[10] Writing long before Berg, Jauss had noted: "Traditional bourgeois as well as orthodox Marxist aesthetics still cling to classical priority of the work over the reader" (138). He goes on to describe an aesthetics of reception in terms of a retrieval of "the rights" of the reader.

or, at least, in constant motion. Thus, we cannot posit a subject-object distinction:

> The reader is in and not in the text. The reader can never be separated from the texts that surround him, partly because "reader" and "text" are interchangeable signs, but also because the reader is an active producer of what she reads. The text exists so that the reader may fill it. The reader exists so that the reader may fill her. Neither the reader nor the text has a single, stable center; both the reader and the text may be endlessly exchanged. For poststructural critics, reading is not what it is for most other critics—that is, discovering meaning or significance, looking over, scanning, decoding a text to arrive at an objective interpretation. Rather, readers read to expose themselves to the flickering significances of the text.... (202)

Biblical studies, then, stands accused of having evaded the implications of a mode of reading it claims to have incorporated into its discipline. That mode of reading, however, exerts a powerfully credible claim to be taken seriously, whether from Gadamer's emphasis on the historicity of all interpretation, from the deconstructionist blurring of the borders between text and reader, from the Ricoeurian perspective of refiguration, or from the Bleichian emphasis on the necessarily interpersonal nature of language-use. All these perspectives combine to root interpretation in concrete human experience, which calls for the disclosure of the explicit reader as part of the interpretation of the "text." Hence, I now move to such a disclosure of myself-as-reader, prior to undertaking a reading of Revelation.

A Real-Reader Reading of Revelation

In the light of all this, I propose that what follows will be, primarily, my reading of the readers in/of Revelation. It will be as "idiosyncratic" as every reading actually is, but I will claim that this does not make it unable to find a "common language" (in the Gadamerian sense) with other (idiosyncratic) readings, largely because shared interests I have with other readings enable our idiosyncrasies to enrich one another's readings, both by the shared ground these interests automatically create, as well as by the necessary plurality of perspectives our differences contain. For example, I have an interest in the political ramifications of the gospel. I come at that interest, though, from a literary perspective which foregrounds the final form of the biblical text. There are other readers with the same political interest who approach the biblical text by foregrounding the historical factors behind their text. These two approaches will lead to radically different (idiosyncratic) readings of any text, but will not prevent our finding common ground for the exploration of our shared interest in the political ramifications of the gospel. "Common language," in other words, is more constructively interpreted in terms of shared interests than in terms of interpretative agreements. Furthermore, in accepting the necessary idiosyncrasy of all readings, I obviously eschew the (false) claim to scientific objectivity in interpretation. Nonetheless, I am committed to a "dialogue" with the text, that is, to taking the claims of the text seriously and to using all the skills and training I have had in the process.

Essential to a real-reader reading is the acknowledgement that I am more than one reader in my reading. In fact, the "interminably slow" readings of scholarship certainly encourage a necessary focus on the multiple situatedness of the actual reader.[11] Let me illustrate from my own reading of Revelation, in which I have been conscious, without a great deal of pondering, of being at least the following "readers." I present these "readers" randomly, with no attempt to prioritize them, nor with any claim that these describe the complete range of "readers" I am.

First, I am a *South African political/reader*, participating in a struggle for justice, which leads me to foreground the political polemic of Revelation in a variety of ways, as well as to read the book with an emphasis on what it tells us about living as Christians now, rather than on the eschatological End. In this reader-persona I am also consciously and deliberately intent on exposing the readings of the North American Right, which have been influential in the church in South Africa.

Second, I am a *priest/reader and a pray-er/reader*, deeply moved by the liturgical worship which plays such a large part in the narrative, and by its passionate quality. In this respect, my reading is accepting, uncritical.

Third, I am a *suspicious/reader*, especially suspicious of claims to unmediated divine knowledge, which means that I want to deconstruct the narrator's claim to possess that knowledge. I have this suspicion because of Christianity's record of failure in South Africa to know and speak the mind of God, as well as secular authority's claims to divine knowledge, enforced by censorship, detention, house arrests, and murders. This affects my reading of the letters, for example, in which my suspicion leads me to find aporias in the text which justify my suspicions of the narrator's integrity and his claims. I find an intense conflict between this "reader," who effectively denies the motivating drive behind the text (the narrative as divine revelation) and my previous reader who wants to respond to the text by joining the worship. My suspicion takes other aspects too, for example, the privileged position accorded the Christian community vis-a-

---

[11] I would argue, against Berg, that "interminably slow" readings are not necessarily unreaderly. In fact, the characteristic reading methodology of Christians (and probably all religious people who have sacred texts) is to read and reread the same sacred texts, so that it is true to say that the Bible is read "interminably slowly." This is the same thing, in a different gear, as Berg's "interminably slow" scholarly readings.

vis the End-time catastrophes of the seal, trumpets, and bowls. This privilege seems to me to deconstruct the narrative's demand for political justice.

Fourth, I am a *pastor/reader*, intent on examining how a church leader deals with his people. In this "reader-persona," I find much evidence for a deep pastoral concern in the narrative, which is more important to me than the End. But I also find this pastoral concern to be ambiguous in the all-important letters, as well as in the dismissal by Judgment of all outside the Christian community. This is a particular problem for me as a South African reader conscious of the incompatability of the aims of religious exclusivism with those of building a common, plural society.

Fifth, I am an *institutional-church/reader*, conscious of the fact that institutional religion and apocalyptic religion live in different thought-worlds (see Wilson 1981:223–4). In this "reader-persona," I wonder what Revelation can say to the now-institutional church in South Africa.[12]

Sixth, I am a *middle-class-white/reader*, living in a context in which sixty percent of the population is poverty-stricken. In this aspect, I find myself confronted in Revelation by an absolute assault on wealth, which confronts me also as a preacher and pastor of a largely middle-class white congregation. Yet I am also intrigued by the fact that paradise is narrativized in Revelation in images of opulent wealth, so I find myself confronted by the evil of wealth while at the same time seduced by its association with the central hope offered in the narrative.

Seventh, I am a *male reader*, embedded in a still-patriarchal Bible and Church, though I am encouraged by, and seek to influence, my Church's struggle to grow past its patriarchy. In this aspect of my reader-presence I am confronted by the powerful inclination of the gender imagery of this book towards patriarchy.

Finally, I am a *church/Academy* reader. By this I mean that I have three feet (as it were) in the church and one foot in the Academy. My belonging to the church encourages me to read through the eyes of faith, while the Academy encourages me to separate faith from critical reading. I find this dual membership a source of some tension, partly attracted to the indifference to faith which underlies much scholarly work, while remaining committed to the relationship of faith I entered into some twenty years ago.

Thus, my interpretative stance has the aspect of self-disclosure, in which is revealed the complex, often contradictory, web of social and structural relations in which I find myself (like everyone) embedded. A glance back at my listing will indicate that contentment with, and strug-

---

[12] See my reply (1993) to du Rand.

gle against, are distributed through the network of embeddedness which I disclose in my reading of the text of Revelation. These contradictions especially are often painful to acknowledge to myself, let alone share with anyone else, but they will have definite effects on the way I enter the text and my engagement with it. In short, the "world" I-as-reader bring to Revelation is a world of struggle: faith struggles with doubt and scepticism; past experience struggles with the "world" of the text and with the demands of building a new society; male interests struggle with female ones; contemporaneity with antiquity, and so on.

A Reading of Revelation 2.1–7

I now move to a reading of Revelation, with an eye to the question of how my actual-reader presence "in" the text affects the narrative, so that a Christian praxis is born in this engagement, rather than found through reception of something discovered in the text and picked out for application in my context. For the sake of manageability, I confine this discussion to the encounter between the narrator,[13] the Christian community(ies) of chapters 2–3, and myself as the actual reader. I take Revelation 2.1–7 as my basic text, though my discussion will include a detailed examination of 3.7–13, as well as comments on other aspects of the narrative.

In this discussion I foreground an important narrative movement or tension central in this encounter: a movement from a single, compliant readership (1.9) to the diverse, seemingly troublesome, and complex readership of chapters 2–3, and back to a single-community readership from chapter 4 onwards. I will suggest that this movement may be a strategy of control on the narrator's part, an attempt to bring under greater control the diverse and troublesome relationship with the Christian communities of chap. 2–3.[14] His narrative method, I will show, is to

---

[13] I use the singular for convenience, here remembering Derrida's point that naming is a way of searching for full presence. Analysis of the narrative's presentation of the "narrator" would quickly show him to have a multi-dimensional identity(ies) similar to my analysis of myself-as-reader. For example, his name, "John," immediately suggests by its commonness an essential unknowability; and in the portion of *Revelation* I analyse in this essay he is indistinguishably human prophet/ divine Christ, as well as loving pastor/bully-judge. See Boring and Michaels for analyses of the complexity of narrative voices in this book.

[14] Notice that I carefully phrase this assertion to acknowledge that I am talking about a motive which I can only assert the narrator may have. At other points in my reading I will present evidence to justify this assertion, but it is important to recognize the difference between attributing motives (to a character in a narrative) and to reading the intentions of the narrative (or character). Here I am using Brett's distinction between the "communicative intention" of a text (i.e. what is said) and its "motive" (i.e. why it is being said). See Brett, whose argument is that interpreters constantly confuse "communicative intentions" with "motives."

sweep aside the diversity, complexity, and differentiation he encounters initially by creating a single, textual community which is utterly compliant to his will.

The place to begin this exploration of reader-relationships in/outside the text is with 1.9, in which the narrator addresses his reader(s) as "your brother who share with you in Jesus the persecution and the kingdom and the patient endurance...." In this way, he establishes a wholly compliant reader who shares completely his faith and situation. The narrator and the Christian community are one family, wholly-united in relationship, commitment, and situation. This actual reader, by virtue of being a Christian, is able to share[15] this point of entry into the narrative with the readers in the text.

From this beginning to the relationship among the readers in/outside the text, the narrative moves to the seven churches of chapters 2–3. All sorts of questions arise as to whether they are the actual, historical readers, or intra-textual constructs, but I bypass these to locate my interest in the diversity of these readers. In social location they range from poverty (Smyrna, and possibly Philadelphia) to wealth (Laodicea), with some whose social location is indeterminate (Ephesus, Philadelphia, Pergamum, Thyatira, and Sardis). In attitude to their situation they range from a living faith that embraces suffering (Smyrna, and some in Pergamum, where there has been an experience of martyrdom, and Philadelphia) to the hypocrisy and complacency, subtlely differentiated, of Sardis and Laodicea. Further, there are different attitudes within particular communities, with some who are ready to accommodate themselves to the surrounding culture, including its religious practices and beliefs, while others resist in exemplary fashion (Pergamum and Thyatira; Ephesus possibly falls into this group, too, though for very different reasons). In addition, as we shall see, they vary in attitude and relationship to the narrator.

Even this picture of the diversity of readers in chapters 2–3 is a simplification, for the narrative subtlely differentiates even where there are similarities. Thus, for example, although Smyrna and Pergamum both share the narrator's commitment to suffering, only Pergamum, it seems, has experienced actual martyrdom among its ranks. To take another example of a similar subtlety (only one among many): Sardis and Laodicea share a clear hypocrisy and complacency, as I have indicated; yet where

---

[15] Not necessarily completely, though. If the narrator's rather mysterious self-description at 1.9 refers to his persecution and imprisonment, then this actual middle-class reader enters the narrative at a certain distance. If, on the other hand, "tribulation" in this verse refers more generally to the problems of resisting the surrounding culture, which it is the book's purpose to make its readers more sensitive to (a possibility many interpreters have suggested), this middle-class reader would be able to identify very closely indeed.

Sardis seems to have worked hard to appear alive: "you have a name of being alive" (3.1), Laodicea has been contentedly "neither cold nor hot" (3.15).

On the generalized level of a shared faith, these readers share the compliance of the "ideal" reader of 1.9, but as I ponder the narrative, I see that there are numerous gaps between the narrator and these readers, some of them downright troublesome, and some of those apparently almost uncontrollable. The weave of the text, then, presented at 1.9 as perfectly unified, with narrator and audience of one mind, heart and purpose, begins to stretch and tear early in the narrative.

Before I proceed to explore this "stretching and tearing," it will be useful to note how the tripartite structure of each letter functions to narrativize both the narrator/reader unity and disunity. Each letter begins with an "address" ("and to the angel...") which binds the risen Christ, the narrator, and the community addressed into one. Both the narrator and the community accept Christ as Lord, the words spoken are Christ's, but also the narrator's by virtue of his being the vocal instrument of Christ's message; thus the expectation is created, particularly in view of the unity established at 1.9, of the community's giving the same obedience to the message which the prophet exemplifies in the giving of it. Particularly powerful in achieving this fusion of the narrator's voice with the Lord's is the τάδε λέγει formula ("These are the words...") with which each letter begins. The fusion is complete, moreover, so that it is not possible to separate their voices. The τάδε λέγει are at one and the same time the prophet's words, because he has written them under his own name, and the words "of him who holds the seven stars..." (2.1), which repeats some of the details of the vision of the Risen Christ a few verses back, and so in a very direct way makes the words the words of Christ. This is a brilliant literary stroke, the narrator placing himself at one with the deity with deft economy. Its most immediately obvious effect, on a rhetorical level, is to present the narrator's message as the perfect Word of the Lord, beyond criticism or question. The sevenfold repetition of the τάδε λέγει formula ensures that the book's receptors never forget that God is speaking to them in this man.

In the middle section, the "message," a rupture of some kind—these ruptures are varied, as I shall have space to do no more than indicate—occurs in all seven letters. In the final section, the "exhortation/promise," the narrator acts to repair the rupture and restore the absolute unity of 1.9. This movement from unity to rupture to unity is a repetition on the micro level of the book's movement on the macro level. The significance of this movement or tension is that it questions the very purpose of the narrative, which is presumably that the actual readers should unproblematically accept the narrator's visions as complete truth. What I am demonstrating is that I-as-reader, because of the suspicion I bring to my reading (to point merely to one relevant factor from the list above), have seized on this "stretch" in the narrative and begun to pull at it, to make it more evident, if you like. In doing this, the weave is altered. What was a barely noticeable stretch has become a tear, and I-as-reader have "rewritten" the text.

For reasons of space, I now move to examine one of these ruptures in detail, Ephesus (2.1–7). The first striking thing about Ephesus is the wealth of qualities she has. In verses 2–3, "and" (καί) recurs nine times, separating positive qualities on each occasion.[16] This is very powerful, but added to the power of repetition is the fact that this Church has the critical qualities, "works" (τὰ ἔργα), "toil" (τὸν κόπον), and "patient endurance" (τὴν ὑπομονήν), as well as discernment—"you cannot tolerate evildoers; you have tested those who claim to be apostles but are not, and have found them to be false" (2.2). "Works" seems to be a general term for the church's life and quality, defined less by any intrinsic meaning than by immediate context (see also 2.19; 3.1, 15). One of its defining terms is "patient endurance,"[17] added to which is Ephesus' discernment, her watchfulness against threats of evil, and especially her ability to discern false leadership (2.2 and 6).[18] In other words, Ephesus possesses a second quality of ultimate importance (when compared with the other cities in chapters 2–3).

How surprising it is, then, to find that such a Church faces an imminent threat of destruction: "If not, I will come to you and remove your lampstand from its place, unless you repent"(2.5). The reason for this threat is "that you have abandoned the love you had at first" (2.4). Apparently this fault overrules all the virtues for which the Ephesian Church has been praised.

But there is a double surprise in this letter. The first we have seen, that ultimate sanctions should threaten a Church which seems to have so many vital qualities. The second surprise is the vagueness of the fault which overrules all these positive qualities. What is this "first love" which

---

[16] Smyrna and Pergamum have καί three times each in the parallel parts of the letters; Thyatira has it five times, Sardis has no positive qualities, Philadelphia has καί twice, and Laodicea, of course, also has no positive qualities.

[17] Which Thyatira (2.19) also has, as does Philadelphia (3.10). In the latter case, this quality is of ultimate importance, guaranteeing the Philadelphian church protection from the "hour of trial which is coming on the whole world" (3.10).

[18] The very opposite absence of this adherence to the truth characterizes the churches at Pergamum and Thyatira, where these churches' inability to discern correctly will be, the prophet warns, the cause of judgment falling upon them (2.16, 22–23).

the community has forsaken? Is it love for God, for one another, for the prophet? In the context of the Christian gospel a failure in love is obviously serious, but the threat seems out of all proportion here.

Furthermore, would the Ephesians have known what the narrator was talking about? That the narrator knows that "you hate the works of the Nicolaitans, which I also hate" (2.6), suggests that the reader is to imagine a prior relationship between John and the Church, which makes the supposition that they would know what he is talking about plausible. But the accusation is so vague, while the comment on their hatred of the Nicolaitans is so specific. Such a contrast might suggest that we are not necessarily to imagine that the Ephesians possess knowledge of what they are being accused of. What is certain is that, in the text as it stands, we have a devastating criticism made of this Church, couched in deliberately vague terms, given the narrator's proven ability to be specific when he wants to be.

This "double surprise" creates a "gap" for the reader, which (s)he may fill in a variety of ways.[19] Narratively the vagueness of the threat, and its ultimate character are perhaps strategems of control. Remembering that Revelation was read aloud, and that the first-time hearer/reader is extremely vulnerable to the emotional controls of the narrative, it is probable that the narrator's intended effect would strike home with great force. The Ephesians would be flattered by the praises lavished upon them, and nervous of the hugely serious, but undefined, crime of which they are accused. Add to this the identification of the narrator's voice with the Divine voice (in the τάδε λέγει formula) and what has been created is a community securely under the narrator/seer's control.

Furthermore, a question mark has been raised by this way of dealing with the Ephesian community about the identification of the narrator's voice with God's: is this the way God deals with God's people? (Of course, it may be. All the critiques levelled at the narrator could be levelled at God, particularly in view of the textual identification between them. However, as *pray-er/reader* I have "prejudiced" myself against such a reading.) So the illusion the narrator has fostered that his calling has delivered him from being human has already begun to dissolve. The "gap" exists to cast an ironic eye on the narrator's performance, and to enable the knowledgeable reader this time to share in the irony. In other words, the narrative functions as a critique of the very claims it makes.

---

[19] An historical critic such as Schüssler Fiorenza, for example, has filled it by reconstructing a situation of struggle behind the text, in which John is pictured as being engaged in a battle for control of the communities in which the Nicolaitans, Balaamites, and followers of Jezebel appear. The leaders of these groups in Schüssler Fiorenza's reconstruction are rival prophets.

The "gap," then, does two things: it highlights the helplessness of the first-time hearers who are unable to perceive the irony (or are at least unlikely to), at the same time as it highlights the need for the community to have the opportunity for reflection, so that they can share in the irony and free themselves from being so helpless.

As the first letter in the sequence, the Letter to Ephesus creates a situation of crisis in which beliefs and actions have ultimate consequences. Both the rewards offered (2.7, the promise of a return to Eden) and the sanctions applied (2.5, destruction of the church) are final. In addition, knowledge of human success or failure in the call to obedience is beyond rational comprehension, known only to God and the narrator. From a literary point of view, the crisis about which so much has been written is rhetorical, the device, in other words, by means of which the narrator/seer's "world" imposes itself on the "world" of his receptors. Put differently, the narrator/seer creates crisis by means of the narrative. We must also remember that the book's first-time listeners from other Churches heard this message first, and so would have fallen under the narrator/seer's influence before their own situations were presented to them.

What I have acknowledged is myself as-reader entering the drama of the narrator's relationship with the Christian communities in the text, showing how the narrator's initial presentation of himself in secure authority over, and unity with, these communities has crumbled under the pressure of the concrete relationships as they have revealed themselves in the narrative. Not only that, but we have also seen how the narrator himself experiences a fracturing of his identity in the heat of exercising his calling.

It is important also to point to the features in the South African context which have contributed to this engagement with the text: on the one hand, I am the product of a largely "Christian" society which believes deeply in the Bible as the Word of God; on the other, I have seen that status abused for sectional and even inhumane interests, so that struggling with acceptance is a profound scepticism and distrust of authority that claims to be beyond or above discussion or question. I fear the powerlessness, in other words, which the narrator attempts to structure into his relationship with the Christian communities. Narratively, there is a rupture between the narrator's stated pastoral intention and the way he carries it out, which echoes ruptures of a similar sort in my experience between the gospel and praxis. In such a context, reading Revelation does not involve accepting the authority of the prophet in an unquestioning way, but rather engaging with his "performance" critically, in which way a disempowered community may discover that faith grows with its questions. Ephesus becomes an image of every disempowered community, bowing its head under an all-controlling authority. Faith for such communities surely involves engagement with the disempowerment inherent in their situation, rather than a meek and ready acceptance of the structural position they are told is God's will for them. God's "word" is partly the discovery that a "suspicious" stance towards authority has been proved to have been entirely justified.

I will now briefly examine the letter to Philadelphia (3.7–13) to add force to the argument I presented in dealing with Ephesus, but also because this letter draws me-as-actual-reader into a different mode of relationship from the other letters. Where hermeneutical suspicion has been the dominant mode thus far—and would continue to dominate a discussion of Pergamum, Thyatira, and Sardis—Philadelphia draws me away from that suspicious stance into the mercifully restful acceptance which I as priest-and-prayer reader long to give the narrative as well. Philadelphia strikes the reader most immediately as similar to Smyrna. Like Smyrna, it is exemplary in its faithfulness to the Lord; despite outward lack of strength, it has problems with the "synagogue of Satan," and it is exhorted to maintain its faithfulness. However, there are also important differences between the two, these relating to the greater privilege offered this church.

Firstly, Philadelphia is the only church to receive a promise in the middle section, after the phrase "I know your..." (οἶδά σου...) with which the actual address to each church begins: "Look, I have set before you an open door, which no one is able to shut" (3.8). The meaning of the "open door" has been the subject of considerable debate, but as a promise it seems clear that Bousset is correct in understanding it as referring to the community's certain entry into messianic glory (cited in Charles (1.87); see also Beckwith (480) and Mounce [117]). This interpretation also fits best with the dominant concern of the letter which is to assure this church of "little power" of the Lord's protection.

The second privilege is that no other church receives so many promises of the Lord's help than Philadelphia. Apart from this early promise of the "open door, which no one can shut," the Lord promises that the members of the synagogue will "come and bow down before your feet" (3.9), and that he "will keep you from the hour of trial that is coming on the whole world..." (3.10). Smyrna, by contrast, receives only one promise at the end: "I will give you the crown of life" (2.10). The seer pours promise upon promise upon Philadelphia, in a lavish display of special affection and care. Only in this letter does the Lord proclaim his love for a church, which he does in intimate, personal terms: "I have loved you" (ἐγὼ ἠγάπησά σε [3.9]).

Furthermore, this church is required to do absolutely nothing itself, except "hold fast to what you have" (3.11). It seems that this church has done everything expected of it, which is stressed in the symmetrical use in 3.10 of the verb, "to keep" ($\tau\eta\rho\dot\eta\sigma\omega$) to refer to the community's and the Lord's actions: the seer says, as "you have kept my word" ($\dot\epsilon\tau\dot\eta\rho\eta\sigma\alpha\varsigma\ \tau o\upsilon\ \lambda o\gamma o\upsilon\ \tau\hat\eta\varsigma\ \dot\upsilon\pi o\mu o\upsilon\hat\eta\varsigma\ \mu o\upsilon$), so "I will keep you ..." ($\sigma\epsilon\ \tau\eta\rho\dot\eta\sigma\omega$). Here, the use of the same verb and the "tit-for-tat" nature of the promise powerfully suggest the perfection of the church's quality of life. This is a church which is eschatologically prepared. Nothing remains to be done, except to wait for the Lord's eschatological action. Seen in this perspective, Philadelphia is clearly superior to Smyrna or, to compare them in different terms, less in crisis than Smyrna.

The question is what role this letter plays in the narrative. On one level, its tender note of divine love, and its abundant promises of divine protection in the eschatological moment act in the narrative as a whole, as well as in this letter, as an incentive to faithfulness. Philadelphia is where every church should be, in a state of readiness for the parousia. It is significant that 3.11 begins with just that promise, "I am coming soon" ($\H\epsilon\rho\chi o\mu\alpha\iota\ \tau\alpha\chi\dot\upsilon$), the particular wording of which anticipates the ending of the book (see 22.7, 12, 20) and draws further attention to Philadelphia as the exemplary community.

It is important that the readiness of Philadelphia is accepted and presented in the light of its weakness. Philadelphia, we are told, has "little power" ($\mu\iota\kappa\rho\grave\alpha\upsilon\ \H\epsilon\chi\epsilon\iota\varsigma\ \delta\dot\upsilon\upsilon\alpha\mu\iota\upsilon$ [3.8]), yet this observation at no time offsets the divine opinion that this church is absolutely ready for the Lord's coming. Narratively, this brings the hope of eschatological fulfilment closer for all the churches, striking a note of pastoral concern and sensitivity which has been absent in the narrative up to this point. As I have suggested, it shifts the relationship of me-as-reader from suspicion to prayerfulness, preventing a break in relationship between the narrator and me-as-reader, which the analysis so far has made a possibility, and introducing a different dimension of faith into my response.

However, it is also true that something of the incomprehensibility of the narrator's attitudes so far is continued in this letter. We know virtually nothing about this church after reading the letter, which makes it difficult to understand why Philadelphia should be so richly privileged. What we have, then, is a reversal of previous puzzles: whereas in some of the other letters we found it difficult to account for the harshness of the Lord's judgement on these churches (Ephesus, Thyatira, Sardis), here we find some difficulty in accounting for the love lavished on Philadelphia. Admittedly, we are told: "You have kept my word and have not denied my name" (3.8), which is repeated in 3.10 with the important addition, "my word of patient endurance." Unquestionably there is a strong affirmation, intensified by the repetition of this church's adherence to the central values in the book of "keeping" and having "patience," but there is no explanation of why Philadelphia is unique in this respect and deserving of special love, praise, and protection. After all, these values were also present in Ephesus (2.2), in Smyrna (by implication), in Pergamum, and in Thyatira. If we account for the narrator/seer's special attitude to Philadelphia on the grounds of the absence of negative qualities, then we have to ask what privileges Philadelphia above Smyrna, particularly in the light of that church's participation in the martyrdom-value, which is an equally central value in Revelation's story.

This letter, then, shows a pastoral tenderness little evident in any of the others, but makes little attempt to motivate the narrator's unique attitude. In this way, the narrative continues to demonstrate an "irrational" relationship between the narrator/seer and the Christian communities. This "irrational" element is part of the narrative structure of the book's apoclayptic genre, portraying a narrator/seer/Lord who is above accountability in his dealings with human beings, whose part is to submit unquestioningly to the superior/perfect knowledge of the divine word. Thus, I as pray-er/reader am thrust back into a questioning stance, though the pastoral qualities mentioned earlier remain dominant in this letter.

Had I space, I would demonstrate that three other letters, namely, those to Pergamum, Thyatira, and Sardis, reveal surprising ruptures between the narrator and the communities of a similar order to the ones I have examined in the letter to Ephesus and to Philadelphia. Broadly speaking, though, these ruptures, which show themselves in the Greek text more clearly than in English translations, are of two kinds. First, there is a profound lack of clarity about precisely who is being addressed. On the one hand, each church is addressed as a singular unit; on the other, some churches appear also to contain different groups. In those letters in which praise and blame are apportioned, it is often difficult to understand who is being praised and who blamed and for what. For example, in Thyatira (2.18–29) the same group (apparently), addressed by the singular, "your" (σου), which has been praised for its "works" (τὰ ἔργα) is also dammed for "tolerating the woman, Jezebel" and presumably being numbered among her "children" (τὰ τέκνα αὐτῆς) who will be killed. Thus, the same people who are praised for their faithfulness to the highest values of the narrative are accused also of adhering to idolatry, the narrative's most profane value. It is important to emphasize at this point that I am not arguing for some failure of communication in the text: rather, I am arguing that the frequent incomprehensibility and apparent irrationality of the narrator's attitudes are integral to the narrative and part of its meaning.

The second kind of rupture has to do with contending perspectives on spirituality. It is clear, in the letter to Sardis, for example, that the narrator has a very different perception of the church's spirituality from that held by the church itself. This would be true also of a fifth letter—to Laodicea. The significance of this lies in the suspicion the narrator's pastoring "style" occasions that he is seeking to leave the relevant communities with little choice but to accept his perceptions.

The Christian community in these letters is characterized by variety, imperfections, weaknesses, and holiness. The series in chapters 2–3 underlines the dependence of the community on the beneficence of the Lord (narrator). This dependence is increased by the concluding section of each letter, which, as I indicated, seeks to mend the ruptures of the middle section. I mean by this that acceptance is always conditional, applying to "The one who conquers" (ὁ νικῶν). Thus, in these concluding sections, acceptance and the threat of exclusion mingle together. The apparently-confident note with which each letter concludes, "Let anyone who has an ear hear..." (ὁ ἔχων οὖς ἀκουσάτω) suggests that the narrator's "ideal" reader will fully accept the prophetic message. However, the aporias I have identified in the middle sections suggest the opposite, that the narrator has had to work hard to "manipulate" possibly recalcitrant audiences into a submissive response. The struggle between and mingling of these opposites of acceptance and exclusion is the locus for a contextual theology of prophetic and pastoral care. The essence of such a contextual theology is dialogue (in the Gadamerian sense), in which all participants share on equal terms. The narrative of these messages reveals, for this reader, that the will of the Lord is found in dialogue, which is achieved in struggle.[20] The narrator's stance, though, is anti-dialogue, designed to ensure that no dialogue takes place. In the South African context, reading the biblical text must counter the notion that the will of God is found in unthinking submission to some truth supposed to be found in the text and recoverable by someone who claims to reveal it in pure, non-ideological form. Rather, interpreting the biblical text should create opportunities for all readers to engage in dialogue.

I-as-reader suggest, then, that such engagement by the "ordinary reader" is what is projected by the "world" of Revelation. That this is so would be suggested more powerfully had I the opportunity to examine the narrator's reduction of the complex readership of chapters 2–3 to a

---

[20] See Mosala 1986 and 1989 for the notion of the text as a "site of struggle."

single, ideal reader.[21] This reduction occurs immediately when chapter 3 ends, and separate addressees are thereafter absent. From chapter 4 to the end, the narrative addresses no one in particular or, rather, reverts to the addressee of 1.9, who is "your brother who share[s] with you in Jesus the persecution...." Thus, simply by being a reader, every reader shares the invitation extended to the narrator and accepted by him at 4.1–2. And by virtue of never being addressed specifically again in the narrative, the readers who had raised voices of protest in 2–3 are continually silent.[22] In this narrative context, this actual reader acts to resist this enforced silence of the Christian reader. Most of the readers-I-am combine to say that reading this biblical text involves recovering its silenced voices.

In tribute to the marvellous artistry of this book, I should also mention the rich complexity expressed in this narrative move. For by the move he makes from chapter 4, the narrator, on the one hand, widens the gap between himself and the communities with whom he is in relationship. In this way, as I have suggested, he opens up new opportunities for manipulation. On the other hand, this same move draws him closer to his communities by enabling him to mediate the inaccessability of the divinity. In other words, the community is able to share in the wonderful experience of living in the presence of God. Thus narrator and audience are united in a unique experience; and this unity is narrativized in a variety of other ways through the book, which is why Revelation is rightly seen as a resource for understanding and sharing worship.

Conclusions

On one level, what I have done in this paper is nothing new—it is a commonplace today that readers make or contribute to the making of the meaning of their texts. On another level, though, I have sought to acknowledge my presence in the reading and note the impact of the reader-I-am on the meaning I find in the text—to take a step where reader-response criticism has declined to move, in other words. I hope that such a step is seen to be as serious and careful an engagement with the text as in conventional criticism. I also hope that it is clear that the idiosyncrasy which the actual reader must bring to a reading does not conflict with the aim of careful attention to the text itself. In reality, "dialogue," as Gadamer conceives it, insists that all voices present in an encounter be fore-

---

[21] There are indications, scattered through the narrative, that the narrator remembers the individualized readers of chaps. 2–3. These are found in brief reminders that only the faithful will qualify for the rewards (see 14.12; 15.2; 21.27; and 22.15).

[22] There are other voices of protest in the text, the most significant of which are the martyrs at 6.10.

grounded, not hidden. Biblical studies, even of the reader-response variety, has continued to "hide" the voice of the actual reader, thereby impoverishing its dialogue with the biblical text and with other readers.

WORKS CONSULTED

Anderson, Janice Capel
    1985   "Double and Triple Stories, the Implied Reader, and Redundancy in Matthew." *Semeia* 31:71–89.

Aune, David E.
    1987   *The New Testament in Its Literary Environment*. Ed. Wayne Meeks. Library of Early Christianity. Philadelphia: Westminster.

Aune, David
    1990   "The Form and Function of the Proclamations to the Seven Churches (Revelation 2–3)." *NTS* 36:182–204.

Bauckham, Richard
    1993   *The Climax of Prophecy: Studies on the Book of Revelation*. Edinburgh: T & T Clark.

Beckwith, Isbon T.
    1979   *The Apocalypse of John: Studies in Introduction with a Critical and Exegetical Commentary*. Twin Brooks Series. Grand Rapids, MI: Baker <1919>.

Benstock, Shari, ed.
    1988   *The Private Self: Theory and Practice of Women's Autobiographical Writings*. London: Routledge.

Berg, Temma F.
    1989   "Reading In/To Mark." *Semeia* 48:187–206.

Bleich, David
    1975   *Readings and Feelings: An Introduction to Subjective Criticism*. Urbana, IL: National Council of Teachers of English.
    1976   "The Subjective Paradigm in Science, Psychology, and Criticism." *New Literary History* 7:313–34.
    1988   *The Double Perspective: Language, Literacy, and Social Relations*. New York and Oxford: Oxford University Press.

Boring, Eugene M.
    1992   "The Voice of Jesus in the Apocalypse of John." *NovTest* 34:334–57.

Brett, Mark G.
    1991   "Motives and Intentions in Genesis 1." *JTS* 42:1–16.

Caird, G. B.
   1984   *The Revelation of St John the Divine*. 2nd ed. Black's New Testament Commentaries. London: A & C Black <1966>.

Charles, R. H.
   1920   *A Critical and Exegetical Commentary on the Revelation of St John*. Vol 1. ICC. Edinburgh: T. & T. Clark.

Derrida, Jacques
   1976   *Of Grammatology*. Trans. by Gayatri Chakravorty Spivak. Baltimore and London: The Johns Hopkins University Press.
   1982   *Margins of Philosophy*. Trans. Alan Bass. Chicago: Chicago University Press.
   1986   "But, Beyond...(Open Letter to Anne McClintock and Rob Nixon)." Trans. Peggy Kamuf. *Critical Inquiry* 13:155-70.
   1991   "Living On: Border Lines." Pp. 256-68 in *A Derrida Reader: Between the Blinds*. Ed. Peggy Kamuf. New York: Columbia University Press.

Dostal, Robert J.
   1990   "Philosophical Discourse and the Ethics of Hermeneutics." Pp. 63-88 in *Festivals of Interpretation: Essays on Hans-Georg Gadamer's Work*. Ed. Kathleen Wright. Albany: State University of New York Press.

Durand, J. J. F.
   1993   "Theology and Resurrection—Metaphors and Paradigms." *Journal of Theology for Southern Africa* 82:3-20.

Fetterley, Judith
   1978   *The Resisting Reader: A Feminist Approach to American Literature*. Bloomington: Indiana University Press.

Ford, J. Massyngberde
   1975   *Revelation*. AB 38. New York: Doubleday.

Freedman, Diane P., Olivia Frey, and Frances Murphy Zanhar, eds.
   1993   *The Intimate Critique: Autobiographical Literary Criticism*. Durham and London: Duke University Press.

Gadamer, Hans-Georg
   1989   *Truth and Method*. 2d ed. New York: Crossroad.
   1989a   "*Destruktion* and Deconstruction." Pp. 102-13 in *Dialogue and Deconstruction: The Gadamer-Derrida Encounter*. Ed. Diane P. Michelfelder and Richard E. Palmer. New York: State University of New York Press.
   1989b   "Hermeneutics and Logocentrism." Pp. 114-28 in *Dialogue and Deconstruction: The Gadamer-Derrida Encounter*. Ed. Diane P. Michelfelder and Richard E. Palmer. New York: State University of New York Press.
   1989c   "Text and Interpretation." Pp. 21-50 in *Dialogue and Deconstruction: The Gadamer-Derrida Encounter*. Ed. Diane P. Michelfelder and Richard E. Palmer. New York: State University of New York Press.

Garrett, Jan Edward
    1978   "Hans-Georg Gadamer on 'Fusion of Horizons.'" *Man & World* 11:392–400.

Gerhart, Mary
    1992   *Genre Choices, Gender Questions.* Oklahoma: University of Oklahoma Press.

Hans, James S.
    1980   "Hermeneutics, Play, Deconstruction." *Philosophy Today* 24:299–317.

Hemer, Colin J.
    1986   *The Letters to the Seven Churches of Asia in Their Local Setting.* Sheffield: JSOT.

Hendrickson, William
    1982   *More Than Conquerors: An Interpretation of the Book of Revelation.* Grand Rapids, MI: Baker <1940>.

Holland, Norman
    1975   *5 Readers Reading.* New Haven and London: Yale University Press.
    1976   "'The New Paradigm': Subjective or Transactive." *New Literary History* 7:335–46.

Hoy, David Couzens
    1990   "Legal Hermeneutics: Recent Debates." Pp. 111–35 in *Festivals of Interpretation: Essays on Hans-Georg Gadamer's Work.* Ed. Kathleen Wright. Albany: State University of New York Press.

Jauss, H.-R.
    1978   "Theses on the Transition from the Aesthetics of Literary Works to a Theory of Aesthetic Experience." Pp. 137–47 in *Interpretation of Narrative.* Ed. Mario J. Valdés and Owen J. Miller. Toronto: University of Toronto Press.

Ladd, George Eldon
    1972   *A Commentary on the Revelation of John.* Grand Rapids, MI: Eerdmans.

Lategan, Bernard
    1984   "Current Issues in the Hermeneutical Debate." *Neotestamentica* 18:1–17.

Long, T. M. S.
    1993   "Reading the Book of Revelation in South Africa: Some Methodological and Literary Observations in Response to Du Rand." *Journal of Theology for Southern Africa* 83:78–86.

Michaels, J. Ramsey
    1991   "Revelation 1.19 and the Narrative Voices of the Apocalypse." *NTS* 37:604–20.

Michelfelder Diane P. and Richard E. Palmer
    1989   *Dialogue and Deconstruction: The Gadamer-Derrida Encounter.* Albany: State University of New York Press.

Moore, Stephen D.
    1989   *Literary Criticism and the Gospels: The Theoretical Challenge.* New Haven and London: Yale University Press.

Mosala, Itumeleng J.
    1986   "The Use of the Bible in Black Theology." Pp. 175–99 in *The Unquestionable Right to Be Free.* Ed. Itumeleng Mosala and Buti Tlhagale. Johannesburg: Skotaville.
    1989   *Biblical Hermeneutics and Black Theology in South Africa.* Grand Rapids, MI: Eerdmans.

Mounce, Robert H.
    1977   *The Book of Revelation.* ICC. Grand Rapids, MI: Eerdmans.

Pellauer, Mary D.
    1993   "The Moral Significance of Female Orgasm: Toward Sexual Ethics That Celebrates Women's Sexuality." *JourFemStudRel* 9:161–82.

Phillips, Gary A.
    1985   "History and Text: The Reader in Context in Matthew's Parables Discourse." *Semeia* 31:111–38.

Pilgrim, Walter E.
    1989   "Universalism in the Apocalypse." *Word & World* 9:235–43.

Ricoeur, Paul
    1975   "Philosophical Hermeneutics and Theological Hermeneutics." *Studies in Religion* 5:14–33.
    1976   *Interpretation Theory: Discourse and the Surplus of Meaning.* Fort Worth, TX: The Texas Christian University Press.
    1984–88   *Time and Narrative.* 3 vols. Trans. K. Blamey and D. Pellauer. Chicago: University of Chicago Press.

Risser, James
    1989   "The Two Faces of Socrates: Gadamer/Derrida." Pp. 176–85 in *Dialogue and Deconstruction: The Gadamer-Derrida Encounter.* Ed. Diane P. Michelfelder and Richard E. Palmer. SUNY Series in Contemporary Continental Philosophy. Albany: State University of New York Press.

Rogers, Robert
    1982   "Amazing Reader in the Labyrinth of Literature." *Poetics Today* 3:31–46.

Schüssler Fiorenza, Elisabeth
    1985   *The Book of Revelation: Justice and Judgment.* Philadelphia: Fortress.

Staley, Jeffrey L.
    1991   "Stumbling in the Dark, Reaching for the Light: Reading Character in John 5 and 9." *Semeia* 53:55–80.
    1992   "Reading with a Passion: John 18:1–19:42 and the Erosion of the Reader." Pp. 61–81 in *SBL Seminar Papers.* Ed. Eugene H. Lovering, Jr. Atlanta: Scholars.

1994 "The Father of Lies: Autobiographical Acts in Recent Biblical Criticism and Contemporary Literary Theory." Paper presented at a Conference on "Rhetoric and Religion" at UNISA, Pretoria, 15 August 1994.

Swete, Henry Barclay
1977 *Commentary on Revelation*. Kregel Reprint Library. Grand Rapids, MI: Kregel.

Tolbert, Mary Ann
1991 "A Response from a Literary Perspective." *Semeia* 53:203–11.

Weinsheimer, Joel C.
1985 *Gadamer's Hermeneutics: A Reading of Truth and Method*. New Haven and London: Yale University Press.

West, Gerald Oakley
1991 *Biblical Hermeneutics of Liberation: Modes of Reading the Bible in the South African Context*. Cluster Monograph Series. Pietermaritzburg: Cluster.
1993 "The Interface between Trained Readers and Ordinary Readers in Liberation Hermeneutics—a Case Study: Mark 10:17–22." *Neotestamentica* 27:165–80.

III
"READING WITH" WOMEN

READINGS OF *SEMOYA*[1]: BATSWANA WOMEN'S INTERPRETATIONS OF MATT 15:21–28

Musa W. Dube
University of Botswana
Botswana

ABSTRACT

This paper will present some interpretations of Batswana women readers of Matt. 15:21–28. In keeping with the theme of this volume, the aim of presenting their readings is to take seriously the subjectivity and agency of their own interpretations. I shall first give the historical background of these readers and then briefly touch on the methods used to acquire these readings and their framework. Thirdly, I shall present the findings of a questionnaire and the tape-recorded sermons. In conclusion, I shall employ a post-colonial feminist perspective to ask what are the useful models of reading to be drawn from their interpretations.

THE BACKGROUND

The interpretations of Matt 15:21–28 were drawn from women belonging to African Independent Churches in Botswana (henceforth AICs).[2] AICs denote a movement of churches that initially rose in protest against the white-only leadership in the missionary-founded churches of the nineteenth century (Ngubane, 1986:71–90). African Christians walked out of the Western churches and began their own where they could serve God with all their gifts and freedom. Their protest was not only closely tied to the beginning of political liberation movements against colonial rule; it was in itself resistance to Western cultural imperialism.

The rise of AICs was also a search for a spiritual fulfillment. In the Western, missionary-founded churches Africans were presented with a gospel alien to their context, thinking, and needs, primarily because the missionary presentation of the gospel was intolerant of African religious world views and cultures as a whole. In keeping with the modernist thinking of the time, Western Christianity was prepackaged and imported

---

[1] *Semoya* is a Setswana word, which means "of the Spirit." The people of Botswana are called Batswana and their language is Setswana.

[2] I am grateful to the University of Botswana, which provided the funding for this project during the summer of 1994.

to the colonies and expected to be a good fit universally. As J. B. Ngubane points out, colonial preachers "appeared determined to instill in their converts these Western values and a distaste especially for traditional religious values and culture, which were considered inferior and primitive. African converts were expected to adopt a new identity based on the Western-Christian order" (75).

Part of this alienation included an underestimation of simple but important issues such as song, dance, drama, and ritual, which are meaningful forms of discourse for articulating life. Furthermore, "Africans as a whole were not convinced about the inferiority of their religious and cultural values"(Ngubane: 75). Their continued appreciation of African religious worldviews in the face of structured derogation was an act of political resistance against cultural imperialism.

The rise of AICs therefore marked the first groups of African Christians who freely sought to yoke the wisdom of Christianity and African religions in the service of life and diversity. In keeping with the discourse of song, drama, dance, and ritual, such a creative integration was hardly characterized by a systematic theological debate according to theological orthodoxy. Instead, the integration unfolded itself, informed, guided, and justified by perceptions of what enhances and restores life in God's creation. This perspective has made the AICs the biggest church on the African continent in terms of number, distribution, and growth rate. Its membership represent not only those who have a high appreciation of both African religious perspectives and Christianity, but primarily those who will not let cultural imperialism stand in the way of serving life in God's diverse creation.

Various studies of AICs show that pneumatology is central to the theology of these churches. *Moya* or the Spirit is an ever-present agent of God among all the believers. Women and men receive the Spirit, which empowers them to prophesy, heal the sick, assist those searching for jobs, restore family relations, ensure good harvest, good rains, and good reproduction of livestock, and to dispel the ever-intruding forces of evil from people's lives. Healing, as a manifestation of the presence of the Spirit, is an act of restoring life as a whole. The centrality of *Moya* as an agent of restoration through healing has earned these churches the name, *"dikereke tsa Semoya,"* that is, Churches of the Spirit, while the healing manifestation of the Spirit has also earned them the name of *"dikereke tsa phodiso,"* that is, Churches of Healing.

Interestingly, women have always played a central role in these churches as founders, bishops, archbishops, prophets, faith-healers, preachers, and ministers. The rise of AICs and their spirit of protest and integration of religious cultures is traced to a woman from the eighteenth century, Kimpa Vita, a Congolese Catholic Christian who was renamed Donna Beatrice at baptism. Kimpa Vita proclaimed that the Spirit of St. Anthony had taken possession of her. Empowered by the Spirit, Kimpa Vita's preaching became "a powerful protest against the Catholic Church" (Daneel: 46) and colonial government. She wanted all crosses, crucifixes, and images of Christ to be destroyed because, as she said, they were just as good as the old fetishes. She proclaimed that God will restore the subjugated kingdom of Kongo (Daneel: 46). Of significance, however, was Kimpa Vita's articulation of a culturally integrated Christianity. Vita held that Christ came into the world as an African in Sao Salvador and that he had black apostles. Daneel places this proclamation within the proper anti-imperialist context by observing that, "her proclamation gave expression to a deep yearning: the yearning for a Christ who would identify with the despised African;" for "how could the White Christ of the Portuguese images, the Christ of the exploiters—how could he ever help the suffering African, pining for liberty?" (46).

With this radically subversive proclamation for both the colonial church and government, Kimpa Vita was recognized as a dangerous thinker. She was thus condemned to death and was burnt at the stake in 1706. The centrality of women in AICs, however, could not be ended with the crucifixion of Kimpa Vita. A line of other women have ever since heard and responded to the word of the Spirit of God to serve as church founders, leaders, prophets, and faith-healers. Outstanding among these are Ma Nku, Grace Tshabalala, Alice Lenshina, and Mai Chaza, who became founders and leaders of some massive AICs movements in the first half of this century in Southern Africa (Daneel: 46–59; Sundkler, 1976:79–93).[3] Moreover, the women in this study, being leaders and founders, attest that this tradition of women responding to the word of the Spirit remains alive.

For the most part women leaders in the AICs attribute their leadership to a revelation, a vision—which normally reoccurs, instructing one to preach, heal, and prophesy—or to the experience of divine healing after a long illness (Hope and Young: 194). The Spirit that reveals and gives one a vocation and power operates with a significant independence from the written word. This point was underlined by Bishop Virginia Lucas when we asked, "Why are you a female church leader when the Bible seems to suggest otherwise?" She responded:

---

3 Sundkler (1976:79) acknowledges the centrality of women in AICs although he brackets the subject noting, "here is an exciting task awaiting the new generation of African women scholars."

I have been asked this question several times before. I always tell people that when God spoke to me through the Spirit, God never opened the Bible to me. Instead, God's Spirit told me to begin a church and heal God's people, which is what I am doing.[4]

It is against this historical background—political protest of racial and religious discrimination, a search for cultural liberation through integrating Christianity into African religious views, and an experience of God's Spirit empowering both women and men to serve creation—that the following interpretations of Batswana AICs women should be understood. As Daneel has ably expressed in the title of his book, the AICs' approach should be seen as a *"Quest for Belonging."* More importantly, their approach should be seen as a resistance and a demonstrated will to map their own identity in diversity in a world where discrimination against race, gender, and sexual and religious orientation are too often justified at the expense of nurturing difference and life.

Methods of Acquiring the Readings

The interpretations of this paper were acquired through a fieldwork project carried out during the summer of 1994 in Botswana. I was assisted by three research assistants, Fidzani Mafa, Keitumetse Sekhute, and Tsholofelo Matswe, all of whom were Botswana University students at the time. We interviewed over two hundred AICs women from various ethnic groups and geographical areas. Their educational level ranged from complete lack of formal education to seven years of primary school level. Consequently, we often read to them while they listened. Because of their low formal education, most of these AICs women automatically belong to the lower class of the society. This low literacy rate of our respondents is quite consistent with the AICs general membership, and is not surprising given that in colonial times formal education served as an imperialist tool of cultural alienation and assimilation.

We acquired the interpretations in three different ways: administering a questionnaire, recording sermons, and conducting a follow-up seminar on issues that were not adequately addressed. I shall confine their interpretations to the first two methods.[5] First, the questionnaire concerning Matt 15:21–28 was administered to the targeted group. We visited AICs women in leadership positions and asked them to interpret the passage

---

[4] Virginia Lucas is a founding member of the Glory Healing Church in Mogoditshane, Gaborone. Her quoted words are translated inclusively from Setswana.

[5] I am leaving out the seminar findings because this paper will deal with the questionnaire and sermon findings of sixteen women from one particular area, while the seminar involved more women from a wider geographical area.

for us by answering our questions. Except on a few occasions, when we found two or more women together, the questionnaire was administered to women individually. Second, we requested church leaders to preach on Matt 15:21–28 on particular Sundays or on Thursdays, when women's services were held. We recorded their sermons and then analyzed the transcripts.

I chose the passage with the interests and position of AICs women in mind; particularly, the issues of healing, race, gender, and land. These are also my interests, since I am not a complete outsider to the political, social, economic, and cultural experiences that have molded their thinking and practice. Therefore, in approaching the respondents for the interpretations of the passage, I and my research assistants always clearly stated, "We have come to learn from you." This assertion was a genuine search, which in part acknowledges my own difference; that is, it recognizes my Western academic interpretive communities that inform my biblical interpretation and estrange me from their perspective. It was also an acknowledgement of my position and their position as belonging to the suppressed knowledges, and an attempt to subvert the dominant discourses through bringing in different interpretive communities. In short, I was searching for modes of reading that are subversive to imperialistic and patriarchal domination, and I was suspicious of my own training.

The acquired readings were from many different perspectives. Some of them were self-contradictory, a factor which to some extent reflects the difficult nature of the passage. What is presented here is therefore just a fraction of their many interpretations, and it represents a selection on my part given the limitation of space. In fact my very presence as a university researcher affected their interpretations.[6] With this summary of the methods of inquiry, I shall now present the most common reading framework we found amongst the AICs.

A READER'S GRID TO BIBLICAL PASSAGES

The perspective that I wish to present in this paper is one that we encountered several times among our respondents. After reading the pas-

---

[6] The fact that most of the women interviewed were respected for their leadership tipped the power relationship in their favor. However, the historical beginning of the AICs was characterized by censorship and scorn from both the state and church historians. Consequently, most respondents did not understand why we wanted their interpretations. It seemed logical to them that we should seek better interpretations from the mainline churches; that is, missionary founded churches with more educated people. Although we always emphasized that we had come to learn from them, there were times when it was obvious that they felt obliged to give what would be a correct and acceptable interpretation in our eyes.

sage aloud to our respondents, we would begin to ask questions designed to solicit their interpretations of the passage. Frequently, the respondents defined the boundaries of our discussion by pointing out, "*Kana re bua ka dilo tsa Semoya,*" that is, "Remember, we are discussing issues of the Spirit." As mentioned above, *Moya* is a central element in AICs. It is the Spirit that chooses and empowers women and men to be prophets, faith-healers, church founders, and leaders in the service of life.

Semoya (of the Spirit) was thus a prevalent perspective among these sixteen AICs women[7] of Old Naledi, Mogoditshane, and Maruapula, all of which are low income residential areas in and around Gaborone. *Moya* as God's agent of empowerment and communication with people justified the position of these women. As the above conversation with Bishop Virginia Lucas shows, *Moya* is regarded as an ever-present and new word of God.

The interpretations which follow are from sixteen AICs Batswana women readers, most of whom were in leadership positions. The questions are presented in the sequence in which they were asked, and each question will serve as a sub-heading for their interpretations.

The Framework of *Semoya* and Matt 15:21–28

"*Why do you think Jesus went to Tyre and Sidon?*" (v. 21). Eleven readers held that Jesus was following his daily routine of preaching, teaching, and healing. The remaining five held that he was particularly led by *Moya*, the Spirit, to go there in order to meet and heal the daughter of the Canaanite woman. They all assumed that Jesus went to do good. This assumption set the tone for their interpretation of the story.

"*Why did Jesus not respond to this woman's request?*" Six readers said Jesus was testing the faith of this woman. When we questioned this, the respondents held that the act of testing her faith does not indicate a lack of knowledge on the part of Jesus, nor was such an act unusual in matters of faith. Abraham and Job were cited as some of the examples of people who were tested because they already had faith. That the Canaanite woman's faith was tested proves that it was great faith to the AICs readers (v. 28).

Three other respondents also attributed Jesus' silence to a testing of faith. However, they said Jesus was testing the faith of the disciples. In

---

7 I am grateful to the following sixteen women and their churches for providing the interpretations of this paper: Bishop Boitumelo Ngwako, Bishop Virginia Lucas, Bishop Mokgele, Bishop Mmautlenyane, Bishop Mmangwedi, Bishop Mmamadisakwane, Bishop Grace Galetshetse, Mme Mmadipina, Mmamoruti Christina Kasai, Steward Mmamarumo, Mme Mmakokorwe, Moefangedi Mmatshiping, Mme Mmajarona, Mme Mmasebokolodi, Mmamoruti Mmaletsholo, Mme Catherine Kgwefane.

this case, Jesus wanted to see what the disciples would do to help this woman. If this was to test the disciples, they probably failed the test, since we are told that "his disciples came and urged him saying, "Send her away for she keeps shouting after us," (v. 23).

Three respondents said Jesus knew that this woman would finally receive her request, while two said that Jesus was still praying to God to heal her daughter. One respondent said Jesus was in the habit of remaining silent sometimes, as at his trial and crucifixion. Another one pointed out that Jesus was still debating whether to help this woman or not because she was not his follower.

"*Why did Jesus say, "I am sent only to the lost sheep of the house of Israel," (v. 23), and what did he mean?*" The response to this question can be divided into two groups. The first group concentrated on the phrase, "I am sent only to the lost sheep." These held that Jesus was responding to the disciples' request that he dismiss the woman (v. 23). Rejecting their view, Jesus was pointing out that, on the contrary, he could not possibly send this woman away because he was sent to people who were lost, such as this Canaanite woman.

We frequently had to push the respondents to address the specificity of Jesus' statement; that is, "to the lost sheep of the house of Israel." This was not a disturbing question to most of them. "Israel" was interpreted to mean "those who believe." Several respondents asserted that "the lost sheep of Israel" were lost believers. The Canaanite woman was identified with believers, because she came to Jesus with faith (v. 21, 28), but she was also "lost" because her daughter was possessed by demons (v. 21).

Those who accepted that Jesus was neglecting this woman asserted that Jesus was sent to the "lost sheep of Israel," that is, those without faith; this woman, however, had great faith (v. 28). Consequently, Jesus thought this woman was wasting his time because she had all the faith she needed to heal her daughter successfully.

"*Jesus answered the woman and said, "It is not good to take the children's food and throw it to the dogs" (v. 26); Who are the children and who are the dogs? a) Israelites b) Canaanites c) other.* Thirteen out of sixteen held that "children" referred to the Israelites. This interpretation must be understood from their perspective; that is, "Israel" referred to all those who believe in the God of Israel. On the basis of the woman's faith, three held that "children" also referred to the Canaanites.

Concerning the identity of "dogs," most respondents emphasized that Jesus always spoke *"ka ditshwantsho,"* that is, "in parables." This emphasis was a warning that the meaning of his words was not always apparent nor to be taken literally. The answers to this question were more varied. Six said the "dogs" were the Canaanites. One said the "dogs" referred to "the lost sheep," that is, the Israelites. In other words, believers who have now lost their faith. Seven of them held that "dogs" could refer either to the Israelites or the Canaanites, but it generally refers to those who do not have faith. One respondent held that Jesus was challenging this woman to faith since she was not yet one of his believers. Another one said Jesus was just testing this woman's faith.

"Do you think this woman is among the dogs or the children?" While the previous question focused on the nations, Israel versus Canaan, this question focused on the woman herself. Eight respondents were of the opinion that the Canaanite woman was one of the children on the basis of her faith. The other half was of the opinion that she was among the "dogs" for various reasons. Two of them attributed this label to her nationality because the Canaanites did not know God's law. The majority said "dogs" referred not to the woman, but to the demonic spirits. The latter held that Jesus was challenging the woman to believe first, and thus to become a child, before she could receive the children's bread.

Bishop Mmangwedi, one of the respondents, gave this saying of Jesus an ironic interpretation; that is, Jesus was agreeing with this woman and saying, "Indeed it is not good to take the children's food and throw it to the dogs. Rather, it must go to those who deserve it, like you!" This reader used the whole ministry of Jesus to substantiate her ironic reading, holding that generally Jesus was ready and willing to heal and restore life. Another respondent held that the distinction between the "dogs" and "children" should not be overemphasized because both of them designate dependents in the house.

"What does the Canaanite woman mean when she says, "Yes, Lord yet even the dogs eat the crumbs that fall from their master's table" (v. 27)? The majority of the respondents held that this woman perceived how Jesus felt that she did not deserve the children's food, either because of her nationality, inadequate faith, servanthood, demonic spirits, or a lack of faith in the God of Israel. However, the Canaanite woman was insisting that regardless of the nature of her inadequacy, she was not incapable of improving, that is, of picking up the crumbs. Therefore, the woman was insisting that nothing could make her a permanently undeserving child, despite her current inadequacy.

One respondent held that this woman was insisting that she was also a child of God just like the Israelites. This respondent held that through her very word, "even the dogs eat the crumbs," the Canaanite woman became one of the children.

Mmamosebeletsi Mmadipina, a woman who had worked as a domestic servant in South Africa, held that people tend to look down upon other races. Mentioning a few local oppressed groups such as the Basarwa and Bakgalagadi, she pointed out that this woman was humbling herself in the face of humiliation. She found a correlation between the dogs/children, crumbs/food of the passage and the South African apartheid system.

For Bishop Mmangwedi, the interpreter who found irony in this story, the words of the Canaanite woman serve to underline the words of Jesus. That is, while Jesus' answer was negative to the disciples who asked for her dismissal, this woman was actually saying, "Yes, I am one of the deserving children, yet even those inferior outsiders—the dogs—deserve something." In other words, the Canaanite woman's response endorsed and surpassed that of Jesus by holding that no one was totally undeserving.

"What did Jesus mean when he said, "Woman, great is your faith. Let it be done to you as you desire"? (v. 28). Their response hinged on two aspects: *boitshoko le tumelo*, that is, "perseverance and faith." Jesus' words and the healing of the daughter were perceived as the recognition of the woman's faith and her perseverance through all that seemed to hinder her wishes. At this point, the response of Jesus was said to express his appreciation of the sincerity of her faith, which was not shaken by silence, the disciples' requests, or Jesus' statements.

"*Is this story a case of racism between Canaanites and Israelites?*" The answers were yes and no, for different and contradictory reasons. Six of the eleven who affirmed that it was racism did not substantiate their answers. The other five gave various observations. One of them said, "But what is important is that we should overcome racism as it is overcome in the story." One of them said this story served to show us that apartheid was real in the world. While another identified the passage as a racist case, she also held that the story showed that Jesus had come to do away with it. Two of them identified the discrimination of the passage as pertaining to those with faith and those without, between good and evil rather than between two different races.

Two of the five respondents who denied that this was a case of racism did not give any reason for their answer. Three others said the story was about testing the woman's faith to help her understand her own standpoint.

Regardless of whether the respondents identified racism in the passage, they consistently emphasized that Jesus came for all people.

INTERPRETATION THROUGH SERMONS

It must be noted that in the questionnaire we brought our preset questions and asked respondents to answer back. We were initiators, and to some extent we predetermined our findings. In a sermon setting we were not initiators, but listeners. We wanted to listen to the interpretations as they would occur under normal circumstance without the intrusion of a researcher. Although I cannot claim that our presence did not affect the mode of their interpretations, our findings in these visits were indeed significantly different from those of our questionnaire.

Their sermons were generally characterized by methods of interpretation rather than content. In other words, the meaning of the passage was intricately woven into the acts of interpretation. In presenting these findings, I will speak of communal interpretation, participatory interpretation through the use of songs, interpretation through dramatized narration, and interpretation through repetition.

To begin with communal interpretation, it must be noted that in most AICs preaching is not the exclusive right of one individual during a service. Once the text of the day has been read, all are free to stand up and expound on the text. This communal form of interpretation is inclusive and allows the young and old, women and men, to be heard in the church, if they so wish. Here communal interpretation becomes a ritual of bonding, as all members participate.

Communal interpretation is supplemented with participatory interpretation through songs. While the preacher is expounding the passage, listeners can contribute to the interpretation by occasionally interrupting with a song which elaborates on the theme of the passage according to the way they understand the preacher. Conversely, the preacher herself/himself can pause and begin a song that expresses the meaning of the passage. For example, in the case of Matt 15:21–28, one of the songs interjected was, "*ante Jeso one a mpona ha ke lela jwale,*" that is, "Oh, so Jesus was listening to my plea when I pleaded." The song underlines the Canaanite woman's plea for help and Jesus' positive response. Its use becomes the listeners' way of participating in the interpretation of the passage.

Most interpretations were largely grounded on the assumption that "a story well told is a story well interpreted." This traditional method of interpretation capitalizes on recalling, narrating, and dramatizing the story without explicitly defining what it means. Instead, the meaning is articulated by graphically bringing the story to life through a dramatic narration. Those who lacked the gift of dramatic presentation still laid emphasis on the act of recalling and retelling the story almost verbatim. Although it was particularly striking and confusing that in most cases the dramatic retelling was all there was to the interpretive act, we soon realized that the nuances of interpretation were to be read in the interjected songs and the repeated phrases.

Repetition as another mode of interpretation emphasized a particular point or theme. For example, speakers who viewed the seeking of healing as the point of the story would repeat perhaps two or three times the Canaanite woman's request, her insistence, and the guaranteed healing (v. 22b, 25, 28). Those who found the test of faith to be the main theme tended to repeat Jesus' silence (v. 24), his discouraging statements (v. 24, 26), the disciples' request (v. 23), and, finally, the triumph of enduring faith (v. 28). This mode of interpretation, as an oral exercise, was accompanied by the use of tone, such as a raised, lowered, or whispering voice to underline whatever point the interpreter wished to highlight.

Although I have highlighted communal and participatory modes of interpretation, we encountered several other churches where the pastor was the only speaker of the day while the rest silently listened. Similarly, while dramatic recalling, retelling, and repetition was quite prevalent, it was by no means the only way of reading. There were several other churches who struggled with the metaphors of the story and tried to explicate them. Some employed other biblical stories to interpret the passage, and others drew examples from everyday life. I have called these modes of interpretation traditional, assuming that they arose organically from the culture, but at the end of my research one respondent gave a biblical reason for their guarded ways of interpretation. She read Rev 22:18, which says, "I warn everyone who hears the words of the prophecy of this book: if anyone adds to them, God will add to that person the plagues described in this book."

In sum, the questionnaire and sermon findings highlights the difference in methodological approach. The questionnaire reflects my academically informed approach, which is both Western and textual-centric. The sermons, on the other hand, reflect an approach which is both oral and indigenous. Obviously, my Western training has oriented me toward textual-centric interpretations and leaves me less equipped to give an in depth understanding of oral interpretations. However, it was through combining these two different methods, my own training and their own expertise, that I perceived myself as "reading with" these AICs women.

A Post-Colonial Feminist Perspective

Since the aim of this volume is to take seriously the subjectivity and agency of non-academic readers, what are the strengths and models of reading to be drawn from the interpretations of AICs women? To address this question, I am using a post-colonial feminist perspective. A post-colonial perspective is a framework that takes into consideration the global experience of imperialism: that is, how the eighteenth to twentieth century imperial powers constructed or construct their subjects and themselves to justify colonialism and imperialism, and how narratives are instrumental in this process. As used here, the word imperialism denotes the tendencies of metropolitan centers to impose various forms of domination—military, environmental, religious, economic, and linguistic—on foreign nations on a global scale. Imperialism attempts to impose sameness by suppressing difference. Colonialism, as one of the manifestations of imperialism, denotes the geographical occupation and control of one nation by another.[8]

A post-colonial perspective on the Bible asks what has been the role of the Bible in justifying imperialism and why? It seeks to know how we can read the Bible in the light of its role in imperialism (Banana: 17–29).[9] Such a perspective is not peripheral to the AICs biblical readers, who arose out of colonial oppression, and neither is it avoidable, for on the African continent more so than anywhere else colonialism was justified and effected through the Christian religion (Mishra and Hogde: 288). As the classic approach of David Livingstone eloquently sums up, imperialism and colonialism in African nations was championed through a complex network of "Christianity, Commerce, and Civilization" (Thomas: 67–68). Since African nations are struggling to emerge from the whole experience of being subjected to this dehumanizing oppression and exploitation, one cannot skirt the question of "how can we read the Bible as post-colonial subjects?"[10]

Feminist biblical perspectives hardly require explanation, given their prevalence. Simply put, their frameworks propound various perspectives that take cognizance of the history of gender oppression and seeks to imagine, articulate, and map ways of reading and living which fight gender oppression and affirm the agency of women (cf. Anderson:103–34). Western biblical feminists seek to understand both how the Bible has been used to justify gender oppression and ways of subverting it. For a post-colonial feminist the concerns become wider (Donaldson; Blunt and Rose). Not only does one struggle with the role of the Bible in the oppression and liberation of women, one also struggles with how to read the Bible given its role in the subjugation and exploitation of one's nation and continent. Therefore, a post-colonial feminist seeks to become a decolonizing reader, that is, one who strives to recognize an imperializing text:

---

[8] See Said: 3–186 who gives an in depth analysis on the role of narratives in the justification of eighteenth to twentieth century imperialism.

[9] Banana struggles with the same issues and suggests that other religious traditions are equally valid and should be recognized.

[10] Said (43–61) argues that imperialism constructed both the colonizer and the colonized. Thus he holds that a post-colonial critic of narrative belongs to both Western and non-Western literary departments.

how it represents other lands and people, how it claims a self-justifying power to travel, to enter different nations, to observe and to teach them, and how it uses gender to legitimize the exploitative imposition of universal standards. A decolonizing reader strives to arrest the violence of an imperializing text by exposing its effect and seeking ways of perceiving and promoting difference. Put differently, a post-colonial feminist is concerned with ways of reading that counteract various forms of imperialism and gender oppression rather than bracket or perpetuate them.

A post-colonial feminist approach does not hope to repeal the history of imperialism, but neither does it easily subscribe to the often unquestioned assumption that Christianity is universally sound for the whole globe (Kwok Pui-lan: 25–42). Instead it asks the following questions: does history show us that this universalism has been achieved through respect for various cultures? If not, how can the Christian gospel interact with other cultures' perceptions of the divine? A post-colonial feminist approach seeks to know who is served by the universalism of Christianity: is it the imperial centers or the subjugated? These are some of the questions and concerns confronting a post-colonial feminist reader of the Bible, yet I believe that these AICs women readers offer us strategies of interpretation that are born out of a struggle with issues of both imperialism and sexism. In their interpretations we encounter a will to define and promote a gospel that restores and affirms difference in the lives of Canaanites and Israelites, of women and men, of blacks and whites, of African religions and Christianity, of the word of the Spirit and the written word. In short, we encounter a search for decolonizing and for healing.

SUBJECTIVITY AND AGENCY OF AICs READERS: A POST-COLONIAL FEMINIST ANALYSIS

What then are the strategies of reading offered by AICs for today's world? I define today's world as a multi-cultural global village, where different cultures are increasingly forced to live with each other. Through the history of eighteenth to twentieth century imperialism and on into current forms of communication, we are increasingly thrown into contact with one another. Thus the need to develop better forms of dialogue and interaction is imperative. To answer the above question, I shall look at four aspects of their readings: the framework of *Semoya*, the wisdom of a creative integration of different religious traditions, a feminist model of liberation, and healing as a political struggle. I shall conclude by asserting that the AICs' approach articulates a commitment to the restoration of life in our diverse creation.

To begin with the framework of *Semoya*, what strategies of reading does it offer us? It is important to recall once again that *Moya*, the Spirit, is central to the AICs. It is *Moya* that empowered them to reject the discriminative leadership of missionary founded churches and to begin their own churches. From the beginning, *Moya* revealed to them the beauty of the gospel, its justice, and its inclusiveness over against the discriminative tendencies of the colonial church. Consequently, when they rejected the discriminative colonial church, they took upon themselves the responsibility of interpreting the gospel from a *Semoya* perspective. A *Semoya* framework, therefore, is a mode of reading that resists discrimination and articulates a reading of healing: healing of race and gender relations; of individuals, classes, and nations.

As the above interpretations show, a *Semoya* framework presupposes that there is something good for all people within the gospel. This is apparent in the first response when readers understand Jesus as going to Tyre and Sidon on his daily routine of healing, teaching, and preaching. Concerning the Canaanite woman who came to meet Jesus, a *Semoya* perspective also assumes the prophetic operations of the Spirit that revealed and led Jesus to this region in order that he should meet the Canaanite woman and heal her daughter.

In keeping with their historic beginnings, that is, the AICs' rejection of a discriminatory gospel and their move to creatively define a gospel of healing, a *Semoya* framework is inclusive. The inclusiveness of a *Semoya* reading is apparent in the respondents' interpretations of "Israel" and "Canaan." Israel has become an all-inclusive category for all those who believe in God. Their inclusive reading also became evident when we raised the question of discriminatory nuances in Matt 15:21–28. Respondents emphasized that *Jeso o tletse batho botlhe*, "Jesus came for all people." There was a stern refusal to give in to racial discrimination between Israel and Canaan. Such a standpoint was even underlined by the group which acknowledged racial discrimination, but pointed out how Jesus overcame it; hence, emphasizing that we are also challenged to overcome it.

This insistence on reading for healing of relations, and the belief in the inclusiveness of the word of God was brought home to me when one reader explained the relation of Canaanites and Israelites. "Israelites were taken from Egypt, where they were enslaved," said the respondent, "and sent to Canaan, a land that flowed with milk and honey. This Canaanite woman with great faith illustrates for us what it means that their land flowed with milk and honey." This imaginative interpretation articulates the power and will of their inclusive vision.[11] By asserting that the land of the Canaanites was rich both materially and spiritually, this reading is a subversive post-colonial reading; it invalidates the imperial strategies that employ the rhetoric of poverty and lack of religious faith among the colonized to justify dominating other nations. It is a reading that confronts a story that has been extensively used to justify imperial imposition and apartheid to articulate a reading that affirms liberating interdependence and healing between different races.

Second, their approach exhibits the wisdom, the courage, and the creativity of integrating different religious faiths in the service of life and difference. Historically born within the imperial times, which proceeded by dispossessing people of their cultural and religious integrity through promoting Christianity as the universal religion, the AICs subvert this imperial strategy. They reject the imposition of Christianity as the one and only valid religion and they freely cull from both religious cultures whatever wisdom these traditions offer in the enhancement of life and nurturing difference. For today's multi-cultural and multi-faith global village, a mode of reading that allows one to encounter and to acknowledge the strength and weaknesses of our different cultures, and to respectfully learn cross-culturally is imperative. These AICs women readers offer just this mode of reading.

One may be asking what is the aspect drawn from African religious views in this paper? First, the emphasis on healing; its approach and its function, which I shall further elaborate below, is a thoroughly African religious world view. Second, I have constantly referred to *Moya* or Spirit, without adding its biblical adjective "Holy."[12] I have maintained this expression, because it is how the AICs women readers generally spoke. More importantly, the Spirit as the divine agent, which enters and empowers women and men, is quite prevalent in African religious spirituality. Therefore, in the claims of *Moya* we encounter a perfect example of the integration of two religious traditions, a fact well-documented by AICs' scholars (Sundkler, 1976:237ff.). This validation of two different traditions is both a strategy of resistance and healing from imperial cultural forces of imposition, which depends on devaluing difference and imposing a few universal standards. Their anti-imperial strategy does not subscribe to the artificial cultural dualisms and hierarchies that are constructed for the interest of domination and suppression of difference.

---

[11] Weems (71) notes that the fact that some "factors are suppressed in the reading process says more about the depth of human yearning for freedom than it does about lack of sophistication on part of the readers."

[12] Hinga (191) speaks of the centrality of the Spirit in AICs without explicitly saying the "Holy" Spirit.

More importantly, this creative integration offers a positive model for today's multi-cultural and multi-faith global village: how difference can be encountered, critiqued, and nurtured.

Third, the *Semoya* strategy of reading does not only resist imperial forces of imposition and domination, it also offers a feminist model of liberation. The AICs women insist the written word is a tradition of wisdom, which has goodness for all, but they are by no means limited to it. They maintain that God's agency is contained but not limited to the written word. They experience divine communication directly through God's Spirit, and they have experienced God's Spirit empowering them for human service. As Virginia Lucas said, when God spoke to her, "*God never opened the Bible.*"

Through listening to the word of the Spirit, the AICs women offer a feminist strategy that breaks free from the patriarchal and canonical constraints of biblical traditions. It allows them to claim divine empowerment and leadership despite their gender. Moreover, this feminist model of reading is by no means ungodly or less biblical. It is biblically grounded, since such books as John provide for a direct dependence on the Spirit (Jn 14:26). It is also godly because it is guided and justified by whether the word of the Spirit empowers one with the responsibility to restore and enhance life through leadership and healing.

Fourth, healing among the AICs is an articulation of political resistance and survival. Before I expound on this aspect, let me elaborate a few points about their healing activities. To start with, most AICs are also healing centers. Their healing services are open to members and non-members, believers and non-believers, that is, the community in general. Healing practices are not miraculous or limited to prayer and laying of hands. Rather it involves drinking holy water, taking cleansing baths, offering sacrifice, using ashes, oil, candles, sea water, and techniques of massage and internal cleansing, etc. Another significant factor about their healing practices is that healing embraces all aspects of one's life; that is, it includes tackling unemployment, breakdown of relationships, bad harvests, lost cows, evil spirits, bodily illness, and misfortune. In short, healing becomes an act of restoring and maintaining God's creation against all forces that inhibit the fulfillment of individuals in society.

Evidently, this use of healing is a political struggle against structural forces behind unemployment, breakdown of family relationships, poverty and lack of success. Through their claim that God's Spirit empowers them to heal these social ills, AICs join hands with God in a constant struggle against institutional oppression. They offer the promise and the solution. This space of healing becomes their political discourse of confronting social ills, not as helpless beings who are neglected by God, but as those who are in control and capable of changing their social conditions. This confrontation of the social ills has undoubtedly made AICs the biggest and most popular churches, for they address the political struggles of Africa and offer solutions.

Conclusion

In conclusion, a *Semoya* reading is a framework that since its historical beginnings witnesses to God's agent, the Spirit, empowering people of different religions, cultures, classes, races, and gender. This framework refuses to accept defeat, rejection, imperialism, unemployment, breakdown of relationships or any form of incapacity; that is, *even dogs can pick up the crumbs*. Thus a *Semoya* reading relies on the direct agency of the Spirit, which by its revelations and power equips different people to participate creatively in the daily process of restoring and empowering God's diverse creation to its fulfillment. Reading from a *Semoya* perspective, therefore, is an act of reading the written word for healing and hearing the word of the Spirit for empowerment.

Works Consulted

Anderson, Janice Capel and Stephen D. Moore, eds.
    1992   *Mark & Method: New Approaches in Biblical Studies*. Minneapolis: Fortress.

Appiah, Kwame A.
    1992   *In My Father's House: Africa in the Philosophy of Culture*. Oxford: Oxford University Press.

Banana, Canaan
    1993   "The Case for a New Bible." Pp.17–29 in *Rewriting the Bible: The Real Issues*. Ed. L. Cox and I. Mukonyora. Gweru: Mambo.

Blunt, Alison and Rose Gillian, eds.
    1994   *Writing Women and Space: Colonial and Postcolonial Geographies*. New York: Guildford.

Chrisman, Laura and Patrick Williams, eds.
    1994   *Colonial Discourse and Post-Colonial Theory: A Reader*. New York: Columbia University Press.

Christensen, Torben and William Hutchinson, eds.
    1982   *Missionary Ideologies in the Imperialist Era: 1880–1920*. Denmark: Forlaget Aros.

Cox L., I. Mukonyora, and F. J. Verstraelen, eds.
  1993   *Rewriting the Bible: The Real Issues*. Gweru: Mambo.

Daneel, Inus
  1987   *Quest for Belonging*. Gweru: Mambo.

Donalson, Laura
  1992   *Decolonizing Feminisms: Race, Gender and Empire-Building*. London: University of North Carolina Press.

Felder, Cain Hope, ed.
  1991   *Stony The Road We Trod: African American Biblical Interpretation*. Minneapolis: Fortress.

Fraser, Jendayi, ed.
  1994   *Africa Today: Resistance and Rebirth in South Africa* 41/1.

Hope, Marjorie and J. Young
  1981   *South African Churches in Revolutionary Situation*. Maryknoll, NY: Orbis.

Hinga, Teresia M.
  1992   "Jesus Christ and the Liberation of Women in Africa." In *The Will to Arise: Women, Tradition, and the Church in Africa*. Ed. Mercy Oduyoye and Musimbi R. A. Kanyoro. Maryknoll, NY: Orbis.

Kwok Pui-lan
  1989   "Discovering the Bible in the Non-Biblical World." *Semeia* 42:25–42.

Mishra, V. and B. Hodge
  1994   "What is Post(-)colonialism?" Pp. 276–90 in *Colonial Discourse and Postcolonial Theory: A Reader*. Ed. Laura Chrisman and Patrick Williams. New York: Columbia University Press.

Mosala, Itumeleng J. and Buti Tlhagale, eds.
  1990   *The Unquestionable Right To Be Free: Black Theology from South Africa*. Maryknoll, NY: Orbis.

Mudimbe, V. Y.
  1988   *The Invention of Africa: Gnosis, Philosophy, and the Order of Knowledge*. Indianapolis: Indiana University Press.
  1994   *The Idea of Africa*. London: James Curry.

Ngubane, J. B.
  1990   "Theological Roots of the AICs and Their Challenge to Black Theology." Pp. 71–100 in *The Unquestionable Right To Be Free: Black Theology from South Africa*. Ed. Itumeleng Mosala and Buti Tlhagale. Maryknoll, NY: Orbis.

Oduyoye, Mercy A. and Kanyoro Musimbi, eds.
  1992   *The Will to Arise: Women, Tradition, and the Church in Africa*. Maryknoll, NY: Orbis.

Oosthuizen, G. C.
  1968   *Post-Christianity in Africa*. London: C. Hurst.

Said, Edward W.
    1993   *Culture and Imperialism*. New York: Alfred A. Knopf.

Schüssler Fiorenza, Elisabeth, ed.
    1993   *Searching the Scriptures. Volume 1: A Feminist Introduction*. New York: Crossroad.

Segovia, Fernando F. and Mary Ann Tolbert, eds.
    1995   *Reading From This Place. Volume 1: Social Location and Biblical Interpretation in the United States*. Minneapolis: Fortress.

Setiloane, G.
    1976   *Images of God Among the Sotho-Tswana*. Rotterdam: A. A. Balkema.

Sugirtharajah, R. S., ed.
    1991   *Voices From the Margin: Interpreting the Bible in the Third World*. Maryknoll, NY: Orbis.

Sundkler B.
    1961   *Bantu Prophets in South Africa*. London: Oxford University Press.
    1976   *Zulu Zion and Some Swazi Zion*. Oxford: Oxford University Press.

Thiongo, Ngungi
    1986   *Decolonizing the Mind: The Politics of Language in African Literature*. London: James Curry.
    1993   *Moving the Center: The Struggle for Cultural Freedoms*. London: James Curry.

Thomas, Norman E., ed.
    1995   *Classic Texts in Mission and World Christianity*. Maryknoll, NY: Orbis.

Weems, Renita J.
    1991   "Reading Her Way Through the Struggle: African American Women and the Bible." Pp. 57–77 in *Stony the Road We Trod: African-American Biblical Interpretation*. Ed. Cain Hope Felder. Minneapolis: Fortress.

Engaging Popular Religion:
A Hermeneutical Investigation of Marian Devotion in the Township of Mpophomeni

Megan Walker
University of Natal
South Africa

ABSTRACT

This paper investigates the meaning of Mary for a specific group of people on the margins of the church and society. It seeks to find out whether and how the Marian texts of faith may become sources of a contemporary liberative Mariology. It seeks to locate the worlds which Mary opens up for people through examining the expressions of Marian devotions in KwaZulu-Natal and at the meaning which the figure of Mary conveys to those who take part in such devotions, and engaging these meanings in critical conversation.

Introduction

I have argued elsewhere that the figure of Mary, when viewed from a feminist perspective, has at best functioned ambiguously in Christian tradition (1991a:153). This, after all, is hardly surprising for the dominant Marian texts of faith, like all dominant texts, are distinctly ideological, i.e. they are the product of a kyriarchal, patriarchal, androcentric, and clerical world that was often misogynist and which used the figure of Mary to perpetuate its own ideal of "the feminine." Given this, theologians are left with the question of how we may legitimately speak of Mary in a way that does not perpetuate the oppressive use to which she has been put. How are we to claim continuity with the faith of the church in a way that will allow alternative and liberating readings of the Marian texts?[1]

The best way forward is to engage in a dialogue between the tradition, critical feminist scholarship, and the faith of ordinary people, especially those who are on the margins of church and society (Walker, 1991a:157). I suggest we use what West (155ff.) describes as an "in front of the text" hermeneutic that locates the meaning of Mary in the world which she opens up for her receivers; in order to locate this world we need to consider the role played by popular religion.

---

[1] I am using "text" here in Ricoeur's sense of meaningful action as text (1981d: 197ff.).

I am consciously seeking an "interested" as opposed to "interesting" reading of the Marian tradition.² In other words, I view the potential of the Marian tradition to promote human liberation and wholeness as a key interpretive category. By way of introduction I discuss an appropriate hermeneutic for theologising about Mary and the role of popular religion in such a hermeneutic. The bulk of the essay investigates the role of Marian devotion in a specific context. Out of this discussion I suggest ways forward in our ongoing task of theologising about Mary.

Hermeneutics for a Liberative Marian Theology

The question that I bring to Marian theology is the same question that Sandra Schneiders has asked of the New Testament (3), namely, how can a text that is oppressive of women function as both foundational and normative for its readers? How are we to claim continuity with a tradition that has functioned to define and control women according to its essentially patriarchal and androcentric ideals? In responding to this dilemma Schneiders proposes a hermeneutic that locates the meaning of the text in the world that it opens up for those who receive it. She argues, following Paul Ricoeur, that understood in this way, even an intrinsically oppressive text can function in a way that is liberating for those who receive it.

For Ricoeur the various texts of a tradition assume a certain autonomy with respect to the intention of their author, their original cultural situation and the social conditions that affected their production, and their original addressees (1981a:91). Ricoeur argues that texts become freed from their original context in such a way that they can take on new meaning as they are interpreted in new contexts. Here we find the possibility, according to Schneiders, "not only of multiple valid interpretations but of the text's exploding the very world out of which it came and whose prejudices and errors it ineluctably expresses" (7). As Ricoeur says,

> An essential characteristic of a literary work, and of a work of art in general, is that it transcends its own psycho-sociological conditions of production and thereby opens itself to an unlimited series of readings, themselves situated in different socio-cultural conditions. (1981b:139)

So, for him,

> A hermeneutics of the power-to-be thus turns itself towards a critique of ideology, of which it constitutes the most fundamental possibility. Distanciation, at the same time emerges at the heart of reference: poetic discourse distances itself from everyday reality, aiming towards being as power-to-be. (1981a:94)

---

² For a discussion of the difference between "interesting" or detached and "interested" or committed readings see West (51ff.).

We can see that for such a hermeneutic the real referent of the text is located in front of the text in the world which the text opens up for people. Ricoeur says that "what is sought is no longer an intention hidden behind the text, but a world unfolded in front of it" (1981a:93). It is this world that the text is finally about (Schneiders: 8).

For Ricoeur, then, the properly hermeneutical moment arises when one turns one's interrogation towards the sort of world opened up by the text. This is the world that the reader has to appropriate. The text, which has been decontextualised by the process of distanciation, becomes recontextualised as it is appropriated by contemporary readers who explore and exploit its surplus of meaning (Schneiders: 7). Appropriation does not involve the projection of oneself into the text but rather receiving an enlarged self by apprehending the proposed worlds which are the genuine object of interpretation (Ricoeur, 1981c:182).

If the focus and the authority of the text lies in the world which the text opens up for people, then it becomes essential to know what that world is. We need to ask what meaning Mary gives to the lives of those who receive her.

POPULAR RELIGION AS THE HERMENEUTICAL LOCALE[3]

Moreover, within a liberationist paradigm, we need to ask what worlds Mary opens up for those who are on the margins of church and society. Theologies of liberation require that we not only make an "option for the poor" but that we also accept the "epistemological privilege of the poor." This involves an epistemological paradigm shift in which the poor and oppressed are seen as the primary interlocutors of theology (Frostin: 6).

Looking for liberating Marian meaning in popular expressions of Marian devotion is not without contradictions, for the world of those who are poor and oppressed has been and continues to be distorted by the ideological interests of the dominant. We need to grapple with the question of whether and to what extent popular religion is a reflection of social alienation and furthers such alienation, or whether it is a site of resistance and struggle. In other words, is it oppressive or liberatory?

The early liberation theologians were often hostile to popular religion, because they saw it as serving to entrench further situations of oppression and alienation. A catechesis magazine published in Medellin in 1968 stated:

---

[3] I am indebted to Scannone (222) for this phrase.

> The manifestations of popular religiosity—even if they sometimes show positive aspects—are, in the rapid evolution of society, the expression of alienated groups—that is, of groups that live in a depersonalized, conformist, and noncritical manner and do not make efforts to change society. (Cox: 234)

Such a position is understandable, for popular religion can and sometimes does lead to a resignation that simply reinforces an oppressive status quo. As a "strategy for survival" popular religion takes on the character of a supernatural power to help or console the individual. Thus it can act as a factor of adaptation to domination and reinforces the fatalism of "poverty culture" leading to popular resignation and alienation (Parker: 30). In this way the people themselves transmit their own oppression from generation to generation, because they have "incorporated their enemy and tyrant into their own religious structures" (Dussel: 86).

While there is undoubtedly truth in such an analysis, this is not the only way in which popular religion functions. Dussel has remarked that "the field of popular religion is not totally in the hands of the shamans; it also has room for prophets. It is a field of conflict, and for that reason, can serve the interests of the dominated classes, in other words, liberation" (87). It would seem that popular religion can, at least in certain circumstances, also motivate people for acts of liberation. In Latin America popular religious cults, often those surrounding Mary, have played an important role in motivating people to political action (Dussel: 92f.).

The positive significance of popular religion may be seen also as it constitutes a crucial aspect of people's identity and has supported and sustained this identity over and against those who seek to undermine it. Elizondo claims that, while popular expressions of faith function in different ways in different contexts:

> For a colonised/oppressed/dominated group, they are the ultimate resistance to the attempts of the dominant culture to destroy them as a distinct group either through annihilation or through absorption and total assimilation. They will maintain alive the sense of injustice to which the people are subjected in their daily lives. (37)

In the same way that people have often incorporated their enemy and tyrant into their religious structures and symbol systems, they have also, perhaps at the same time, incorporated symbols of resistance. Parker argues that people collectively produce symbolico-religious representations and practices by a process that shows both their oppression and their relative autonomy. "By means of a process of meaning-production, which both conditions and is conditioned, the different sectors and subordinate classes express through their manifold religious activities, a *symbolic protest*" (29).

I am therefore arguing for an extension of the hermeneutical method outlined above. This method locates the meaning of the Marian tradition not only in the worlds which Mary opens up for her receivers, but more specifically in the worlds which Mary opens up for those who are marginalised and oppressed. This is not to limit her to these worlds or to deny the possibility of other meaning, but it is to give them a certain privileged position in our interpretation of the person of Mary. It is to understand her primarily through the lenses of those who are the victims of history.

Marian Devotion in KwaZulu-Natal and in Mpophomeni

Writing from the South African context, Takatso Mofokeng has argued that the African Independent Churches are the South African institutional home of popular religion. Like popular groups in Latin America they enable the lower working classes to "survive the stressful social, economic, political, and psychological contradictions of an emerging industrial society that is permeated by aggressive racism" (15). In addition, various groups within the mainline Churches provide powerful examples of popular religion, for example, within the Catholic Church the various sodalities, such as the Women of Saint Anne and the Legion of Mary, as well as popular practices such as Marian pilgrimages. These are largely outside of clerical control and on the margins of the official structures of the church.

In what follows I describe research undertaken in 1991 in KwaZulu-Natal at both a regional and parochial level. I focused on the Marian pilgrimages and on the role of Mary in the sodalities, especially the Legion of Mary. In this research I consciously adopted a phenomenological and qualitative approach, because I was concerned with the meaning of Marian devotion for the people from Mpophomeni whom I interviewed, rather than with the extent of such devotion or with an "objective" account of it.

The Marian Pilgrimages

Situated in the Archdiocese of Durban, the people of the Mpophomeni parish have been influenced by developments both in that diocese and in the Diocese of Mariannhill. Indeed many of the people in Mpophomeni originally came from areas in the Mariannhill Diocese. The process of evangelisation in these dioceses, and the region that they represent, was heavily impacted by the Oblates of Mary Immaculate and the Missionaries of Mariannhill (originally Trappists). Both of these congregations had a strong Marian devotion: given this, it is not surprising that both dioceses should develop specific Marian pilgrimages. It was these two pilgrimages, at Kevelaer and at Nshongweni, that I investigated during 1991.

Kevelaer: Consolatrix of the Afflicted

Kevelaer Mission, situated near Bulwer in southern KwaZulu-Natal, was founded by the Trappists of Mariannhill in 1888 and was named after the Marian shrine of Kevelaer in the German Rhineland. In the 1940s the parish priest, Father Vitalis Fuchs, CMM, obtained a copy of the famous medieval picture which was venerated in Kevelaer in Germany and built a pilgrimage Church to house it, turning Kevelaer into the pilgrimage shrine of the diocese of Mariannhill. From 1947 onwards pilgrims have been regularly flocking to Kevelaer (Weinmann: 123f.).

Although smaller group pilgrimages occur at various times, the main diocesan pilgrimage takes place annually in August around the Feast of the Assumption. In 1991 the pilgrimage began with people sitting on the ground in a large square between the Church and a sanctuary area in the front. It officially started with Mass at approximately 6 p.m. at which several bishops were present and warmly welcomed. There was then a break of a couple of hours, followed by sermons, and then just before midnight most of the participants lit their candles and went on a candle-light procession. Praying the rosary as they went several thousand people walked approximately two kilometres. After another break of a couple of hours, the concluding Mass was held shortly before dawn.

During the night queues of people filed past the shrine to pray and to leave letters, petitions, and gifts, at the statue of the Pieta. The people have little relationship with the holy picture brought from Germany, which they were originally intended to venerate, but have a visible relationship with the statue of the Pieta with which they seem more able to identify (Weinmann interview). This is perhaps not surprising for the title under which Mary is venerated at Kevelaer is that of Mother of the Afflicted or Consolatrix of the Afflicted, the one who consoles those who are suffering. Clearly, as we will see below, their understanding of Mary as someone who has also suffered, strengthens people's identification with her and, it may be argued, increases her importance for them.

During the course of the night there are also many priests available to hear confessions, and many people make their confessions. Many people also bring plastic containers, which they fill with water from a fountain outside the Church. This water, which has been blessed during the pilgrimage, is considered to have special powers and there are reports of it, or simply of the "Mother of Kevelaer," helping them with their sickness and problems (Weinmann: 125 and interview).

Since its inception in 1947 the Kevelaer pilgrimage has grown in size with many people coming from beyond the borders of the diocese. Weinmann estimates that in 1984 there were approximately twenty-two thousand pilgrims (127). While numbers have declined due to violence and other factors in recent years, there were nevertheless several thousand people present when I attended in 1991. One prayer of petition was said in English at Mass; otherwise the whole pilgrimage was, to the best of my knowledge, in Zulu.

One interesting feature was the presence of non-Catholics at Kevelaer. While I have been told that there are also increasing numbers of non-Catholics attending the Nshongweni pilgrimage, they were not obviously visible, whereas at Kevelaer I saw several people wearing the distinctive dress of the various African Independent Churches as well as a few Methodist *Manyano* women, complete with rosaries.

Nshongweni: Our Lady, Mediatrix of all Graces

The Nshongweni shrine and pilgrimage also came into being in the late 1940s. The parish priest of Nshongweni, Father H. Wagner, OMI, had already been encouraging devotion to Mary among his parishioners before he was called up to serve in the French army during World War II. His parishioners prayed to Mary for his safe return, and he made a vow that if Mary brought him safely back to the Nshongweni mission, he would propagate her cult by establishing a pilgrimage shrine (Weinmann: 129 and Khumalo interview).

On his return in 1942 Father Wagner acquired two old statues, one of Mary and one of Saint Joseph. He stored them away intending to use them later. His parishioners discovered them and gathered before the statue of Mary to pray to her. Although Father Wagner discouraged them at the start and said that they should rather pray before the big statue of Our Lady of Lourdes, which was in the Church, they persisted and came as pilgrims for every Marian feast (Weinmann: 129).

Slowly during the late 1940s and early 1950s the pilgrimage shrine became established at Nshongweni. In 1952 the statue was placed on a basement of granite stone so that the crowd could see it from a distance. Later a new amphitheatre was built to accommodate the growing number of pilgrims who started to come from as far afield as what was then the Transvaal.

The annual pilgrimage is held on the weekend nearest to the 31st of May to mark the Feast of the Visitation, or, as Bishop Khumalo puts it, the Feast of Mary the helper. Mary is venerated at Nshongweni under the title of Our Lady, Mediatrix of all Graces. She is seen as the one who assists people in obtaining God's graces. Believing that she will assist them in getting God's help people come to her and pray for their various needs. Many testify to the ways in which Mary has helped them as a result of going on the Nshongweni pilgrimage.

A concern on the part of the organisers is that the pilgrimage should provide an opportunity not only for people to bring their needs to Mary but also for those who have perhaps lapsed in their Christian life to come and make a good start again. Hence the emphasis on rousing sermons and the availability of priests to hear confessions (Khumalo interview).

The pilgrimage started at about 6 p.m. when a group of mostly women on the platform-cum-sanctuary at the front of the natural amphitheatre began leading those present in songs to Mary. We were then welcomed by a priest. This was followed by several sermons, interspersed by hymns to Mary. One of the sermons in particular was geared to helping people prepare for confession, and many priests were available to hear confessions. After the sermons and some singing, the rosary began with a hymn being sung between each decade. Mass followed at about midnight at which the Archbishop presided and preached. After Mass there was the blessing of the sick, followed by another sermon. After this, sometime around about 2 a.m., the candlelight procession began. This must have lasted a couple of hours as thousands of people processed behind the statue of Mary that was carried through the fields near the mission. Once everyone had returned from the candlelight procession the last service, Benediction of the Blessed Sacrament, began. This ended shortly after 5 a.m. after which people departed.

Reflections on the pilgrimage experience

In opting to go with people on the pilgrimages I was taking on the role of a participant observer (Walker, 1985:6). Thus I went as a pilgrim as well as an observer. I prayed the rosary and carried a candle in the candlelight processions, as well as observing, and trying to work out the meaning of, what was going on. Of course, the extent of my participation varied from activity to activity.

The two pilgrimages have distinct orientations. Nshongweni, as that of Our Lady, Mediatrix of all Graces, enables people to bring their requests to Mary, as well as calling them to conversion. Kevelaer, as that of Mary, Consolatrix of the Afflicted, enables people to see Mary as identifying with them as they, also, bring their petitions to her.

I found Kevelaer to be more controlled by the hierarchy; there was a great fanfare when the bishops arrived, which did not happen at Nshongweni. There also seemed to be a greater lay participation at Nshongweni. While these are only impressions, they may reflect differences not only between the different pilgrimages, but between the dioceses themselves.

The difference is also reflected in the different structure of the two pilgrimages. The programme at Kevelaer had large gaps between events, whereas at Nshongweni everything followed one after the other. While the gaps at Kevelaer were no doubt intended to give people the chance to pray privately, to go to confession, or to visit the statue (all of which people did anyway while other things were going on at Nshongweni), I got the impression that they had quite a disruptive effect. It also gave the impression, to me at any rate, that people's participation, in a communal sense, was dependent on priests (or bishops) saying Mass or preaching. This was in contrast to the common participation at Nshongweni where, in between other things, catechists led people in praying the rosary together.

However, even at Nshongweni, I sensed a certain disunity between the private and public prayers of people and the message that was being preached. While the preaching apparently focused on justice and peace with particular reference to the centenary of the papal encyclical *Rerum Novarum*, and while people were clearly praying for peace and justice, it was unclear how this related to Mary. While Bishop Khumalo, chairperson of the organising committee, insisted that everything, including justice and peace, comes through Mary, I did not get the impression that there was any particular Marian content to the message being proclaimed (Khumalo interview).

Thus a dichotomy seemed to exist between the act of praying in which Mary is all (or nearly all) important, and the content of people's desires, which did not seem to relate particularly to Mary. This can be seen as linked to Weinmann's comment that although Mary is important for people personally, she is not usually seen as linked to social or national life (interview). This is an issue that we will return to later.

We must note, nonetheless, the importance and influence of ordinary people in both pilgrimages. Despite the pilgrimage having been organised by the hierarchy, it is the people who make the pilgrimage and who were, particularly in the case of Nshongweni, responsible for the emergence of the event. It is also the people who give the pilgrimages their distinctive meaning. For example, the people have not venerated the images which the priests intended them to, but have rather persisted in the veneration of other statues, which they were better able to relate to and which the priests were consequently forced to accept.

Mpophomeni: The Parish of Saint Anne

While the pilgrimages are the most prominent expressions of Marian devotion at a regional level and attract people from various parishes, I was concerned with pursuing the meaning of Mary for people from one local parish. I therefore opted to follow up research on the pilgrimage with interviews with people from Saint Anne's parish in Mpophomeni.

The township of Mpophomeni is located about fifteen kilometres from Howick in the midlands of KwaZulu-Natal and serves as the main Howick township. It came into existence in the early 1970s, although a number of different groups of people were moved into it at different stages after that. It was particularly affected by the strike at BTR Sarmcol in Howick in 1985 in which just under a thousand workers were dismissed and by the ensuing consumer boycott. These events united the community, and it developed a reputation of supporting NUMSA (National Union of Mineworkers of South Africa) and COSATU (Congress of South African Trades Union). In these struggles the Catholic Church was seen as supportive of the strikers, and the then parish priest, Father Larry Kaufmann, CSsR, was among those detained in the security police crackdown in 1986.

Between 1986 and 1990 Mpophomeni was subject to a number of attacks from Inkatha vigilantes, beginning with an attack in December, 1986, in which four residents were abducted and killed. The community's experience was that the police, instead of protecting them from the attackers, were involved in harassing and assaulting them. They did succeed in getting a court order against the police. Saint Anne's Church was, on one occasion, set fire to during an attack.

During the second quarter of 1990 it seemed that peace was returning and vigilante attacks stopped. The community focused on rebuilding the township. It had grown significantly, with vast numbers of refugees moving in. In May 1991 violence again broke out, this time between different groups of youth in one of the wards. Although both were officially supporting the ANC (African National Congress), there were allegations of both police and Inkatha involvement. Things quieted down after May, but they flared up again in early July with several people being killed and a number of houses burned. The township was quite tense when I did my interviews, and the people were clearly concerned about, but also confused by, the violence around them.

Marian devotion in the parish

The primary expressions of Marian devotion in the Mpophomeni parish centre around the pilgrimages, the common praying of the rosary, occasional hymns at Mass, and the activities of the Legion of Mary (St. Amour interview). The pilgrimages are high points of the year for many people, although fewer people attend them than in many other parishes. The rosary is the primary form of devotion for many people, who pray it either individually or in common. During the violence the practice was started of praying the rosary for peace at noon. The Church bell was rung daily and people were expected to pray for peace; at least some of them coming together in neighbourhood groups to do so. The rosary is also prayed in common in the various sodalities, as we shall see below.

The sodalities, with particular reference to the Legion of Mary

Within the parish, but also extending to an international level in some cases, there exist four sodalities. These are the Legion of Mary, the Sacred Heart of Jesus Association, the Saint Anne's Women, and the Catholic African Women's Association. These sodalities need to be understood in terms of people's need for group association and the support, as well as the status, that this brings. It is common for members to belong to more than one association at the same time, thus acquiring extra papal indulgences (Sempore: 49; Weinmann: 94).

While sodalities traditionally were encouraged by the Church, contemporary Catholic ecclesiology and pastoral planning is more hesitant about them and sees them as representing a somewhat elitist notion of the Church in which they are seen as, according to Pope Pius XXII, the prolonged arm of the hierarchy (Prior: 18). The Lumko Missiological Institute discourages sodalities and prefers the vision of Church offered by that of Small Christian Communities in which the Church is seen as a communion of communities (Prior interview). According to Father Edgar Weinmann, CMM, then parish priest of Mpophomeni, the activities of the various sodalities in the parish, while good in themselves, are the sort of things that should be happening anyway, preferably through Small Christian Communities (interview).

The sodality which I discuss in this paper is the Legion of Mary. It was founded in 1921 by an Irish layman and describes itself

> as an association of Catholics, who, with the sanction of the Church and under the powerful leadership of Mary Immaculate...have formed themselves into a Legion for service in this warfare which is perpetually waged by the Church against the world and its evil powers. (Graef: 151)

It is organised along military lines, and its members place themselves at the total service of Mary, becoming "a slave of Mary" (Graef: 151).

The Legion of Mary first came to Natal in 1937 when it was established in the Mariannhill parish. Today its local headquarters are in Umlazi, Durban, although it still comes under the international movement whose headquarters are in Ireland. Weinmann sees the Legion of Mary as, internationally at any rate, a fairly reactionary movement, although it does not function this way in Mpophomeni (interview), and claims that its manual "is not yet influenced by the recommendations of the Vatican Council II and is not taking into account the justified longing of people to be autochthonous in their Church structures and to be able to express one's faith in one's own culture" (115).

The Legion of Mary takes on a life of its own in the Mpophomeni parish which does not seem to be particularly influenced from the outside. It meets every Sunday after Mass to pray the rosary and other prayers of the Legion; during the week its members are involved in various apostolic activities, such as visiting and praying with the sick, caring for the old, consoling bereaved families, instructing children, visiting lapsed Catholics, etc. It sees its mission as bringing people to Mary so that she can lead them to Jesus, and as doing the work of Mary (Lavuna interview). It also seems to be involved in organising and motivating people to go on the pilgrimages.

Central to the Legion is its prayer, particularly the rosary and the Magnificat. Although there are also special Legion prayers, its members are obliged to pray the rosary and the Magnificat every day. They also encourage Marian prayer in the parish, getting people to pray the rosary before Mass on Sunday and carrying popular devotions into people's homes.

Many of the people whom I interviewed in the Mpophomeni parish belong to the Legion of Mary and so we shall further consider its impact on people's lives and faith below.

The Meaning of Mary for the People of Mpophomeni

We have seen that Marian devotion is clearly an important religious phenomenon in KwaZulu-Natal and in Mpophomeni. In the research which I did with a group of people from the Mpophomeni parish I sought to understand the meaning of Mary for them. I was particularly concerned with the extent to which Marian devotion can function in a liberating and life-giving way.

Description of Research

My main research tool in this task was depth interviewing. The depth interview has been described by Walker as "a conversation in which the researcher encourages the informant to relate, in their own terms, experiences and attitudes that are relevant to the research problem" (1985:4). A depth interview is not bound by a rigid questionnaire as the researcher is free to follow up ideas introduced by the person being interviewed. It does not lack structure; the researcher has some broad questions in mind, although these are adapted to each situation (Jones: 46ff.). The analysis of depth interviews, moreover, is clearly an interpretive activity in which the researcher is an active participant.

I interviewed twenty people from the Mpophomeni parish. Most of the interviews were in Zulu, hence the need for interpretation. Although three people were able to respond in English, at times two of them needed an interpreter. In this I was assisted by a woman from the parish, Mrs. Hilda Lavuna, who took me around, introduced me to people and arranged for me to interview them, and, in some cases helped with interpreting. A theological student, Sister Maxentia Mkhize, FSF, did most of the interpreting for me.

The length of interviews varied, but on average they lasted about an hour and were conducted in people's homes. I tape-recorded them and worked with transcripts in seeking to analyze and interpret them.

I wanted to find out what the dominant "texts" of faith are for people and what messages they convey about Mary. I was also particularly concerned with how people understand Mary in relation to their sociopolitical and economic context, and particularly her relationship to situations of violence and poverty, as well as with the extent to which they can see her identifying with them.

All of the people whom I interviewed welcomed us warmly and spoke of the interviews as a chance of renewing their faith. They clearly saw us as part of the Church and identified with it, and some insisted on praying before the interview began. The people interviewed were not a representative cross-section of the parish but people selected by Mrs. Lavuna whom she thought would be helpful. An unrepresentatively large proportion of them belonged to the Legion of Mary, which reflected both her own involvement in the Legion as well as our particular research interests. I did not have a problem with this for I was attempting not a neutral or positivist collection of data, but rather an interpretive theological exercise.

The Research Findings

Expressions of Marian devotion

The most widespread form of Marian devotion which I found among the twenty people I interviewed was praying the rosary. Almost everybody seemed to pray it regularly, and one person described it as the best way of getting in touch with Mary. Another person, who described his troubled life, said that he survived through praying the rosary. A couple of people spoke of how they would pray the rosary at any given opportunity, such as when they travelled on the bus, or when going to sleep. For most people the rosary seemed to function as their most basic form of prayer. As one person put it, when it is time for them to pray, they pray the rosary. It is the primary way in which people present their requests to Mary and share with her their troubles and sufferings. It is also used as a way of giving thanks and praise to Mary.

There were also several other prayers to Mary which people said were important to them. The one most often named was "Khumbule Maria":

> Remember, O most gracious Virgin Mary, that never was it known that anyone who fled to thy protection, implored thy help, and sought thy intercession, was left unaided. Inspired with this confidence, I fly unto thee, O Virgin of virgins, my Mother. To thee I come, before thee I stand, sinful and sorrowful. O Mother of the Word Incarnate! despise not my petitions, but in thy mercy hear and answer me. Amen.

Other prayers named were the "Hail Mary," "Hail Holy Queen," "We fly unto thee our Patroness," and the various prayers of the Legion of Mary. One person also spoke of the practice of making novenas, a set of devotions stretched over a period of nine days.

Several people also spoke of having their own private prayers which they said to Mary from their hearts. They expressed the importance of just speaking to Mary, and telling her everything, especially when they are afraid. Some people described the results which they had seen through praying the rosary and other prayers to Mary. One woman said that if she was troubled and she prayed the rosary, her troubles were solved after just one mystery. A number of people claimed that Mary had protected them in times of danger. She was also said to have helped people to find jobs, pass at school, find the right husband, and settle domestic quarrels.

Almost all of the people I interviewed had been on at least one of the pilgrimages although they were not necessarily able to go regularly. Some people spoke of financial and health constraints that made it difficult for them to go. Of the ten people who regularly go on the pilgrimages, six of them go to both pilgrimages while three go to Nshongweni and one to Kevelaer.

Those people who go on the pilgrimages regarded them as an opportunity to renew their faith. Several people described the pilgrimages as a chance to give praise and thanks to Mary and to express their love and devotion to her. The pilgrimages also provide them with a chance to pray and to present their petitions to Mary and to share their needs and sufferings with her. As one woman put it: "It means to be with her and to tell her all what I am and all what I am pondering in life." A couple of people explained the importance of the communal nature of the pilgrimages and said that the other people there also prayed for them and that they gained strength through other people's prayers. One man said that it had been important for him to take his children on the pilgrimages and present them to Mary. People stated the results of having gone on the pilgrimages. Not only did they feel renewed, but several people related the way their circumstances had changed after the pilgrimages.

While two people stated the importance of praying at the statue of Mary, and one of the importance of touching the statue, for most of the people it seemed that the experience as a whole was important. The opportunity and the challenge of spending the night in prayer was something direct and personal, outside of the realm of clerical mediation. As one man said, it is a time when nobody can ask for him. He is asking for himself, irrespective of whether a priest is saying Mass or preaching sermons. The clerical activity is not important; it is rather the whole experience in which he actively participates that is important.

The texts of faith

When asked how they come to know about Mary, most people said that they come to know about her through the Scriptures or through Bible (and other) stories. They did not have a particularly literate knowledge of Scripture, with a couple of people not being able to specify a biblical story about Mary, and one person saying that she was unable to read, immediately after saying that the Scriptures were her primary source of information about Mary. Indeed one Biblical reference quoted was clearly inaccurate, referring to Mary of Bethany rather than Mary of Nazareth, while another, that of Mary crushing the head of the dragon, not only mixed up a dragon and a snake, but clearly presumed a certain ecclesial interpretation of Scripture. Thus it seems that while Scripture is given a symbolic importance as a source of truth, people's actual beliefs about Mary are passed on more through a multi-faceted, and primarily oral, network.

This can be illustrated by looking at what was by far the most important biblical motif for most people, namely the story of the Annunciation. The Annunciation is also the subject of a hymn, "*Kwake Kwathi uMaria*," which describes Gabriel's visit and Mary's response. This hymn was regarded as being particularly meaningful for people. Furthermore, people are made aware of the story of the Annunciation through the recitation of the rosary, of which it comprises a decade, as well as through the Hail Mary, the dominant prayer recited in the rosary, for it recalls the angel's words to Mary.

It is therefore not surprising that other sources that people gave for their knowledge of Mary were songs, catechetical instruction, sermons, prayers, and advice from their elders. Of these, songs and sermons seemed primary. Nobody cited pictures or statues as important for conveying information about Mary. When questioned about them, some people gave examples of pictures that they liked. In the same way the people did not seem to pay very much attention to the picture of Mary in the Church (Weinmann interview).

Thus it does seem that Marian meaning is conveyed through a primarily oral network. We should not see this in isolation however, for many of the Marian practices, through which the oral messages come, clearly involve a ritual dimension. They clearly also involve more than just a cerebral knowledge but enable people to enter into a relationship with Mary which they experience as both helpful and empowering.

Mary's importance for people

It is clear that Mary is an important person for all of the people interviewed. She is seen as a great woman, the great mother, and the Queen of heaven. She has conquered evil and is seen as the mediator between people and God, as the only mother who can help us. Mary, it was claimed, can do anything for people.

Mary is seen as important because she brought Jesus, the saviour, into the world, and therefore she plays a crucial role in salvation. For most of the people I interviewed her primary importance lies in her ability to intercede for them to God, to help provide for them and protect them. Mary was compared both to an ancestor, through whom one normally goes to God, and to a mother in a family, through whom one normally goes to the father. People spoke of the way in which they turned to Mary in any type of need and the way in which she protected them, healed them of sickness, helped them find work, helped them pass in school, and defeated evil spirits. As one woman said, "Mary is able to help us all if we ask her, and she can give us anything that we're asking from her, because she is the important person who is in the place of helping other people."

Seen in these terms, Mary's importance seems to lie in her Goddess-like attributes. This fits more with pre-Vatican II mariology, which stresses Mary's privileges and sees her on the divine side of the divine-human divide, than it does with post-conciliar mariology, which sees Mary as representative of the Church.[4] Such "maximalist" mariology could be criticised not only on the grounds that it diminishes the impor-

---

[4] See Tambasco (10) for the distinction between Christotypical or "maximalist" and Ecclesiotypical or "minimalist" mariology.

tance of Christ as well as enforcing patriarchal stereotypes, but also on the grounds that it encourages resignation in the face of injustice and oppression. While such a mariology may offer a very real and possibly legitimate source of support and a tool for survival, by positing Mary as the great provider it tends to diminish people's responsibility to take control of their own lives.

Mary is important to people for further reasons. Several people spoke of the importance of Mary having suffered. They cited the way she had been forced to give birth to Jesus in a stable and live in a situation of poverty, as well as the way in which she had seen her son condemned to death and crucified. This image of the suffering, sorrowful mother is clearly one with which people feel able to identify and from which they derive strength. Several people spoke of difficult circumstances in their own lives in which they were able to identify with Mary. That Mary stayed with her son as he was dying and persisted in her faith in the face of death, rather than running away, is both an encouragement and example to people in situations of suffering and violence. As one woman said, "Even if the guns are shooting we must keep on praying to Mary, ask her because she knows what it is to suffer, she underwent such things."

Several of the women I interviewed were able to identify with her because she was a woman, and, in some cases, also, because she was a mother. One woman said that "as Mary is a woman who went through what we are going through, like sufferings, like perseverance, I think that for us women we do need to have that strength and perseverance in facing sufferings."

Some of the women also spoke of the importance of Mary being a mother and of their ability to identify with her in that. It was important to them to know that Mary knew what it was like to be pregnant and to give birth. Thus the common experience of motherhood seemed to establish a bond between these women and Mary.

For one woman, Mary's womanness and motherhood tended to undermine and denigrate her own sexuality and motherhood. She said that she appreciated the fact that Mary was a woman but said "I can't identify with Mary. I just feel ashamed because my own womanness is for this world and for Mary it is for heaven." A similarly negative attitude to sexuality was apparent in another woman who could not see how Mary could provide an example for her as she was not a virgin or a religious. She seemed to limit following Mary to those select groups.

A more positive attitude was expressed by one woman who seemed to see Mary as legitimising women's participation in the life of the church. A convert from Lutheranism, she claimed that the presence of Mary in the Catholic church meant that women could stand up, speak, and witness in the church, something which she had not experienced as a Lutheran. Thus there seemed to be, for her at least, some correlation between feminine Marian imagery and a certain freedom for women.

Thus, while Mary's primary importance for people seemed to be as a great mother, Goddess-type figure, who sometimes served to enforce patriarchal views about both motherhood and sexuality, there are also other ways in which she is seen as important. Along with the role of provider, there is also an emerging role of fellow-sufferer through which some people are able to relate to Mary as one who strengthens and supports them and even, in one case, legitimises their identity as women in the church.

Mary in a context of violence and oppression

The situation of violence in which they found themselves was clearly a cause of great concern for the people interviewed. It was also a cause of some confusion since they didn't know who was behind it, although they had some suspicions, or what to do about it. Everybody I interviewed thought that Mary was upset about the violence and saw her as sharing their sorrow. One woman thought that "even if Mary is looking down to Mpophomeni she is crying even as we are crying. Maybe she is even saying 'Oh, my poor children, just look how you kill each other.'"

People were generally uncertain what Mary could tell them to do about the violence, other than praying to her. Everybody insisted that they should pray to Mary to end the violence. One woman claimed that the violence was due to people not having prayed to Mary (citing some apparition where Mary is said to have warned people of coming disaster if they did not pray the rosary). Most people were generally clear that Mary wanted the killing to stop. They understood her as wanting people to love and respect one another and be reconciled with one another. They saw Mary as wanting to bring love into the situation so that people could live in unity.

People were also fairly clear that Mary was opposed to situations of poverty and oppression. They thought that if Mary could speak to the rich and powerful she would tell them to stop oppressing the poor. One person pointed out that it was not the poor's fault that they are poor. Most people were clear that the rich had a duty to help the poor and also that the poor needed to pray to Mary for help. However, while five of those interviewed maintained that Mary does not side with either the rich or the poor but loves all of her children equally, the bulk of those interviewed saw Mary as clearly on the side of the poor, and four people quoted the Magnificat where Mary claims that God has cast down the mighty and exalted the lowly.

Most of the people interviewed saw Mary as someone who could identify with them and who could even come and live among them; indeed, as one person insisted, Mary is already among them although they do not necessarily realise it. For some, this was related to Mary's particular option for the poor. Mary was seen as herself a poor person who knows what it is like to be in their situation; therefore, she could be with them and struggle with them. As one person said:

> I think that Mary can come to this place and identify with the people because I know that Mary knows what it is to suffer. She herself suffered in this world. I remember the time when Mary had to give birth to Jesus. She had no place and she used a terrible place, the stable, to give birth to Jesus. And after that Herod persecuted Jesus; he wanted to kill this child. And Mary, it was painful to Mary to know that, so much that she had to leave the place and go to another place as she went to Egypt. So I believe that Mary can come and stay with the people and suffer with us...I have no doubt that Mary loves those who are suffering most.

For another woman, Mary's identification with the poor and the fact that God chose Mary, who was a poor woman, is a statement about how God works. She says that

> it can be a lesson to our society if Mary takes sides with the poor, showing the people that God also comes to the poor people, because Mary, being poor herself, she is the very one who brought Jesus into this world. God sent the angel to Mary. And there were rich people; and the people in the place, I think that they were all expecting Jesus to be born from a rich family, but that never happened.

I had gathered from some priests and pastoral workers, and from my own experience in another parish, that any attempt to introduce works of art depicting Jesus or Mary as black was often met by resistance from the people, who could only see them as white, as this was how they had always been depicted. Moreover, all of the statues and pictures that I saw in people's homes, and the icon that was in the Church, clearly depicted Mary as a white woman. I was therefore concerned to see whether Mary's identification with people extended to their being able to see her as black.

With the exception of one woman who could not conceive of Mary as anything other than white, everybody else could quite happily see her as a black woman. Some people stressed that Mary is for all people. Therefore she will adapt herself to whatever people are. As one woman said: "if you are black, she's black; if you are white, she's white. It's what you are then she is that thing what you are." However some people also seemed to see her as more specifically related to them. As one woman said "because I'm speaking of her as my mother...so my mother is a black, so she is a black."

I was also concerned with the extent to which people related to Mary exclusively as a mother, or whether they were also able to relate to her in other ways. Cavalcanti has noted the predominance of mother imagery, over and against sister or companion imagery, in the Latin American context, although Gebara and Bingemer note that this is changing and that the image of the great mother is giving way to the image of Mary as a companion along the way (162ff.). Although the dominant imagery for the people I interviewed was mother imagery, and while six of the people interviewed could not conceive of Mary in any other way, the bulk of those interviewed could also relate to Mary as a sister, or as a friend, or as a companion, or indeed in various other ways. Some people spoke of being able to share things with Mary that they wouldn't be able to share with a mother. One person gave Mary's friendship with Elizabeth as an example of the sort of sharing relationship which she has with Mary.

The potential for liberation

Here we come, in a sense, to the heart of the matter, namely, whether Mary remains simply an object of devotion who can dispense favours to people from her heavenly throne, or whether there is the potential for her to become a companion who inspires and motivates people's earthly faith and struggles. While the primary importance of Mary for the people interviewed clearly seemed to relate to her importance as an object of devotion, I believe that we can also see an emergent image of Mary as fellow-sufferer and fellow-struggler.

I have noted Mary's importance as the great mother who is the object of veneration, answerer of prayers, protector, healer, and mediator between people and God. Although she may well fulfil legitimate needs of people in this role, it is in many respects problematic.

From a purely orthodox theological point of view, in this role Mary runs the risk of overshadowing Christ as mediator between God and humanity and reflects a position which sees Christ as remote and somewhat inaccessible, similar to the way in which the humanity of Christ was downplayed to such an extent in the Middle Ages that people turned to Mary as a substitute. While such a position would appear to fit in with a traditional African view in which, as one person said, Mary is a good ancestor, we need to ask whether it is legitimate to displace the central importance and the crucial humanity of Christ.

For, although Mary's importance obviously reveals a need on the part of people for a mother figure, or at least for a feminine aspect to the divine, I have argued elsewhere (1991a:146ff.) that to see Mary as a substitute Goddess tends only to entrench further ideas of male dominance and female dependency. Several people explained Mary's importance through reference to the family structure in which the mother is the way to the father. Thus Mary's importance as intercessor and mediator arises out of a fundamentally patriarchal world-view.

Furthermore, we need to question the extent to which Mary, as an object of devotion, can really empower people to take control of their own lives. The view of Mary as the great provider to whom people pray for their needs can be said to encourage passivity and can easily be exploited by those in power in either Church or society. Linked with this is what Weinmann terms the emphasis on Mary's privileges at the expense of her virtues (interview). The veneration of Mary for that over which she had no control (her virginal motherhood, Immaculate Conception, etc.) tends to remove her from the sphere of imitation and example. While most of the people interviewed were able to talk of following Mary, doing so was a secondary concern, and some were unable to see Mary as setting an example to be followed.

Thus the dominant view of Mary as object of devotion and great provider is problematic, but it would be simplistic to write it off entirely. Not only does it provide consolation and support for many people, it also represents a complex system of meaning production that, whatever its distortions, does provide people with experience of the divine. We need to note its dangers and to look for alternative and complementary Marian meaning.

Mary as fellow-struggler

Mary is also seen as someone who is identified with people in their sufferings and struggles. She is someone who, after the example of the Magnificat, takes an option for the poor. As a poor woman she suffered with her son when he was crucified. She stands as an example to people to stand firm in the face of oppression and suffering.

I grant that this is not the dominant view of Mary found among those interviewed. It was present, to a greater or lesser degree, in the majority of cases even though it was often intertwined with other views. Thus it can be said to present a possibility and a starting point for developing a liberating theology of Mary.

Drawing the Dialogue Together: Groundwork for a Theology of Mary

I now consider some of the hermeneutical questions that this study has raised before outlining a possible framework for theologising about Mary.

Questions of hermeneutical method

An important feature of popular religion is that it is a form of religious expression that is owned and controlled by the people themselves, rather than by a select group of clergy or intellectuals. The Marian devotion which I researched is relatively free of clerical control and mediation, and it may even contain within itself the seeds of protest against such control. It is, moreover, a phenomenon that is sometimes viewed with suspicion, and even distaste, by some clergy and intellectuals.

While acknowledging the importance of people's involvement in defining and controlling their own religious expressions, this also raises some problems. Popular devotion is not simply the "pure" religious expression of the people themselves, but also reflects various outside influences and interests, which may have been internalised, as well as beliefs which may have arisen from the people themselves but which are not necessarily liberating. If one follows Scannone (231ff.) in arguing that the role of the theologian is to assist the people in discerning truth and distortion in popular religion, then one needs to be clear about one's basis for doing this and the criteria used.

The question of outside influence

The very introduction of the element of criticism involves introducing a certain outside influence. The ideal found in certain Latin American theologians in the mid-seventies, namely that of simply structuring and defending the faith of the people (Segundo: 23), an ideal which Nolan also seems to subscribe to (165), is not really feasible. Indeed Segundo has shown that the very theologians who espoused this ideal found that they were not really able to hold to it (19).

Criticism needs to be exercised with great sensitivity and with a great respect for the faith of the people, which must be our theological starting point. For example, my analysis presupposes a feminist and liberationist perspective which is suspicious of the ways in which people's images of Mary may have been distorted to further the interests of the dominant. On this basis I have seen greater liberating potential in the images of Mary as fellow-sufferer and fellow-struggler, than I have in those of her as a great provider. Nonetheless I would not want simply to condemn that image of Mary or deny that such an image may disclose truth.

What I want to do is to select one particular view of Mary as my primary starting point for theologising about her. Although the one I choose is not the dominant view, it is the one in which I find the most potential for a liberating interpretation of Mary. Such a selection is human, fallible, and historically situated. Different Marian traditions are not necessarily mutually exclusive (Gebara and Bingemer:18) although we do need to engage them in a process of on-going discernment.

The dichotomy between people's faith and official theology

Even so, we should be concerned at the gap which exists between official theology, and specifically that which predominates in progressive Catholic circles, and the faith of ordinary people. During the course of my interviews in Mpophomeni I discovered a certain resentment among people toward what was perceived as a neglect of Mary by the official Church; in the same way I have become aware of a certain dismissal of popular Marian devotion on the part of certain representatives of the official Church.

This raises the question of the relationship which ought to exist between academic theology and the faith of ordinary people. Though academic theology has its own role which must include discernment and criticism, it needs to be accountable to the faith of ordinary people, and specifically the marginalised and oppressed. The ideal way for this to happen would be for the trained theologians and "experts" to emerge from the people themselves and to remain linked to them, along the lines of Gramsci's understanding of organic intellectuals (see Joll: 90ff.). This would obviously have far-reaching implications for the Church's religious and theological formation programmes as well as for its pastoral praxis.

It also raises the question of the extent to which the official Church should take Mary and Marian devotion into account in its catechetical and evangelising mission. While the danger of Mary being co-opted by both the ecclesiastical and political right-wing does not seem as great a danger in South Africa as it is in parts of Latin America, we still need to ask whether the relative silence on Mary on the part of the official Church does not deny us a strong possible source of liberating meaning with which many people would be able to connect. Would the use of Marian sources not provide a more accessible motivation to liberative action than endless sermons and pastoral letters on papal encyclicals?

A possible framework for theologising about Mary

This essay has not sought to produce a final, comprehensive theology of Mary. I need to note, however, as ought to be clear from the discussion above, that I am not the best person to fulfil this task and that what I say can only be seen as tentative. I cannot claim to be an organic intellectual or even to theologise on behalf of the people with whom I researched, which I would regard as the ideal, and whose faith I regard as the starting point from which Marian interpretation should happen. I can only say I would theologise with them as my primary dialogue partners. What I attempt below is to provide a rough sketch of a possible direction in which a liberative interpretation of Mary might develop.

Starting point and method

Mariology is our interpretation of the texts concerning Mary as they come to us through the tradition, and as we interpret them in particular contexts today. As the Marian texts intersect with the lives of people today, they take on meaning for us. The starting point for any Marian theology therefore lies in a specific context, in this case the context of South Africa, KwaZulu-Natal, and, that of those people in Mpophomeni with whom I did research.

Mary who identifies with the poor

The starting point for such a theology, like those which have developed in various Latin American contexts, would be with Mary as the poor woman of Nazareth, who identifies with people in their sufferings, and with whom people can themselves identify. Mary is the one who was forced to give birth in a stable and live in a situation of poverty. She was forced into exile in Egypt. She is the mother who watched while her son was arrested and executed. In all of this Mary stayed faithful to what she believed was God's plan with which she had agreed to cooperate. Her "yes" to God in the Annunciation was a "yes" to the yearnings of her people for freedom and is best expressed in the words of the Magnificat, which from this perspective must be seen as a central text for understanding Mary. Thus Mary not only identifies with the poor, she also proclaims a social reversal in which they will be exalted while the rich will be pulled down from their thrones.

Mary who reveals the reign of God

Mary is therefore important not simply for her own sake, but for her participation in bringing about the reign of God, and for what she reveals both about it and about God. As the one who brought Jesus, the saviour, into the world, she plays a crucial role in salvation history. As the location of the Incarnation, she also shows us that us the location from which God's redemptive mission occurs. As a woman I interviewed said, the fact that God chose Mary, a poor woman, shows us something about how God works. Moreover, to see Mary as a type of the Church, as Vatican II did, involves acknowledging the social identity of the Church, the preferential position of those who are marginalised and oppressed within it, and the eschatological yearning of the Magnificat with which the Church identifies.

Mary who reveals the truth about humanity

Most contemporary Catholic mariology sees Mary as symbolic of the Church. She can also be seen as symbolic of all humanity. Mary is the one who reveals to us the deepest truth about human nature and human destiny. From her Immaculate Conception, which shows us that sin and alienation is not the final word about humanity, through to her Glorious Assumption, which speaks both about the importance of material reality and the final victory over the forces of death, the person of Mary can be seen as a normative example of what it means to be human. The person in whom this normative humanity is revealed is none other than the poor woman who suffered the same sort of fate with which many of those on the margins of society today can identify. Thus the figure of Mary holds out the hope of a different reality, but also utters a judgment on present human reality.

Mary and the revelation of God

As I have indicated above, I am suspicious of views (such as those of Boff and Greeley) which present Mary as the feminine face of God on the grounds that they have not been sufficiently critical of the extent to which our overall theological structure has been distorted by patriarchy. Mary cannot properly represent God unless it is recognised that it is God her/himself, and not merely Mary, who is seen as feminine.

It is in and through the human that we come to know about the divine. Individual human beings may and do reveal divine reality to us. Thus the saints, and in this case Mary, can reveal God to us. She is both a revelation of God and also, if we are to follow the Eastern tradition on deification, someone who has been incorporated into God (Ware: 236).

Thus Mary can function in the mother-provider type role of helper and protector insofar as she both reveals and participates in divine reality. We should be clear, however, that mariology still starts "from below." Insofar as Mary is identified with us, and reveals the truth about human reality and human destiny, she reveals the "more" about created reality and the point at which the created and the uncreated meet.

Conclusion

Ultimately there can be no final word on Mary. The texts of faith, while definitive, are constantly encountering new contexts, which continue to draw new meaning out of them as they intersect with the lives of people today. That they are at times ambiguous and even oppressive has been clearly shown. I hope that I have also shown that they are capable of transcending the oppressive worlds out of which they arose, and of providing us with access to Mary who can be a source of liberating faith for us today.

Works Consulted

Boff, Leonardo
    1979   *The Maternal Face of God: The Feminine and Its Religious Expression.* London: Collins.

Cox, Harvey
    1989   "Seven Samurai and How They Looked Again: Theology, Social Analysis, and Religion Popular in Latin America." Pp. 229–39 in *The Future of Liberation Theology: Essays in Honor of Gustavo Gutierrez.* Ed. M. Ellis and O. Maduro. Maryknoll, NY: Orbis.

Dussel, Enrique
    1986   "Popular Religion as Oppression and Liberation: Hypotheses on Its Past and Present in Latin America." Pp. 82–94 in *Popular Religion.* Ed. N. Greinacher and N. Mette. Concilium 186. Edinburgh: Clark.

Elizondo, Virgil
    1986   "Popular Religion as Support of Identity: A Pastoral-Psychological Case-Study Based on the Mexican American Experience in the USA." Pp. 36–43 in *Popular Religion.* Ed. N. Greinacher and N. Mette. Concilium 186. Edinburgh: Clark.

Frostin, Per
    1988   *Liberation Theology in Tanzania and South Africa.* Lund: Lund University Press.

Gebara, Ivone and Maria Clara Bingemer
    1989   *Mary. Mother of God, Mother of the Poor.* Tunbridge Wells, Kent: Burns & Oates.

Graef, Hilda
    1965   *Mary. A History of Doctrine and Devotion.* Vol. 2. Westminster: Christian Classics and London: Sheed & Ward.

Greeley, Andrew
    1977   *The Mary Myth: On the Femininity of God.* New York: Seabury.

Joll, James
    1977   *Gramsci.* Glasgow: Collins.

Jones, Sue
    1985   "Depth Interviewing." Pp. 45–55 in *Applied Qualitative Research*. Ed. R. Walker. Aldershot: Gower.

Maldonado, Luis
    1986   "Popular Religion: Its Dimensions, Levels and Types." Pp. 3–11 in *Popular Religion*. Ed. N. Greinacher and N. Mette. Concilium 186. Edinburgh: Clark.

Mofokeng, Takatso
    1990   "Popular Religiosity: A Liberative Resource and a Terrain of Struggle." *Journal of Black Theology in South Africa* 4:14–23.

Parker, Cristián
    1986   "Popular Religion and Protest against Oppression: The Chilean Example." Pp. 28–35 in *Popular Religion*. Ed. N. Greinacher and N. Mette. Concilium 186. Edinburgh: Clark.

Ricoeur, Paul
    1981a   "Hermeneutics and The Critique of Ideology." Pp. 66–100 in *Hermeneutics and the Human Sciences*. Ed. J. Thompson. Cambridge: Cambridge University Press.
    1981b   "The Hermeneutical Function of Distanciation" Pp. 131–44 in *Hermeneutics and the Human Sciences*. Ed. J. Thompson. Cambridge: Cambridge University Press.
    1981c   "Appropriation" Pp. 182–93 in *Hermeneutics and the Human Sciences*. Ed. J. Thompson. Cambridge: Cambridge University Press.
    1981d   "The Model of the Text: Meaningful Action Considered as a Text." Pp. 145–64 in *Hermeneutics and the Human Sciences*. Ed. J. Thompson. Cambridge: Cambridge University Press.

Scannone, Juan Carlos
    1975   "Theology, Popular Culture and Discernment" Pp. 213–39 in *Frontiers of Theology in Latin America*. Ed. R. Gibellini. London: SCM.

Schneiders, Sandra M.
    1989   "Feminist Ideology Criticism and Biblical Hermeneutics." *BTB* 19:3–10.

Segundo, Juan Luis
    1985   "The Shift Within Latin American Theology." *Journal of Theology for Southern Africa* 52:17–29.

Semporé, Sidbe
    1986   "Popular Religion in Africa: Benin as a Typical Instance." Pp. 44–51 in *Popular Religion*. Ed. N. Greinacher and N. Mette. Concilium 186. Edinburgh: Clark.

Tambasco, Anthony
    1984   *What Are They Saying About Mary?* New York: Paulist.

Walker, Megan
    1991a   "Mary of Nazareth in Feminist Perpective: Towards a Liberating Mariology." Pp. 145–60 in *Women Hold up Half the Sky. Women In the*

Church in South Africa. Ed. D. Ackermann, J. A. Draper, and E. Mashinini. Pietermaritzburg: Cluster.

1991b   Tradition, Criticism and Popular Religion: A Hermeneutical Investigation of Marian Theology with Special Reference to the South African Context. Unpublished M.A. dissertation, University of Natal, Pietermaritzburg, 1991.

Walker, Robert
1985   "An Introduction to Applied Qualitative Research." Pp. 3–26 in *Applied Qualitative Research*. Ed. R. Walker. Aldershot: Gower.

Ware, Timothy
1963   *The Orthodox Church*. Harmondsworth: Penguin.

Weinmann, Edgar A. N.
1985   *Mary in the Evangelisation of the Zulus*. Licentiate in Missiology Thesis, Pontificia Universitas Urbaniana, Rome.

West, Gerald
1995   *Biblical Hermeneutics of Liberation: Modes of Reading the Bible in the South African Context*. Pietermaritzburg: Cluster and Maryknoll, NY: Orbis.

IV
"READING WITH": INCULTURATION READERS

BIBLE STUDY IN AFRICA:
A PASSOVER OF LANGUAGE

John S. Pobee
World Council of Churches
Switzerland

ABSTRACT

What does it mean to speak of Bible study and Biblical Studies in Africa? Using "Passover of Language" as a metaphor, this essay dialogues with First World/Northern Biblical Studies in elucidating some of the elements of Biblical Studies in Africa. These include hermeneutics of culture, socio-politics, mission, ecumenism, pluralism, women, passion-resurrection, the body, and silence.

INTRODUCTION

Although my brief is to address the scholarly use of the Bible and not the popular use of it, I want to suggest that even the popular use says something about the attitude to Scripture which at some point has implications for the scholarly use of it. Let me illustrate with three cases.

First, the faithful have sometimes used the Bible magically. They put a key in it; two people each hold an end of the key. The belief is that if the culprit touches the key, the book turns around the key. I am not interested in denouncing it. But it presupposes the idea that the Bible is such a holy book that it has the capacity to identify evil. It also points us to the view that in Africa the Bible is not just a holy book but that it contains power. For the same reason people have been known to keep it under their pillows to protect against witchcraft, etc. Some magical thinking leads to magical manipulation of the Bible (see Skweres). This strange use of the Bible implies or bears testimony to a view that the Bible is a sacred text for Christians and is not just any book or piece of literature. Remembering the fact that many are non-literate, one way of stating this is that for such people the Bible is the symbol of the presence of God.

Second is the use in political rhetoric. I have elsewhere (1976:129) argued how biblical language and motifs were used in nationalist political rhetoric. I did interpret that to be evidence of the great influence of the Bible—be it its language, themes, philosophy—in Ghanaian society as in other African societies, a fact which reflects the contribution and role of churches in education and health. But let me also acknowledge the critique of a colleague of mine that "parodying religious language with the view of highlighting what is politically desirable could have the effect of undervaluing religious sentiment" (Dickson: 140).[1]

On the use of the Bible in political rhetoric it has sometimes been argued that the Bible was an instrument for the subjugation of African peoples to colonialism with which Christian missions were perceived to be hand-in-glove (Stanley). But the story is more complex; for the centrality of vernacular study and translation of the Bible into the vernacular demonstrably also contributed to the development of nationalism.

The third is a story from East Africa. A so-called simple woman was always found with a bulky Bible. Compatriots teased her for always carrying the Bible of all books. Unruffled, she finally responded: "Yes, of course, there are many books which I could read. But there is only one book which reads me!" (Weber: vii) The comment of Weber on this story is worth quoting:

> This, in a nutshell, is the whole secret of Bible study. People start out by listening to an old message, by analyzing ancient texts, by reading—naively or critically—the biblical documents of antiquity. They experience this exercise as dull or instructive, as something Christians want to do or something they have been led to do by their own historical, literary, or theological interests. Yet a mysterious change of roles can then occur. Listening, analyzing and reading, students of the Bible meet a living reality which begins to challenge them. Out of the biblical stories, texts and documents a person comes to life, the God of Abraham, Isaac and Jacob and even more intimately Jesus of Nazareth in whom the biblical God chose to be present among us. This divine presence starts to question, judge and guide us. Perhaps gradually, perhaps quite suddenly, the book which was the object of our reading and study becomes a subject which reads us. (vii)

That simple woman knew what scholars will express in exalted language. The Bible is like the glass reflectors on the blind corners, helping readers to see the lie of the land of life more clearly.

I start from popular statements to suggest that the scholarly study of Scripture is not an island unto itself; it is answerable to the hopes and

---

[1] John Mbiti also comments in a letter to me: "I wonder whether the frequent use of the Bible by politicians (and other speakers) in Africa arises from its impact or influence on them as such. Surely if the Bible exercised such strong influence, we would see better results in political life, in practical terms. I would rather feel that the quotations come out more because of our oral culture in which, as you rightly point out, proverbs and wise sayings are employed in speech. Quotations of the Bible by politicians do not or may not carry much weight beyond the weight carried by proverbs in daily use. Of course there is a cumulative effect of proverbs in ethics and morals of society, but I do not feel that we could detect a parallel cumulative effect of the Bible upon many politicians."

fears of the society in which it is done. While I have room for erudition and for scholars raising questions which church people may find not really helpful, I do affirm the accountability of scholarship to the community of faith and its hopes and fears. After all, New Testament writings were occasional writings, addressing particular situations in which communities of faith found themselves. It is my submission that the teaching of Scriptures from a people-centred perspective has the power to transform society by reaching even the non-literate. That is why both message and language of the Bible have had profound effects on African society, especially in respect of the worth and dignity of the individual in God's sight and the responsibility of the individual for society and creation. In short, the Bible proves central in and for human transformation in Africa as elsewhere (Pobee, 1984).

Let me draw conclusions from this. First, in the popular view, the Bible is vested with authority of sorts. But as to how that authority is mediated, there is no agreement. Let me dare suggest that the absence of agreement is intimately linked with divisions in society—confessional, ethnic, class, and cultural. The use of Scripture as a theological undergirding of racism in some sections of the Dutch Reformed Church in South Africa, while others in the same society reject that use of Scripture, is one illustration of how other factors actually mediate the authority of Scripture.

Second, context has everything to do with how Scripture is used. We shall later argue how certain elements of context become hermeneutic for the interpretation of Scripture.

Third, Scripture is used for pursuing the identified cutting edges of mission in any context and, therefore, Biblical Studies must have a missiological orientation. The need for Bible study to have missiological orientation is stressed by African scholars. For example, Sister Teresa Okure, a Nigerian Roman Catholic nun and theologian, has argued that the Fourth Gospel took shape in the context of mission, exploring the relationship between the essentially rhetorical and polemic portraiture of Jesus' mission in the Fourth Gospel and the missionary situation of the community from which the Gospel emanated. Further, the Fourth Gospel presupposes Jesus' mission as the ground and all-inclusive category for comprehending the mission of the disciples of Jesus (Okure, 1988b).

Fourth, the Bible is the Scripture of a community of faith, for which it is the source of life and from which they learn of, nay know, the God they claim to serve (see Smit). Theologians are located in their community of faith as its articulate individuals in its womb. This, of course, has some hermeneutical implications.

Passover of Language

To signal this people-centred perspective in Bible study I entitle this essay "A Passover of Language." It is a phrase I have borrowed from Jean-Marc Ela, a French-speaking, Roman Catholic, Cameroonian priest, who writes:

> If the faith of the Africans is not to die, it must become a vision of a world that they can feel is theirs; European cultural orientations must be stripped away. There is an urgent need to reject present foreign models of expression if we are to breathe new life into the Spoken Word. *Our church must express a Passover of Language,* or the meaning of the Christian message will not be understood. One of the primary tasks of Christian reflection in Black Africa is to totally reformulate our basic faith through the mediation of African culture. In place of the cultural presuppositions of Western Christianity, namely *logos* and *ratio,* we must now substitute African symbolism. Beginning with the ecclesial furrow where the language of faith germinates, we must restore the Gospel's power to speak to Africans through the primordial symbol of their existence. (Ela: 44)

Bible study in Africa, therefore, is firmly located in the objective of African theology, i.e. the attempts of Africans to make sense of the Word of God in their varied contexts and situations. And every theology has implied assumptions and presuppositions which are not unrelated to contexts, circumstances, and challenges. And so comes up the significance of the word "language" in our title.

Language

Language designates more than syntax and morphology; it is the weight and vehicle of a world-view. One of the climactic influences on Africa is colonialism—English, Dutch, Danish, Portuguese, or French. So theology and with it the Bible was taught in the colonial languages, in spite of the fact that the Bible was at times also taught in African languages, which are rich with their own symbolism. But while a translation presupposes that the original is inappropriate for the new context, it nevertheless does not eliminate the original; the original often remains the yardstick of the ideal. But this happened not by sheer force of circumstance or convenience, but also because the colonial tongue was believed to be the heaven-sent medium of communication, religion, and civilization. Even when translations were done in the vernacular, the colonial tongue with all its foreign symbolisms was used, including Christendom ideology, a Eurocentric social-Darwinism, and even some anthropological racism, which became most glaring in the Republic of South Africa. African theology has been concerned to discover new and relevant symbols for describing the eternal Word of God so as to hold dialogue with African peoples. Therefore, it is attempting to move from the inherited language and idiom of the North to a new language and idiom relevant for Africa. That is the "Passover of Language" to which I shall return in a little while.

In insisting on the local language, one is questioning the assumption associated with scholarship in the North that peoples everywhere perceive reality in the same way and, consequently, there must be one and the same starting point for theological and biblical reflection. However, I am inclined to the view that it should start from certain social relations and realities. This is a different epistemology, one that begins with the social reality of the poor and marginalized.

Let me make one more point about language. For those schooled in the North, theology is done in a propositional style of language. But African theology, while not denying intellectual rigour, is expressed also in proverbs, art, music, liturgy, poetry, stories, and biography (Klem; Mbiti, 1978; Pobee, 1989). Proverbs, even if they have an anthropological focus and may seem to have a pedestrian nature, help to interpret the cultures of people, by making prosaic subjects stimulating and unforgettable. As such they have a useful place in pedagogy (Olson). In respect of art, we may draw attention to the woodcarving "Thy Kingdom Come" by Martin Loh Nyonka, which was presented to the Commission on World Mission and Evangelism by the Presbyterian Church in Cameroon. Bible study does not need to adopt a propositional style; it can be done with good and forceful effect in story, art, song, poetry, biography. Further, we have rediscovered that the starting point of theology is not dogma; it is and should be gospel, which is a story (see Onwu).

"Passover"

In a little while I will return to the matter of language. For now I wish to turn to the language of Passover. It is hazardous to use the imagery of Passover because its history evolved over a period of time. It was originally a nomadic festival which was incorporated into Yahwism. King Josiah revived it after a long period of time (cf. 2 Kgs 23:21–23). I use it to indicate aspects of what Bible study should be about.

First, Passover is a spring festival. In that light Bible study should foster renewal that brings deliverance. Second, in late Judaism there developed a practice on the basis of Malachi 4:5–6 that a Passover cup was set apart for Elijah, the prophet of the End-time. At some point in the proceedings a door was opened to see whether Elijah was not standing outside. In that light Bible study as a Passover is about opening doors for divine intervention. Third, Passover, alongside the Feasts of Weeks and Tabernacles, was an occasion when the faithful were obliged to appear before Yahweh as well as for feasting and engagement. Bible study must be a happy social experience in which all, especially the poor, are invited to participate.

Thus the description "Passover of language" seeks to argue that Bible study in Africa should be an instrument in the process of renewal of peoples, opening them up for divine intervention and equipping people for joy in the Lord and participation in the Messianic banquet.

CULTURES AS CONTEXT AND HERMENEUTIC FOR READING OF SCRIPTURE

In order to achieve full dialogue, the language of a people's culture, hopes, and fears must be engaged by the Word of God. Let me, therefore, proceed to delineate some of the elements in that culture, experience, and history. First, *homo africanus homo religiosus radicaliter* and, thus, has a religious and spiritual epistemology and ontology. For that reason the tinge of agnosticism so characteristic of the Northern scientific method will not be wholly satisfactory. The inherited culture of *ratio* has to be seen in a renewed perspective. I suggest that theology should be an intellectual habit rooted in the act of faith which allows for growth, and in this habit is Bible study located.

Second, *homo africanus* has a holistic view of reality, i.e. reality is knowing, feeling, and doing. For that reason biblical and dialogical scholarship may not be limited to the intellectual, rational process and for that matter, the propositional style; it has to be praxis. It is this that the story from Kenya signals—theology lives. In other words, the matrix of sound biblical exegesis includes more than the rational criterion.

Third, *homo africanus* has a communitarian epistemology and ontology. That community sense is much broader than in the North; it is the community of the living, the "living dead" and those who are yet to be born, as well as community within nations. Here we stumble on a feature of African biblical theology—there is a compatibility between the Old Testament and African culture lying in a common outlook on life and human experiences, which results in a common experience of reality in such areas as sacred and profane, humanity and community, humanity and nature, sin and disease (Burden; see also Wambudta).

The foregoing elements are factors in any attempt to understand the Bible. People come to the Bible with such baggage in much the same way as theologians from the North come to Scripture with cultural baggage. In this regard let it be noted that for many Africans, church persons and theologians alike, there is no conflict between biblical and traditional African religious beliefs, particularly in the belief in the existence of a spirit world, including evil spirits. That is the rationale in the University of

Ghana for a course on "Old Testament and African Life and Thought." Here we are reminded that any piece of theology is an attempt to discover symbols to hold dialogue with the world, not in the abstract but in the concrete. That is why I am unable to accept the description of African theology as ethno-theology and syncretistic theology (Daidonso; Muthukya).

Culture then is a hermeneutic for reading Scripture. The work of John Mbiti, Modupe Oduyoye, and D. N. Wambudta show the compatibility between Scripture and an African world-view (Mbiti, 1971; Oduyoye; Wambudta; see also Sanneh). That culture should become a hermeneutic is not surprising because religion is, after all, a phenomenon of human culture and a system of symbols which gives an "aura of factuality" to a human community's way of seeing and doing things. These symbols generate strong morals and motivation in people and indicate commitment to what they consider real (Geertz: 90). But the study of religion is a phenomenon of human culture, and has to be done from a phenomenological perspective.

Nonetheless, culture and religion alone are not enough as hermeneutic. For there is ample evidence of how they have been used as instruments of domination (Okure, 1988; Banana; Maimela), legitimatizing the oppression of the outcasts, the poor, etc. For that reason the elements of culture and religion may be used in as far as they are consistent with God's preferential option for the poor, as well as with African anthropology, which is human centred and socially oriented.

Socio-Political Reality as Context and Hermeneutic for Bible Study

In addition to the culture factor, there is the factor of social reality. What was said earlier about the political use of Scripture also reminds us that the way one reads the Bible also reflects one's social location, i.e. gender, class, race, ethnicity. There is also the social reality of poverty. Many in Africa are the victims of exploitation, oppression, marginalization, and violence. The mythical four horsemen of the Apocalypse—conquest, slaughter, famine, and death—are abroad in Africa. Consequently there is a widespread culture of hopelessness, massive public suffering, and the cry of abandonment. They have made their own the cry of the psalmist: "My God, my God, why have you forsaken me?" Their very lives and experiences are a commentary on the words of Scripture. African scholars argue for the necessity of combining the encounter with African cultures and values with the encounter with social issues. For, given the realities of colonialization and its aftermath, war and dictatorships, liberation—the content of the gospel of hope—is not likely without the recovery of deeply rooted cultural values (Bujo).

Against that background of the stark reality of poverty, African biblical scholars, especially those from Southern Africa, have begun to see the option for the poor as a hermeneutic for biblical theology. This is the perspective of the social reality for reading gospel. That perspective emphasizes the gospel values of solidarity, service, simplicity, and readiness to receive God's gift. For African exegetes, this commitment to the poor is a spiritual experience and grows in stages and in relation to crises. Albert Nolan has identified three stages of growth: first, the stage of compassion; second, discovering that poverty is a structural problem; and third, the discovery that the poor must save themselves, through a process of conscientization, which includes the solidarity of committed biblical scholars (Nolan; see also Sobrino: 127).

The issue is how the Bible can be read in a liberative manner, bringing them life in concrete everyday experience, body, heart and mind, and discovering the meaning of what it is to be human. Thus the objective of Bible study is to expand Scripture so that it can be experienced as good news—gospel. The preferential option for the poor demands witnessing from a position of weakness, which means opening oneself to the power available only through faith (Byler).

Because there are conflicting interests in society—social, economic, ethnic—there will be conflicting readings of Scripture. And so those committed to apartheid read Scripture through the spectacles of the ideology of racism. Consequently the "factual" Bible must be distinguished from the "actual" Bible, to use the language of Mosala (1989; 1991). There are, so to speak, different Bibles within the Bible and the task is to seek the "actual" Bible which alone has final authority. Or, as some would put it, every effort should be made to discover a canon within a canon. But in finding a socio-political hermeneutic, it is important that it should not only foster the identity and integrity of one group but also wholeness of the people of God as a human community. That unifying concern I call the hermeneutic of ecumenism; for ecumenism is committed to dialogue and making connections between different and diverse positions.

The hermeneutic of God's preferential option for the poor highlights the perspective of the dominated, a story of pain and suffering. But we should not allow ourselves to forget that authentic praise and authentic theology begin in the matrix of pain. Praise of God and the dignity of the poor represent the intersection of such humanizing acts of sharing in God's bounty and deliverance. Praise and vision grow in the matrix of pain. So the hermeneutic of God's preferential option for the poor is inextricably linked with worship which, after all, was the vehicle for the preservation of the biblical documents.

This sensitivity to the socio-political reality of Africa means that there should be socio-political approaches to the biblical texts. The use of the social sciences in biblical study is not new, going back as it does to the Chicago School and the Social Gospel approaches, but it has recently become part of the mainstream (see Theissen; Horsley). On the African scene, because of the importance of culture and socio-political realities for perceptions of reality, the social-scientific approach to Bible study becomes a natural tool (Ela and Mana; Oduyoye and Kanyoro; Fabella and Oduyoye). However, in their social-political approach African scholars *on the whole* refuse to impose abstract systems of analysis and modern social concepts on the biblical texts, thus avoiding the danger of domesticating gospel or using gospel to refurbish the social *status quo*.

PLURALISM AS CONTEXT AND HERMENEUTIC FOR READING SCRIPTURE IN AFRICA

Another reality in the context of Africa is pluralism. At the end of the day Europe and America have a predominantly Christian culture, a legacy of the Christendom ideology going as far back as at least Theodosius I. That Christian predominance Africa cannot assume, even when Christianity has large numbers. There is political, economic, social, cultural, psychological, religious, and philosophical pluralism. Religious pluralism is very important, especially as it relates in the African context to Christianity, because African Traditional Religions and Islam live together in families and towns. Biblical theology then should be interested in holding dialogue within a context of pluralism. Thus the ecumenical vision becomes yet another hermeneutic, which also becomes a hermeneutic for Biblical Studies, determining how theological issues are stated. For example, in the search for a liberating and African Christology one will not only be concerned to find relevant and meaningful symbols to state biblical Christologies but also have to face the question of the uniqueness of Christ in this context of pluralism.

PATRIARCHY AS CONTEXT AND HERMENEUTIC FOR READING THE BIBLE IN AFRICA

African women too have discovered that the Bible is a patriarchal book, not only because it was written for the most part by men but also because down the centuries it has been interpreted predominantly by men. For that reason voices of women, a substantial part of the community of faith, have been missing, and cultural gaps have occurred which must be captured for the sake of a full humanity. In this task there is a deep religious and theological issue: the necessity to discern between divine and human elements in the biblical material, the distinction between the timeless truths for our salvation and socio-culturally conditioned practices. In this regard Galatians 3:26–28, the vision of a new order restored in Christ is often the guiding principle. For me that is a part of the ecumenical hermeneutic. African women theologians go further to argue that such re-reading

> demands that emphasis be placed on the vocation of women as mother, God's privileged instrument for conceiving and bringing forth life. This emphasis will go hand in hand with sustained efforts to develop and celebrate the motherhood of God....Our celebration of the motherhood of God will help us to approach God and Jesus as compassionate, merciful, tender givers of life, and refuge of sinners rather than as mighty Lords to be feared and appeased. (Okure, 1988a:56–57)

Let me draw some threads together. Biblical theology in Africa has inherited the fabrications of the North, shaped according to the Northern ethos and needs. But it is now struggling to speak to *homo africanus*. In that regard it is using a plenum of hermeneutics: culture, preferential option for the poor, pluralism, and ecumenism, which have epistemological implications reaching to the heart of knowing and to ways of being in the world. Received biblical scholarship seems to have cut people off from the power of the text. But Africans are rediscovering the power of the text as a story and, therefore, how to use Scripture in a compelling and liberative manner.

The careful reader may have noticed an oscillation between African theology and biblical theology. This is to signal that biblical theology in Africa is not just an autonomous unit but an integral part of African theology. But it also signals that in the African context there is an emphasis on the biblical basis of any theology (Parratt). Thus the discussion of biblical theology in Africa is a discussion of a renewed style of doing theology: it is to interpret gospel in the light of modern research and contemporary problems and issues.

Bible study, whatever else it may be, is interpretative translation of the Bible into contemporary/contextual language. Just as there is need for a dynamic equivalent translation (and not only a formal one), we need a dynamic equivalent interpretation of the Bible. We may then in our culture and socio-economic situation become contemporary with the biblical text. That becomes our Passover—we are led out of Egypt, not only our ancestors. Scripture becomes the told story which lets us experience the exodus today.

The test of such Bible study is whether it effects echoes in the hearers, so that the Bible offers commentary on their own heritage and circumstances. In that sense I am going back to St. Augustine, who wrote that God wrote two books, the Book of Life and the Bible. The Bible is the second book, written to decipher the Book of Life. Thus the Bible may be regarded as an instrument, criterion, and canon for discerning the presence and revelation of God in the indigenous cultures and religions. But earlier we had raised the question of the canon within the canon; so the task of Bible study is also to help *homo africanus* of today appropriate meaningfully the religious experience, belief, and rituals of other people of the past. It is in the dialogue between the culture and religions of the people, on the one hand, and Scripture, on the other, that the truth and power of Scripture can be discerned and experienced and a Passover experience undergone.

African Emphases in Bible Study

Earlier the case was made for a people-centred perspective in the reading of Scripture. That is what gives significance to the realities of culture, socio-political experience, and pluralism. That has determined the emphases in biblical study. Let us delineate some of the key points in biblical studies, research, and proclamation in Africa.

Salvation

According to John 20:30–31, "Jesus did many other signs in the presence of his disciples, which are not in this book. But these are written so that you may come to believe that Jesus is the Messiah, the Son of God, and that through believing you may have life in his name." For now, let me focus on the theme of life, which is Johannine language for salvation. That is the core of the gospel. But given the socio-political challenge, life becomes a paramount concern and gets added importance.

Whereas in the North salvation is largely understood in individualistic terms, in African exegesis, especially in the African Instituted Churches, life is seen in holistic terms. It is salvation of the soul as well as wholeness of body and mind. Hence the emphasis on healing in African churches. Further, because of the communitarian epistemology and ontology of African peoples, salvation is not only for the individual but also for a people and in community. The debate in 1 Thess 4:13ff. is very much alive in the African context. Communitarian emphasis on salvation means that teaching with regard to salvation and teaching in respect of the church are linked. The model of the church is the family in which there is wholeness. And it is not just a matter of numbers but also a matter of participation in the community, taking seriously its traditions handed down from ancestors and their identity, and it is here that joy is located. The word integration then may be characteristic of the African exegeses of salvation: integration of the individual in the community of faith and of humanity; integration of body, mind, soul, and spirit. In short, salvation of the whole person—a comprehensive concept.

Cosmic Powers

African societies, like the biblical world-view, have a spiritual and religious epistemology and ontology. The human community includes also the "living dead," or those who have finished their course here and gone ahead, and the yet-to-be born. Further, they believe we are surrounded by hosts of spirit beings, some good, some bad, which have the capacity and capability to influence the course of the lives of the living. Added to all this is the sense of finality and vulnerability resulting from the harsh socio-political realities. The intersection of the sacred and the secular unleashes power in the world, some of which is capricious, some benign. Religion then becomes part of the process of harnessing power to one's advantage and salvation. Salvation becomes deliverance from cosmic powers. Unlike Western societies, no effort is made to explain away cosmic powers; African exegetes take seriously the reality of cosmic powers, treating them as some kind of organized disobedience to the will of God, which affect the course of human history.

Against that background certain biblical passages become favourite: Psalm 91, especially vv. 9–13; Romans 8:31–39; Ephesians 6:17; Colossians 2:20. This is especially so in African Instituted Churches (Baeta).

Holy Spirit

Precisely because of the spiritual epistemology and ontology, African churches seem to have an emphasis on the Holy Spirit as the focus of belief and practice. The Holy Spirit is, so to speak, continuous and yet discontinuous with the many spirits of their heritage. But there is a particular emphasis on experiencing the Holy Spirit as power ever holy. The African Instituted Churches have been notorious for their emphasis on the Holy Spirit. But even the historic churches and the theologians of the seminaries and university departments have been working on the subject of the Holy Spirit (Obaje, 1986; 1987).

Christology

In view of the comments about the focus of African Churches on the Holy Spirit, one would be tempted to say Christology is not important in

Africa. That would be far from the truth. A casual visitor to the African Instituted Churches cannot fail to be struck by the frequency with which the leadership shout "Jesus, Jesus, Jesus." Jesus is the name we wish to proclaim; Jesus is the powerful name in which we operate. The whole missiological orientation of theology demands some preoccupation with who this Jesus is to whom Africans are invited to relate—someone who is not from their kin-group and is not even an African. It is that consideration which led to the consultation at the Ecumenical Institution, Chateau de Bossey, Celigny, Geneva, which is now published as *Exploring Afro-Christology* (Pobee, 1991).

One also must draw on the insights coming from the African women biblical scholars and theologians. Théresa Souga, a Cameroonian Roman Catholic writes:

> For me this unconditional belonging to the God of Jesus Christ needs entering into the passion mystery: it is a desire growing deeper into me each day, to know Christ, to commune with his suffering, to open myself to the power of his resurrection, to be open to the action of the Holy Spirit, who builds the Church and the history of human beings. This is a matter of deep attitudes, and of motivations, and of operative meanings. The realism of the cross every day tells me, as a woman of the Third World, that the laws of history may be overcome by means of crucified love. (22)

I dare to suggest that this is a fine exposition of the passion-resurrection hermeneutic mentioned earlier. But it is also arguable that the pervasive suffering of Africa generates particular emphases in Christology in Africa. And women, by virtue of the fact that they tend to be at the bottom of the heap in a general sea of suffering, bring meaningful and tested testimony to the search for a viable Christology in Africa.

The Body

The heart of the Passover of Language should be the body. Body may be a symbol of our contextuality, our conditions of time and space as well as of the wholeness of human existence as a living body which is at once body, spirit, and soul. But it also signals the element of mystery about human living as of our faith. That mystery is borne on me by the fact that whereas many peoples of Africa are confronted by the culture of hopelessness, these same people have retained their humanness, their sense of the dignity of the individual in the context of the community. And where the powerful offer violence and death, these victims mysteriously have no sense of bitterness in them. The late Albert Luthuli, Nelson Mandela, Beyers Naude, and Desmond Tutu of the Republic of South Africa, and the late Bishop Akinyele of Nigeria, remain for me the bodily symbols of that mystery of the power of God's word in a culture of hopelessness. I argue, then, for a hermeneutic of the body.

Jaci Maraschin, an Anglican systematic theologian from Brazil, has words which articulate for me the hermeneutic of the body I am crying for. He writes:

> Christian theology is a critical exercise related primarily to the body. It is done inside the body of Christ, created by the resurrected body of Jesus and developed through the power, the suffering and the hopes present in the body of its members. When we speak of bodies, we are thinking of the unity which is in the body: unity of bones, flesh, mind, spirit, blood, nerves and so on. We think of body as a person, as human being, as God's creature. (36)

And, he later continues, it is this body which Bible study serves:

> announcing in the midst of their suffering and deformations the possibility of the new heaven and new earth, with resurrected bodies. Indeed, the gospel is judging actually the differences shown in our bodies in society. The new heaven and new earth are places for new bodies....We cannot, certainly, go to the heavenly banquet without them (the bodies with the marks of suffering and deformation), we cannot certainly love as in the Song of Songs, without knowing that they are also loving through the same beautiful experience, we cannot rest on the Sabbath Day without their rest, their joy, their renewed and humanized bodies. (Maraschin: 38)

It is here that the vitality and viability of the Word of God can be experienced and made vibrant.

Silence

I began this essay with three case studies, and I now conclude with one, which is from Ethiopia when it went through a dark tunnel in its political life during the rule of Mengistu Haile Miriam. The government claimed to be Marxist and committed to the eradication of religion. It was dangerous to speak the Word of God.

In that context a biblical study was undertaken. The text chosen was not fortuitous. It was chosen because the sentiments there were judged relevant to their situation and salvation. Reading the text itself could communicate God's message. And the Bible study had no commentary. The leader only slowly and sensitively read select and relevant portions of Psalm 22:

> 1. "My God, my God, why have you forsaken me? Why are you so far from saving me, so far from hearing my groans? My God, by day I cry out but there is no answer; in the night I cry with no respite" (1–2).

The sentiment was self-evident in their circumstances. They had been brutalized by the government. The faithful were under pressure; their patriarch had disappeared or, more accurately, had been made to disappear. The general secretary of the Mekane Yesu Church also disappeared. Ordinary people were in trouble. Their economic circumstances were desperate. Truly the psalmist told their story.

> 2. "I am a worm, not a man, abused by everyone, scorned by the people. All who see me jeer at me...'He threw himself on the Lord for rescue; let the Lord deliver him, for he holds him dear!'" (6–8).

The sentiments here fitted their situation. Nothingness could be a description of their situation. The jeer was replicated in the taunts of unbelieving soldiers and apparatchiks. A culture of hopelessness was abroad in their circumstances.

In spite of their painful situation, they could resonate to the Psalmist's words:

> 3. "You that fear the Lord, praise him, hold him in honour...revere him...For he has not scorned him who is downtrodden, nor shrunk in loathing from his plight...but he has listened to his cry for help" (23–25).

This is a tremendous affirmation of faith in the one God who holds the world in the palm of the hand.

> 4. "I shall declare your faith to my associates, praising you in the midst of the assembly. You that fear the Lord, praise him...You inspire my praise in the great assembly..." (vv. 22, 23, 25).

They understood that when pain and suffering are subjected to worship they become redeeming, strengthening, and a source of hope. Praise of God and hope are born in the matrix of pain and suffering.

I use this example to register the point that while Bible study is normally exposition on texts, on occasions it can be done silently hearing the word of God. Dare I suggest that God's Spirit sometimes leads us into God's truth without immediate human aid? Dare I suggest that we must learn to cultivate silence before the mystery of God the Word? Dare I suggest the truth of God's Word is on occasions so self-evident and powerful that it can be communicated without human, verbal exposition? But I am also suggesting that Bible study is a tool of liberation. A people's story can be the commentary and exegesis of scripture. The story in the Bible is their story. Their story and that of the Bible fit like a glove. But we must experience the power of silence as exegesis. For after all, before the holy God all mortals should keep silent.

Some may wish to label this case study from Ethiopia intuitive Bible study. I would prefer to describe it as contextual Bible study. For, after all, contextuality is "that wrestling with God's word in such a way as to discern the particularity of this historic moment; and by 'contextualization' we mean the wrestling with God's Word in such a way that the power of the incarnation which is the divine form of contextualization, can enable us to follow his steps to contextualize" (Coe: 7).

I have attempted to articulate exegesis which took the form of silence. The silence was a theological affirmation. The academic theologian's task is to be in the womb of the community of faith to articulate that silence which is the people's exegesis of the text. Here is a very important point: can we hear in our Bible studies, scholarly and scientifically crafted as they are, the echoes of the cry of the people in their context of pain and suffering, exclusion and marginalization, violence and hopelessness? Their Bible knowledge is written on their bodies. Do those ugly features of their situation as well as their hopes make any impact on our Bible study? If not, the Bible study will not be vibrant, life-giving, and alive.

Conclusion

Bible study in Africa is a Passover of Language which seeks to pass over from the language of Euro-centred and Euro-constructed theology to an African-centred and African-constructed theology so as to speak effectively to Africans, body, soul, and spirit, so that they may repent and have life, and that in abundance. To this end there is need to operate with a plenum of hermeneutics—cultural, socio-political, missiological, ecumenical, African feminist, multi-faith, passion-resurrection, the body, and silence. These will be applied in varying degrees depending on context.

This is a very young enterprise and there is a long way to go before we get to anything like a clear picture. But the process has begun in a Passover of language. But that Passover of Language must be guided by the prophetic vocation of the faith and a commitment to freedom of self-expression, thought, and openness to one another and in dialogue with the rest of the *oikoumene*.

Works Consulted

Baeta, Christian
    1962   *Prophetism in Ghana*. London: SCM.

Banana, Canaan S.
    1993   "The Case for a New Bible." A Seminar Paper in Department of Religious Studies, University of Zimbabwe.

Bujo, Benezet
1992 *African Theology in its Social Context*. Maryknoll: Orbis.

Burden, J. J.
1985 "Are Shem and Ham Blood Brothers? The Relation of Old Testament to Africa." *Old Testament Essays* 1:49–72.

Byler, Dennis
1984 "Proclamation and Culture: A Biblical Perspective." *Mission Focus* 12:33–37.

Coe, Shoki
1974 "Contextualization." *Theological Education* 11:1, 7.

Daidonso, ma Djongwé
1983 "An African Critique of African Theology." *Evangelical Review of Theology* 7:63–72.

Dickson, K. A.
1991 "Religion and Society: A Study in Church and State Relations in the First Republic." Pp. 135–51 in *The Life and Work of Kwame Nkrumah*. Ed. Kwame Arhin. Accra: Sedco.

Ela, Jean-Marc
1988 *My Faith as an African*. Maryknoll, NY: Orbis.

Ela, Jean-Marc and K. A. Mana
1993 *Theologie Africain Pour Temps de Crise*. Paris: Editions Karthala.

Fabella, Virginia and Mercy Amba Oduyoye, eds.
1988 *With Passion and Compassion: Third World Women Doing Theology: Reflections from the Women's Commission of the Ecumenical Association of Third World Theologians*. Maryknoll, NY: Orbis.

Geertz, Clifford
1972 *The Interpretation of Cultures*. New York: Basic.

Horsley, Richard A.
1989 *Sociology and the Jesus Movement*. New York: Crossroad.

Klem, Herbert V.
1982 *Oral Communication of the Scriptures: Insights from African Oral Art*. Pasadena: William Carey Library.

Maimela, S. J.
1991 "Religion and Culture: Blessings or Curses?" *Journal of Black Theology in South Africa* 5:1–15.

Maraschin, Jaci
1985 "Theology, Bodies and People." *Ministerial Formation* 31:36–38.

Mbiti, John S.
1971 *New Testament Eschatology in an African Background*. London: OUP.
1978 "'Cattle are born with ears, their horns grow later': Towards an appreciation of African Oral Theology." Pp. 35–51 in *Christian Theology and*

Theological Education in the African Context. Ed. Alison Bares. Geneva: LWF.

Mosala, Itumela J.
1989   *Biblical Hermeneutics and Black Theology in South Africa.* Grand Rapids: Eerdmans.
1991   "Wealth and Poverty in the Old Testament—A Black Theological Perspective." *Journal of Black Theology in South Africa* 5:16–22.

Muthukya, S. M.
n.d   *Africanisation of Christianity.* Nairobi: East Africa Christian Alliance.

Nida, Eugene A. and William D. Rayburn
1981   *Meaning Across Culture.* Maryknoll, NY: Orbis.

Nolan, Albert
1985   "The Service of the Poor and Spiritual Growth." *Grace and Truth* 6:114–22.

Obaje, Yusufu Ameh
1986   *Have You Received the Baptism of the Holy Spirit?* Ogbomosho: Adebayo Calvary Printers.
1987   *The Miracle of Speaking in Tongues: Which Side Are You?* Ogbomosho, Nigeria: Adebayo Calvary Printers.

Oduyoye, Mercy Amba and Musimbi Kanyoro, eds.
1990   *Talitha, Qumi.* Ibadan, Nigeria: Daystar Press.

Oduyoye, Modupe
1984   *The Sons of the Gods and the Daughters of Men: An Afro-Asiatic Interpretation of Genesis 1–11.* Maryknoll, NY: Orbis.

Okure, Teresa
1988a   "Women in the Bible." Pp. 47–59 in *With Passion and Compassion.* Ed. Virginia Fabella M. M. and Mercy Amba Oduyoye. Maryknoll, NY: Orbis.
1988b   *The Johannine Approach to Mission.* Tübingen: JCB Mohr (Paul Siebeck).

Olson, Howard S.
1981   "The Place of Traditional Proverbs in Pedagogy." *Africa Theological Journal* 10:26–35.

Onwu, N.
1985   "The Hermeneutical Model: The Dilemma of the African Theologian." *Africa Theological Journal* 14:145–60.

Parratt, John
1983   "Theological Methodologies in Africa." *Verbum SVD* 24:1, 47–62.

Pobee, John S.
1976   "Church and State in Ghana 1949–1966." In *Religion in a Pluralistic Society.* Ed. John S. Pobee. Leiden: E. J. Brill.

Pobee, John S.
 1984 "Bible and Human Transformation." *Mission Studies* 1:4–12.
 1987 *Kwame Nkrumah and the Church in Ghana 1949–1966.* Accra: Asempa Press.
 1989 "Oral Tradition and Christian Oral Theology: Challenge to our Traditional Archival Study." *Mission Studies* 6:87–93.

Pobee, John S., ed.
 1991 *Exploring Afro-Christology.* Frankfurt-am-Main: Peter Lang.

Sanneh, Lamin
 1992 "Gospel and Culture: Ramifying Effects of Scriptural Translation." Pp. 1–23 in *Bible Translation and the Spread of the Church. The Last 200 Years.* Ed. Philip C. Stine. London: E. J. Brill.

Skweres, Dieter E.
 1982 "Bibelpastorale Publikationen im Frankophonen Afrika und ihre missionsstrategische Bedeutung." *Verbum SVD* 23:177–86.

Smit, D. J.
 1988 "Responsible Hermeneutics: A Systematic Theologian's Response to the Readings and Readers of Luke 12." *Neotestamentica* 22: 441–84.

Sobrino, Jon
 1990 "The Crucified Peoples: Yahweh's Suffering Servant Today." Pp. 120–29 in *The Voices of the Victims.* Ed. L. Boff and Virgil Elizondo. London: SCM.

Souga, Thérèsa
 1988 "The Christ-Event from the Viewpoint of African Women—A Catholic Perspective." Pp. 22–29 in *With Passion and Compassion.* Ed. Virginia Fabella M. M. and Mercy Amba Oduyoye. Maryknoll, NY: Orbis.

Stanley, Brian
 1990 *The Bible and the Flag: Protestant Missions and British Imperialism in the Nineteenth and Twentieth Centuries.* Leicester: Apollos.

Theissen, Gerd
 1978 *Sociology of Early Palestinian Christianity.* Philadelphia: Fortress.

Walls, A. F.
 1992 "The Translation Principle in Christian History." Pp. 23–39 in *Bible Translation and the Spread of the Church. The Last 200 Years.* Ed. Philip C. Stine. Leiden: E. J. Brill.

Wambudta, D. N.
 1981 "Savannah Theology: A Biblical Reconsideration of Salvation in the African Context." *Bulletin of African Theology* 6:137–53.

Weber, Hans-Ruedi
 1983 *Experiments with Bible Study.* Geneva: WCC.

INTERPRETING THE BIBLE IN AFRICAN CONTEXTS: GLASGOW CONSULTATION

John Riches
University of Glasgow
Scotland

ABSTRACT

This article briefly reports on the aims and efforts of integrating academic and popular interpretations of the Bible in a joint project of some African and Western countries. Its aims are to initiate a dialogue between popular and academic readers, to consider the implications of popular interpretations for hermeneutical and pedagogical strategies in the academic setting, and to develop cross-cultural cooperation.

In August, 1994, a meeting was held in Glasgow which drew together thirty biblical scholars from Ghana, Nigeria, Zimbabwe, South Africa, Canada, and the United Kingdom. This somewhat unusual gathering, arose out of research into the relationship between popular and academic readings of the Bible undertaken by the Catholic Institute of West Africa (CIWA) and the Department of Biblical Studies in Glasgow University over the period 1992-1994. The idea of such a joint project was conceived as far back as 1988 when Justin Ukpong of CIWA met John Riches from Glasgow at the International Association of Mission Studies Conference in Rome. A close study of popular readings in the two centres might provide an interesting focus for understanding the differences and similarities between the two cultures and offer important pointers to scholars who wished to inculturate their own work.

Such a joint project did not of course spring entirely out of the blue. On the one hand African scholars have been interested in inculturation hermeneutics for twenty years or more and are more than a little aware of the force of popular readings of the Bible, not least those which come from the African Instituted Churches. On the other hand, teaching students from Africa in European institutions brings home to European scholars the fact that, whatever one's views of the universality of theology, theological education is culturally specific. If it is not to be simply didactic in the worse sense, then it must engage with the cultural assumptions and questions which students bring with them and which inform their understanding of what they hear and read. That is to say, from the start there were both hermeneutical and paedagogical issues which underlay the project. Less clearly stated initially, but appearing very early on, were political, ideological considerations: how is it that the Bible can be both a force for transformation and enslavement? Who controls its use and its readings? How can it become a force for not just individual but also social transformation?

Such were the shared concerns which brought about this cooperative venture. There were also, of course, by virtue of the partnership between different African and European institutions questions to be explored about the interrelationships between North and South, between European and African culture, between methods tried and developed in Europe and those most appropriate within the African context; about, more practically, cooperation in joint programmes of theological education.

Clearly such broad concerns needed from the start to be focused. An initial meeting in Glasgow in 1989 decided that as a necessary preliminary to any theoretical discussions of inculturation and liberation hermeneutics, we should conduct field studies on the existing popular uses of the Bible in the different centres. Initially, we had hoped that there would be four: Harare, Kinshasa, Port Harcourt, and Glasgow. For various reasons, this rapidly became two: Port Harcourt and Glasgow. It had also been hoped to hold local consultations after completing each piece of field work. One such consultation was held in Port Harcourt in 1992, but the political situation made it inadvisable for those from outside Nigeria to attend. Some of those involved in the project were able to meet together at SBL meetings in 1992 and 1993, and the Section on Asian, African, and Latin American Readings of the Bible provided a valuable forum for exchange of ideas. Here contact was made with South African colleagues from the Institute for the Study of the Bible in Pietermaritzburg at a joint session held at SBL in Washington. This also provided opportunity for planning the Glasgow consultation.

It took some time for the project to develop after the 1989 meeting as we faced the problems of finding funds to meet the costs of coordinating the project and funding field work. In the end, the majority of the funding came from Evangelisches Missions-Werk and Missio with further important support from the World Council of Churches, which assisted with travel costs to the Glasgow meetings. Justin Ukpong of the Catholic Institute of West Africa was appointed project co-ordinator, and the project began in earnest in 1992.

The surveys were conducted using focus discussion groups to establish prevailing patterns of thought and practice about the Bible. The Port Harcourt survey was much more extensive than the Glasgow one. In Port

Harcourt trained facilitators were used, and a questionnaire compiled on the basis of the focus discussion groups and then used to interview random individuals. The Glasgow study was carried out by Leslie Milton on the basis of interviews with groups, some of which were already existing Bible study groups, some of which were formed for this purpose.

The results of both surveys are intriguing. The Port Harcourt report tended to show that it was the harsh realities of daily living, of the sheer struggle to survive, which moulded popular readings. The Bible was seen in various ways as the source of succour for those facing personal difficulties. "The belief that the Bible is the word of God has acquired magical dimensions...[It] is used to ward off evil spirits; placed under the pillow at night to ensure God's protection." The New Testament, despite being perceived as culturally more distant from Africans than the Old, and therefore less likely to provide practical guidance and models for liturgical innovation, is still more popular because "it is more powerful than the OT," for the power of Jesus expressed in miracles pervades it. Underlying all this was a clear sense that people turn to the Bible as a source of power to help them survive in a difficult world. "The major motivations for reading the Bible were the search for spiritual support against evil and enemies, and use in prayer." Such views are rooted in a strong sense of the Bible's authority.

The survey in Scotland showed a rather different pattern of use. The Bible was also turned to for consolation and support, but the attitude to its authority and the kind of support it might give differed. Compared with West Africa where use of the Bible is widespread, serious engagement with the Bible appears to be quite restricted. Many of those interviewed had been regular church members for a number of years before they had begun to read the Bible in any sustained way. Often this coincided with a desire to learn more about their faith than was provided by the instruction which they were otherwise receiving, above all in sermons. Bible reading was more easily sustainable as a group activity, and some of the more interesting groups were ones which met for purposes other than Bible study: justice and peace groups, women's groups, etc. Even here there was a certain sense of unease on the part of group members that the use they were making of the Bible may have been relatively peripheral. What does emerge from such interviews is that while there are still strong individualistic readings of the Bible, with people looking to it for consolation and individual support, those who use it for group study may, as they seek to develop their faith, also turn to it for guidance in matters of wider social and political concern. In this they are relatively untroubled at discovering that the Bible is not as unambiguous in its directives as they may have been officially encouraged to believe. There was in many groups a surprising readiness to accept that there might be contradictions in the Bible and to accept that the meanings of particular passages might come clear only in particular settings and contexts.

So much for the preliminaries. The work of the consultation was to reflect on the results of these surveys and to ponder their implications for the hermeneutical and paedagogical strategies employed in the world of seminary and university, as well as to consider ways in which cross-cultural cooperation could be developed.

For those interested in a full report of the consultation, detailed minutes are available from the author. What I propose to offer here are, and can only be, some personal reflections on our meeting.

1. There was, to an outside observer at least, a striking tension between the findings of the Port Harcourt survey and West African colleagues' plans to develop an inculturation hermeneutic. The Marxist sociologist who conducted the survey categorised the popular attitudes to and uses of the Bible as a "theology of survival," which was much less concerned with relating the Bible to African culture than with using it to surmount problems of childlessness, unemployment, sickness, demon-possession, etc. Respondents might recognise that there were closer connections between African culture and the Old Testament, but they still preferred the New because of its greater spiritual power. Thus it might well seem as if the way forward for developing popular readings lay with the "spiritual" churches, which focus on healing and exorcism and prayer for material goods and benefits.

On the face of it, then, there is a clear difference of focus between popular and academic readings. Popular readings are more concerned with using the New Testament as a source of power than with assimilating the culturally closer Old Testament; scholars want to offer cultural readings of the Bible which exploit cultural similarities. Nevertheless, there is a sense of cultural closeness to the Bible among popular readers which needs to be explored, just as there are clearly problems with using the Bible simply as a means of individual survival. African scholars are right, that is to say, to feel that they view the Bible from a different perspective from Western/Northern scholars and that they need to reflect on this and to see what resources the Bible may provide in their search for identity and individual and social well-being. At the same time, those from Southern Africa whose main efforts in the last years of apartheid have been to develop a liberation hermeneutic would argue that there needs to be a critical interaction between popular and scholarly readings and that the individualistic piety of the "spiritual" churches and much popular use of the Bible needs to be counteracted by more critical reflection on the economic, social, and political context in and from which people read the Bible.

2. This dialogue between West and South African colleagues was certainly one of the most encouraging features of the consultation and is something that it would have been difficult to imagine before the end of apartheid, when inculturation hermeneutics was all too easily confused with or coopted by apartheid uses of the Bible. Now there was dialogue and a real interest to cooperate with each other. There was an acknowledged need to relate the concepts of context and culture in any attempt to give cultural readings of the Bible. Cultures have their place within a particular historical continuum (African religious culture has surely been affected by missionary pietism and is, of course, in dialogue and conflict with a broadly scientific/technological world-view). They also have their place within a complex network of economic, social, and political relationships, both on a local and a global scale. The search for human dignity and wholeness, well-being, has to be located within this network of relationships. It is therefore important neither to divorce culture from its wider context nor simply to subsume it under economic, social, and political categories.

3. This in turn suggests that the relationship between popular and academic readings of the Bible has also to be dialogical and carefully structured. Colleagues from the Institute for the Study of the Bible in Pietermaritzburg stressed that they would only enter into partnership with organised groups of the poor and marginalised, partly for fear that they themselves might otherwise have too dominant a role, partly because such groups had already a clear idea of where they stood politically and had their own agenda to bring to the study of the texts. This may or may not be a policy which could be easily applied elsewhere. It makes the point, however, that there is a need for a politically aware group of popular readers, whether such awareness is the result of conscientisation by an "organic intellectual" (Gramschi) or whether such resources for political criticism are already to be found alive and well among the poor and marginalised, as ISB members would be inclined to argue.

4. The survey of attitudes to and practice of Bible reading in the West of Scotland showed up different tensions between academic and popular readings. In one sense it might be said that the most influential popular readings of the Bible, namely pietistic and individualistic ones, do indeed have their roots in the academic teaching of the last hundred years. Scotland was the home of a strong liberal tradition with a deep indebtedness to Ritschl and Harnack. Further, this view of the Bible as a religion of the heart was widely disseminated (across the world!) by William Barclay, who taught for many years in Glasgow University. It was clear from the

survey that such patterns of Bible reading, or at least such broad expectations of what might be derived from Bible reading are still widely present. What the survey also showed was that there were those who were seeking fresh ways of looking at the Bible as part of a wider search for personal growth and development; and that this was often related to attempts to relate personal faith to wider, public issues.

5. This leads directly to two lines of enquiry. The first is to look again closely at the perspectives, cultural and political, from which the Bible has been studied in the history of European academic study. What the consultation brought home to me, more than anything, was the realisation that there is no sharp division between cultural readings of the Bible and "purely historical" readings, or indeed any other kind of readings. European academic readings have been as much driven by major cultural questions and perspectives as any other. What is required is a reassesment of the major paradigms of biblical interpretation to identify the role that cultural analogues and questions have played in the reconstruction and appropriation of the Biblical texts. The second is to initiate a more serious dialogue between popular and academic readers of the Bible. It is important not to make too sharp a distinction here. Those who are academics do not cease thereby to be members of a community of readers, just as those who are not academics are not wholly untutored in readerly skills or indeed in the techniques of biblical studies. The point is more that different people occupy different positions and roles within the community. Some speak out of a situation of marginalisation and struggle; some speak from positions of relative power in church and society; some are engaged in the wider discourses of academia and have their own particular responsibilities here. What we need to discover is how forms of partnership within a particular local community may bear fruit both for academic and popular readings. Part of this may be in a greater ability on the part of the community to appropriate the texts for its own purposes; part may be in opening up new perspectives and questions which can lead to paradigm shifts in scholarly academic readings.

6. One of the outcomes of the consultation was to underline the similarities between Western/Northern readings of the Bible and the goals of African scholars engaged in inculturation hermeneutics. Both groups are engaged in cultural readings of the Bible. Nevertheless, these similarities remain on the theoretical level. Both try to read the Bible from their own perspective and to view it in the light of their own dominant concerns. The effect of this is, in turn, to point to the particularity of such local theologies and to raise the question of how far we can continue to speak of a universal theology, of any kind of commonality among the diversities of theology that will be produced once the cultural hegemony of Western/

Northern readings is broken. The dangers of a simple fragmentation of theology are evident enough. What can be done and what grounds are there to suppose that "polycentrism" in theology, to use a term of David Tracy's, can lead to a deeper sense of the infinity of God?

In one sense this may be the wrong way round to phrase the question. Perhaps we first need to acknowledge the vital importance of local theologies: that what people need to discover is the reality of the living God manifest in their communities and that a "universal" God who is merely the imposition of other communities' apprehensions of God as normative for other communities may be oppressive and serve to conceal God for others. In this sense the quest for "universality" may be simply an attempt to impose totality on others and so be diminishing. In one sense one may argue very properly for the importance of the development of local theologies, as expressions of the living faith of communities in very different situations.

In another way however, we have to be careful not to stress cultural and contextual differences in such a way that we end up denying our common humanity, or lose sight of the sense in which, however much we may stand in different places in the complex web of our world, we are nevertheless all caught in that same web and need to hear each others voices if we are not to deny ourselves by denying our very interrelatedness. It is not just "our" culture which defines who and what we are; it is our belonging to a particular culture in a multicultural world and our responses to that world which ultimately makes us who we are. Denying the existence or importance of other cultures and contexts impoverishes us as much as does the refusal to recognise the importance of our own cultural formation.

And by the same token, to insist on the normativity of our local theologies for all other groups is an impoverishment. It is to deny the very richness, the infinity, of the God whom we claim to experience as living and liberative in our own lives, to deny that this God manifests God-self in a thousand ways and names. But of course that is in no sense a necessary response of those who seek to discover the reality of God in their own readings of the Bible. The very fact that they see the importance of such readings in the life of their own community can only encourage them to assist others in discovering God in this way too. Perhaps the most important aspect of the consultation was the discovery of the possibilities of cooperation, of glimpsing at least some of the ways in which a more polycentric theological community could indeed work together and assist each other.

What then of the future of this group? We planned to meet twice in the next five years: once at International SBL in South Africa (1996) and again in 1999. Plans for the first of these events had to be abandoned when the International SBL meeting fell through; plans for the 1999 meeting will depend on funding which we hope will be forthcoming in conjunction with the development of cooperative programmes between the various centres. During that period we hope to encourage research and publishing in the following areas: the relationship of popular and academic readings of the Bible; the relationship between inculturation and liberation hermeneutics; and the relationship between Western/Northern styles of Biblical studies and African styles. Beyond that we hope that there will be exchange and interchange between our different centres. Already that is happening: members of ISB have been in Glasgow and have been instrumental in establishing a partnership between local Bible study groups and the university department. Cooperation on research continues; visits between South Africa and Nigeria are planned. Pooling of bibliographical information and the development of library holdings is proceeding. All of this can, of course, do no more than provide a base on which development of genuinely creative local theologies can occur.

THE PARABLE OF THE SHREWD MANAGER (LUKE 16:1–13): AN ESSAY IN INCULTURATION BIBLICAL HERMENEUTIC

Justin S. Ukpong
Catholic Institute of West Africa
Nigeria

ABSTRACT

This article reads the notorious parable of the shrewd manager from an inculturation biblical hermeneutic. The cultural context informing this biblical interpretation is primarily that of exploited peasant farmers of West Africa as well as the concerns of the international debt burden of the Two-Thirds World. While most interpretations have read the parable from the perspective of the rich man's economic system, this article reads the story from the perspective of the peasant farmers in the story. This reading proceeds by situating the parable within the theological framework of Luke's critique of the rich and riches and within the social-historical context of the parable.

INTRODUCTION

The parable of the shrewd or unjust/dishonest steward manager[1] has been a *crux interpretum* for exegetes. According to Joseph A. Fitzmyer, "There are few passages in the Synoptic Gospel more puzzling than the well-known story about the dishonest manager (Unjust Steward)....whether a clear and definite explanation of this story will ever be arrived at is hard to say" (Fitzmyer, 1974: 161). L. John Topel echoes similar sentiments about the parable: "The literature dealing with the parable of the unjust steward is staggering, and after all the effort expended its meaning still eludes us. Indeed more than any other parable, it can be expected to keep its mystery for future generations of exegetes for it bristles with difficulties" (216). The celebrated French exegete M. J. Lagrange is reported to have said of the same parable: "I admit that it is not easy to preach on this subject because many people imagine that only an edifying story can be told in church" (Fitzmyer, 1974:161). The parable is puzzling, mystifying, and unedifying because the reader has been

---

[1] The Greek word used is οἰκονόμος, which in its original sense has to do with managing affairs. Since the person was in charge of an estate and not a household steward, I prefer to call him the manager.

conditioned to identify with the rich man in the parable, who is then constructed to stand for God, and from whose perspective the manager is called unjust. But does the rich man in this parable represent God, and is the manager unjust?

Read from the perspective of ordinary West African peasant farmers who live by the world-view provided by their traditional cultures, and who experience economic oppression at the hands of rich middle-men produce traders, the parable evokes an interpretation which differs from Western scholars. What they see is an economic relationship of unequal partners—a rich man in a strong economic position and his employees, peasant farmers, in a weak economic position. From their experience, they know that such an economic relationship generates the exploitation of the weak by the strong. Consequently, they admire the manager who used his discretionary power to grant debt reduction to his customers. For them, he is the hero of the story for granting such a debt reduction to the farmers who needed it far more than the rich man needed the profit. He acted on behalf of the exploited.

My purpose in this essay is not to offer *the* valid interpretation of this parable. For one thing, the methodology which this volume follows eschews the idea of one universally valid interpretation of the biblical text. Rather my purpose is to offer an understanding of the parable from an alternative approach, that is, the inculturation hermeneutic.

Defining Inculturation Biblical Hermeneutic

I have coined the term "inculturation biblical hermeneutic" to designate an interpretation derived from the methodology of inculturation theology. The term "inculturation theology" does not refer to a specific theological discipline. Rather, it refers to a hermeneutical process in theologizing that cuts across all theological disciplines including biblical exegesis. It is a new way of doing theology. "Inculturation biblical hermeneutic" is its application to biblical interpretation.

Although the term is new, it designates aspects that are already familiar. One of these is the attempt to relate the Hebrew Bible's religious culture and African religious culture, a perspective of biblical research that was quite common up to a decade ago (Dickson and Ellingworth, 1969, Dickson, 1979:179–93; Mveng et al.; Ukpong, 1987). An inculturation biblical hermeneutic is an approach that consciously and explicitly seeks to interpret the biblical text from socio-cultural perspectives of different people. This includes both their religious and secular culture as well as their social and historical experiences. This does not mean reading contemporary contexts into the biblical text; rather it means consciously and critically allowing different contemporary contexts to inform the interpretation positively and to influence the type of questions put to the text in the process of interpretation.

Theologians and biblical scholars are increasingly aware that all theological and biblical interpretations are culturally, historically, and socially conditioned (Schreiter: 3–4; Jeffre: 47). It is now acknowledged that the current exegetical methodologies have been developed from perspectives that are specifically Western; that they do not reflect the perspectives and concerns of other cultures; and that each culture has something to contribute to the understanding of the Christian message. As an approach to biblical interpretation, the inculturation hermeneutic seeks to promote the employment of different cultural perspectives in biblical interpretation, and to bring the contribution of various cultural resources to our reading of the Bible. In other words, it seeks to make the different sociocultural contexts the subject of interpretation. It eschews the hitherto dominant classicist approach, which supposes the biblical text to have only one universally valid interpretation, and which assumes that only approaches shaped by the dominant cultures are seen to be valid.

The inculturation biblical hermeneutic supposes that the biblical text is plurivalent and can be validly understood differently according to different contexts and perspectives. But this does not mean that the biblical text can mean anything. Instead it recognizes that there are dynamics built into a text for guiding interpretation, and that these dynamics can function in different contexts to produce different but valid interpretations. Therefore, it advocates a multi-cultural approach to interpreting biblical texts whereby the biblical message becomes available to people of different cultures according to their various contexts. It is a holistic approach to exegesis (McDonald: 547–49).

Interpretation is done within the canon, and comparison with other relevant texts is done in the process of interpretation. The Bible is looked upon as a sacred classic—a book containing norms for Christian living as well as an ancient literary text. Historical critical tools and others are used precisely as tools to aid interpretation and not as ends in themselves (Stuhlmacher, 1979:85–90). With insights from the historical analysis of the text, the text is reread dynamically against the background of a contemporary context. This dynamic rereading of the text involves entering into the text conscious of the present context, with critical awareness, and allowing it to evoke in us responses, reactions, and commitment appropriate to its message and our context. The objective of interpretation is the actualization of the text within today's context.

This is to say that our context as well as that of the text have an important part to play in the process of assigning meaning to the relationship and the interaction of the actors in the text, and in the appropriation of the message. With inculturation hermeneutics there is no question of treating a text merely as an object of analysis. The involvement of the interpreter in the dynamics of the text is demanded.

Inculturation biblical hermeneutics, as used here, is developed from the popular approaches to the Bible, and it is reinforced with Western critical insights of reading. With this brief discussion of inculturation biblical hermeneutics, I now return to Luke 16:1–13.

My interpretation of this parable includes the following assumptions:

1) Parables are plurivalent, hence a parable may have different applications in different contexts. The presence in the gospels of multiple applications of a parable, as in the case of the parable under consideration, attests to this (Croatto: 37).

2) Parables have meaning on at least two levels. One is the historical/social level whereby it expresses what ought to be the proper human relationships in society, or is a critique of societal and individual attitudes and practices in the light of the values of the kingdom. The other is the eschatological level, whereby the eschatological implication of our actions, that is, the God-human relationship at the end time, is expressed.

3) Parables are an invitation to decision and commitment about contemporary situations. Hence they are to be interpreted dynamically in the present context.

Based on these assumptions, I shall interpret the parable of the shrewd manager against a particular context, and I shall seek to identify the social and eschatological messages in the parable and the commitment it evokes in a contemporary context.

Context of Interpretation

I shall reread the parable of the shrewd manager against the background of rural West Africa, specifically that of the palm producers and cocoa farmers. Most ordinary West Africans are peasant farmers engaged in the cultivation of various crops, including the oil palm, from which they obtain palm oil and kernel. They live by the world-view provided by their traditional cultures. According to this world view, there should be no exploitation of fellow human beings. Material wealth is regarded as God's gift to the whole community. Hoarding and profiteering at the expense of others are to be abhorred.

With the coming of Western civilization at the beginning of this century things have changed. A money-oriented economy replaced a barter economy. With this change, new avenues of trade and new means of getting rich quickly developed. For example there arose a crop of rich middle-men produce traders who became rich by buying palm and cocoa produce from farmers at very low prizes and selling them to exporters at very high prizes. This was exploitation since they did not allow the producers of these commodities to get the real values of their produce. They had trading posts at various places run by managers who transacted business for them.

Any peasant farmer in need of agricultural loans went to these managers, who had the power and means to grant such loans. In addition, one could acquire loans for medical expenses and children's school fees. However, all loans were refundable with interests rates ranging from 50–100%. The system operated as follows: for a loan $20.00 a farmer may be required to pledge 8–10 tins (a four-gallon measure) of palm oil, which at the time of the loan may cost $20.00 per tin. The amount of palm oil pledged depended on the leniency of the trader. At harvest time, if oil prices go up, this is not taken into consideration. If, however, the prices of oil go down, the farmer must make up for the difference. This was another form of exploitation, which was very common in the South Eastern Nigeria, Ghana, and other parts of West Africa.

Some Interpretations of the Parable

Interpretations of the parable of the shrewd manager generally have focused on the manager's actions of reducing the debts of his customers. Invariably, the manager of the parable is presumed to stand for God; thus, the manager's action is explained in relation to God's benevolence and generosity. I will identify three mainline interpretations.

One line of interpretation sees the manager as fraudulent but clever. Reported to his master for his fraudulent dealings and about to be dismissed, he engages in a further act of fraud by falsifying the promissory notes of his master's debtors. He is praised, however, not for this act of dishonesty but for his cleverness in taking such a decisive action to avert a future disaster. According to T. W. Manson, with reference to v.8a of the parable: "Whether it is the employer or Jesus that speaks, we must take the purport of the speech to be: 'This is a fraud; but it is a most ingenious fraud. The steward is a rascal; but he is a wonderfully clever rascal'" (292). Thus it is not the manager's fraudulent behavior that is held up for emulation but his prudence.

For those who see the parables as ending at v. 7, prudence consists in general acuteness in taking decisive action in the face of crisis. Hence for J. Jeremias, the manager is a criminal who, threatened with expulsion, adopts unscrupulous but resolute measures to ensure his future security. This clever, resolute behavior in the face of crisis is the moral of the parable. Christians must be aware that they are facing the crisis of the eschaton and must act resolutely (Jeremias: 46–48).

For those who see the parable as ending at v. 8–9, prudence in the use of money is the lesson of the parable. Luke teaches that the Christian can learn from the unjust person that giving material help to the poor can gain one favor in God's sight. Thus the parable teaches the necessity of sharing material goods with the poor in order to be received into eternal life (Hiers: 34; Williams, 1964:294).

This line of interpretation unconsciously identifies with the rich man in the parable. Because its perspective is that of a rich man, the manager is called unscrupulous, fraudulent, criminal—terms which are altogether absent from the text, but which approximate the rich man's assessment of the manager's "unjustness." Because the manager is considered from this perspective, all that can be leant from him is his God-given ingenuity of taking decisive action and giving material goods to the poor, even though this is done in a fraudulent way and for selfish motive. The economic system within which he operates is not critiqued, because to do so would mean critiquing the social and economic foundation of the rich man. The rich man himself is not critiqued because the analysis is done from his perspective. No doubt, the Christian must learn from the manager about taking decisive action at the moment of crisis, and no doubt we must share material with the poor, but why are the poor poor in the first place?

Another line of interpretation seeks to understand the practice of the manager against Near Eastern customs. It is supposed that the manager, according to custom, received no salary but could charge his customers fees. He could keep some or all of these fees, a Hellenistic practice contrary to Jewish law. Therefore, when he was given notice he simply settled with his master's debtors without taking his own fees. This was a prudent way of acting, which the master approved of. The manager used his material wealth in a way that would ensure his future in view of the impending crisis. The crisis requires taking such a decisive action. Thus the shrewd manager becomes a model for Christians who are in a situation which calls for prudent use of material wealth (Fitzmyer, 1974:177–78).

This interpretation rightly focuses on the crisis in which the unfortunate manager found himself. But again, because the interpretation is done from the perspective of the rich man, there is no critique of the unilateral action of the rich man which brought the manager's crisis. Rather such a unilateral dismissal of an employee is taken for granted and implicitly condoned. Those who follow this line of interpretation exonerate the rich man.

Yet another line of interpretation connects this parable and those of chapter 15 and seeks to focus the parable on the rich man's forgiving the manager. According to it, the lesson of the parable is forgiveness manifested in a generosity that seems "unjust" to human eyes. The manager has squandered the rich man's money, just as the prodigal son has squandered his father's money (Lk 15: 11–32). And just as the father forgave his prodigal son, just so in the case of the shrewd manager, the master was not only prepared to forgive him but even to praise the ingenuity of the person who had wronged him. This is a forgiveness beyond human standards. The manager therefore rightly forgives the debtors, just as the older son should have forgiven his prodigal brother. In human eyes, the master's forgiving of the manager is "unjust," "unfair." What the manager does—reducing his customers' debts—is similarly in human eyes "unjust." Yet he is held up as an example for Christians. This is precisely because Christians are being called upon to do what may seem "unjust" means. To forgive seven times a day (Lk 17:3) is far beyond human standards and reveals a higher standard of justice for the kingdom (Topel: 225–27).

While this interpretation, in my opinion, rightly points to the concepts of justice as an important element in the parable, its tying the theme of this parable to that of the parables in chapter 15, and so making forgiveness its focus, is problematic. It is true that he reduced the debts of his customers, and that the master praised him, but this is not enough to indicate the theme of forgiveness in the story. Other factors must be taken into consideration.

Of particular note is the fact that the master did not forgive the manager when the manager was reported as having wasted his goods. Rather he set out to dismiss him. This becomes much clearer when we compare the action of the master with that of the father in the preceding parable of the prodigal son (15:11–32). Both the manager and the prodigal son were guilty of "wasting" property, and while the father of the prodigal son forgave the boy and received him back, the master dismissed the manager. And as we shall see later, the image of the master in our parable stands in sharp contrast to the image of the father in the story of the prodigal son. It is therefore not convincing to hold that the theme of forgiveness found in chapter 15 is continued in our parable.

This brief survey shows that the parable of the shrewd manager has been interpreted mainly from the perspective of the rich man in the story.

For this reason attention has focused mainly on the manager. I contend that the parable has more to offer than a critique of the manager. It is notable that apart from the last approach presented above, no serious effort has been made to relate the parable to one of the great themes of Luke's Gospel namely, Jesus' teachings on riches.

In this study, I shall interpret the parable from the perspective of the peasant farmers in the story. That the farmers are not the main actors in the story provides another vantage point for assessing the activities of the main actors and interpreting their relationship among themselves and to the farmers in the story.

Textual Analysis of the Parable

The parable of the shrewd manager is part of Luke's narrative of Jesus' journey from Galilee to Jerusalem, Luke 9:51–19:27. In this block of material three important themes of Luke's Gospel are found: discipleship, God's mercy, and forgiveness. For Luke the good news of the kingdom is for the poor. The rich are warned against the danger of being excluded from the kingdom by their possessions. They are to use wealth in the right way if they want to enter the kingdom (Marshall, 1984:206). Nowhere else in the Gospel is this theme so well developed as in the section on Jesus' journey to Jerusalem.

The second section opens with the teaching about poverty and detachment from worldly ties as a condition for discipleship (9:57–63). An example of such detachment is given in the Samaritan's use of his own money to care for a stranger (10:25–37). In the story of the prodigal son (15:11–32), detachment from riches is exemplified by the father who acceded to his son's request to give him his portion of the father's property, while the prodigal son exemplifies attachment to and misuse of riches. These stories are not specifically on riches, but aspects of them exemplify Jesus' teaching on riches in the section.

The main teaching on riches is developed in three parables of the section (12:13–21; 16:19–31) and two narratives at the end of it (18:18–30; 19:1–10). What is the focus of this teaching and, by implication, of our parable? The first parable, the rich fool (12:13–21), exposes the folly of hoarding material goods. It is specifically and explicitly a critique of the rich and the societal practice of hoarding material wealth. The parable of the shrewd manager is the second. Its focus is not as clear, but I shall seek to discover it through the comparison with other texts in the section. The third is the parable of the rich man and Lazarus (16:19–31), which exposes the eschatological punishment for not sharing material wealth with the poor. This, no doubt, is a clear critique of the rich; their lack of concern for the poor in society is the object of critique. It is therefore to be expected that the parable of the shrewd manager, which is sandwiched between these two, and treats the same general theme of riches, is also a critique of the rich and the attendant societal attitude associated with riches.

The three parables on riches in the section also have literary connections. Each of them describes the main figure in the parable as a "rich man." This description is not present in the parables of the good Samaritan (10:11–27), the prodigal son (15:11–32), and the pounds (19:11–27), which are also found in the section, and in which material wealth is mentioned, but which are not directly connected with critiquing riches.

For Luke, the phrase ἄνθρωπός τις ἦν πλούσιος (rich man) has a pejorative connotation. It is always found in contexts where material wealth is directly or indirectly critiqued. Apart from the parable of the shrewd manager, there are ten such references in the Gospel. The first is found in 6:24, in which Jesus delivers a curse on the rich, an explicit criticism of riches and the rich. The second is found in the parable of the rich fool (12:16), another context in which material wealth is critiqued. In the third, which deals with invitations to parties of rich people (14:12–13), those who ought to be invited are the poor not the rich. Similarly, the rich are criticized for associating only with the rich. The fourth, fifth, and sixth references are found in the story of the rich man and Lazarus (16:19, 21, 22), which is another explicit critique of the rich and their lack of concern for the poor.

The seventh and eighth are found in the story of the rich noble man who became sad when he was told to sell all his property and give the money to the poor, including Jesus's statement on the impossibility of the rich people to enter the kingdom (18:23, 25). This is perhaps the most poignant pronouncement of Jesus about the rich in the gospels. It was so devastating that even the disciples sought an explanation as to how people could then be saved. Jesus' reply is even more disturbing: to be saved one must be detached from material things, and this is made possible only by God's grace. The ninth reference is about Zacchaeus whose action of making restitution is a critique of riches (19:2). Himself a rich man, Zacchaeus voluntarily restores what he got through extortion. He acknowledges the evil of accumulating wealth while dispossessing the poor. His actions bespeak of self-criticism. The last reference contrasts the offering at the treasury made by the rich to that made by a poor widow whom Jesus commended (12:4). Here the poor widow is preferred to the rich.

In all these stories, the rich and material wealth are held out in one way or another as the object of critique. This means that the use of the term ἄνθρωπός πλούσιος to describe the master of the estate in the parable of the shrewd manager signals that he is to be looked at as an object of critique.

That Luke's presentation of Jesus' teaching on riches in this section is meant to be a critique of the rich and riches is further confirmed by the two narratives on the same theme at the end of the section. These are the case of the rich noble man (18:18–30), which shows how hard it is for those who have riches to enter into the kingdom, and the case of Zacchaeus (19:1–10) where Jesus' words (v. 10) show how the right use of wealth is a precondition for gaining salvation. These narratives serve as practical cases to exemplify and confirm the parabolic teachings in the section.

In terms of proximate context, the two parables in chapter 16 have both literary and thematic continuity. The main figures are described as rich men (16:1; 16:19). Both parables present the rich men against the background of disadvantaged people—the dismissed manager and the peasant farmers in the first story, and the beggar in the second. Both focus on riches. If the second one is a critique of the riches and the rich man, then it follows that the first one should also be a critique of riches and the rich man in the story.

In addition, Luke 16 exhibits elements of discontinuity with the preceding chapter 15. The chapter opens with the words ἔλεγεν δέ, which generally introduces a contrast, and the audience changes from the Pharisees and scribes (15:1–2) to the disciples (16:1). Besides, the main figures in the parables in chapter 16 stand in contrast to those in chapter 15. First, while the shepherd (15:1–7), the woman (15:8–10), and the father (15:11–32) are anxious about and search for what is lost, the rich men in 16:1–13, and 16:19–31 do not care for the marginalized in the society. Second, while the father in 15:11–32 welcomes back his son, who was guilty of wasting goods, the rich man in 16:1–13 dismisses his manager for the same offense of wasting goods. Thus, the main figures in chapter 16 are contrasted with those in chapter 15. This means that while it is reasonable to understand the main figures in chapter 15 as they are generally understood to stand for God, it is not reasonable to understand those in chapter 16 in the same way.

In sum, therefore, the teaching of Jesus on riches in this section focuses on a critique of material wealth and of the rich. The parable of the shrewd manager is a critique of riches, and the rich man in the parable is the object of critique.

In Judaism, the context out which Jesus spoke his parables, the form of the parable comprised the body of the story called the *mashal*, and the moral or commentary on the story called the *nimshal*. (Of course, not every parable had a *nimshal*). Sometimes the same *mashal* could be found with different *nimshalim*, thus pointing to differences in the context of interpretation (Culbertson: 206). In the case of the parable under consideration there is one *mashal* and many *nimshalim* attached to it. This is the common opinion of scholars. There is, however, disagreement as to where the *mashal* ends and where the *nimshalim* start.

The majority of the exegetes see the parables as ending at v.8, and see the other verses as the *nimshalim* on it. (Among those who hold this view are E. Klostermann, A. Descamps, K. H. Rengstorf; see Fitzmyer, 1985:1096.) What is problematic about this view is that v.8b, which is clearly a commentary on the manager's action, is counted as part of the *mashal*. This verse is an exhortation for people to approach their spiritual affairs with the same zeal and seriousness as the approach temporal affairs. Therefore, it cannot be considered as part of the *mashal*, but as a *nimshal*.

According to B. Weiss, W. O. E. Oesterley, J. Fitzmyer, among others, the parable proper ends at v.8a while the rest of the parable (vv. 8b–13) are the *nimshalim* on it (Fitzmyer, 1985:1097). This position rightly recognizes the fact that v.8b is a commentary on the manager's action and hence a *nimshal*. This is the position I shall adopt here.

There are two problems with regard to the understanding of v. 8a. First: to whom does ὁ κύριος in this verse refer? Second is: why did the "master" praise the manager?

With regard to the first question, ὁ κύριος could refer either to Jesus or to the master in the parable. According to some, it refers to Jesus. Jeremias has strongly argued for this position. For him it is doubtful that the master in the parable would praise his deceitful manager. That Jesus is meant here finds an analogy in Luke 18:6 where the same expression (τῆς ἀδικίας) is clearly used by Jesus to qualify the principal figure in that story (Lk 18:1–18). In that text, too, it is clear that with the words εἶπεν δὲ ὁ κύριος the judgment of Jesus inserted into the parable (18:6) should be seen as introducing the insertion of Jesus' words into the parable. Against this argument that the change of subject in 16:9 suggests that Jesus is not the ὁ κύριος of 16:8, Jeremias cites a similar change of the subject in 18:8 (Jeremias: 46–48).

In my view, Jeremias has failed to take into account the fact that in Luke 18:1–8 it is only at 18:4–5, which expresses the comment of the principal figure in the story, that the story is complete, and the rest is a commentary on it. Similarly, in the story in 16:1–13, one needs the reaction of the main figure to make the story complete, and 16:8a is the only possible text expressing such reaction. Besides, from the point of view of the narrative structure of the text, it is only normal that the story which started with the reaction of the rich man to allegations about his manager should end with the expression of his reaction to the further activity of the manager. Along with Fitzmyer and others, I see v. 8a as referring not to Jesus but to the rich man's reaction to his manager's activity (Fitzmyer, 1985:1097), and so the ὁ κύριος refers not to Jesus but to the master in the parable.

With regard to the second question, some authors are of the opinion that the manager is depraved, hence it is only his prudence in facing the crisis that is praised (Jeremias: 46). Fitzmyer has argued that the manager was not fraudulent and that describing him as unjust does not connote depravity. He cites the case of the unjust judge (Lk 18:2–8) in support of this. For him, the manager was praised for both his action and prudence (Fitzmyer, 1974:172–73). In view of the fact that it is the rich man who praised the manager and called him "unjust," it is plausible to see the rich man as condemning the action of his manager yet admiring his prudence. Whether the manager was in *actual fact* fraudulent or not is another matter, which I shall discuss later. But insofar as the rich man was concerned the manager was unjust (v. 8a).

Concerning Fitzmyer's argument, I want to point out that the term "unjust" is used in two different and contradictory senses in the parable of the shrewd manager and in the parable of the unjust judge (Luke 18:1–10). In the former parable, it is the rich man who pronounces the manager unjust. As I shall demonstrate later, his pronouncement is informed by the oppressive society's concept of justice. In the second case, however, it is Jesus who pronounces that the judge is unjust, and he expresses the divine standard of justice. The difference is that in an oppressive society it is taken for granted that the poor people, like the farmers in the first story and the widow in the second, have no rights, and therefore do not deserve to be treated as human. To treat them as human is unjust. This is the connotation of the term in the first story. The dismissed manager gave the poor peasant farmers generous debt reduction, which could bring relief to their poor living conditions. By the standard of an oppressive economic system, which the rich man represents, this was unjust. Poor people have no such rights. Similarly, the judge in the second story shows himself as operating according to an oppressive standard of justice. Because human rights are founded on God and the dignity of humanity as God's creation, by having no respect for God and humanity, the judge shows that he has no respect for human rights. Therefore, he vindicates the woman not because she has rights as a human being, whereby she would deserve to be listened to, but simply because she has pestered him. All this is, of course, unjust by divine standards. Hence, Jesus calls the judge unjust. In other words, what is just by the standards of an oppressive society is unjust by divine standards, and vice versa.

Before going on to discuss the background of the parable of the shrewd manager, it is important to bring together the points that have emerged from its textual analysis. These are:
1) The parable is a critique of riches and of the rich man, the principal figure of the parable;
2) The rich man in the parable stands in continuity with the rich man in the next parable involving Lazarus (16:19–31), and in contrast to the principal figures in the parable of chapter 15, and so he is not representative of God;
3) Four *nimshalim* are attached to the parable as follows, vv. 8b, 9, 10–12, 13;
4) The ὁ κύριος of v. 8a refers not to Jesus but to the rich man in the parable; and
5) The ingenuity of the manager is the object of praise in v. 8a.

Social Historical Context of the Parable

To gain a fuller understanding of the parable, I shall now probe into the economic situation in Palestine reflected in the parable. According to J. D. M. Derrett, the parable reflects Palestinian practices of agency and usury (Derrett: 198–219). A manager of an estate had powers to act on behalf of his master in transactions with third parties such as the renting of a plot of ground to tenant farmers, giving loans against a harvest, liquidation and reduction of debts, and keeping the accounts of such transactions. Even though giving of loans with interests was regarded as usury and forbidden by Jewish law (cf. Deut 17:7–8; 23:20–21; Exod 22:24; Lev 23:36–37), the practice was common. In the promissory notes or bonds of such loans, only the total amount owed (i.e. principal plus interest) was recorded. This made it possible to circumvent the law forbidding usury, for if the amount charged as interest appeared in the bond, the borrower could claim it back in the law court. According to Fitzmyer, the practice of having borrowers sign bonds in which only the total amount owed was indicated was quite common not only in Palestine but also in the Greco-Roman world, Egypt, Syria, and Babylonia (Fitzmyer, 1985: 1097). Josephus records that when Agrippa 1 was almost bankrupt (ca. AD 33–34) he borrowed money from a Near Eastern banker through an agent, Marsyas, who had to sign a bond for 20.000 Attic drachmas, though he had actually received 2500 drachmas less (*Ant.* 18.6, 3.157). A similar practice was known to have been in vogue in India early this century (Gibson: 334).

Against this background, the parable of the shrewd manager depicts a situation where a rich man, probably the owner of a Galilean *latifundium*, entrusted the management of his estate to a manager (Fitzmyer, 1985:1097). During the normal course of his business the manager made loans to people. Since these loans were repayable in kind—in agricultural produce (vv. 6–7)—they could have been loans against a harvest, and the practice was to pay them back with interest. Only the total amount to be paid back, comprising the principal and the interest on it, was indicated in the bond. The manager could also have rented out portions of his master's land to tenant farmers, with the rent to be paid back in kind.

Would the master have approved of all this? Since this was part of the normal course of the business of the estate and since such practices were apparently common at the time, it is likely that the master approved of it. In support of this is, he dismissed the manager for "wasting" his goods, which among other things would mean that he was not making enough profit. In 19:12–27, Luke tells of another master who punished one of his managers for not having made profit. This indicates that the master himself was a shrewd businessman who kept an eye on his business and who would regularly require accurate accounting from the manager. Besides, the text indicates that the money was owed to the master (vv. 5–7). Legally, however, the master could plead innocent in the law court since all the transactions were done by an agent. But that would not exonerate him from moral involvement in the transactions. In other words, the rich man must be seen as morally involved in the usurious deals that took place in the estate.

Was the manager unjust? The text does not provide the precise nature and details of the offence for which the manager was dismissed. It only says that he was guilty of "wasting" his master's property (16:2). In Luke 15:13, the prodigal son is guilty of the same offence. In this text, the offence is expatiated as meaning living a useless life, or living in an extravagant way, $\zeta\hat{\omega}\nu$ $\dot{\alpha}\sigma\dot{\omega}\tau\omega\varsigma$. This could have been the offence of the manager, but it is not indicated. In any case, this does not necessarily involve defrauding his master. It would be implausible then to conclude that wasting the master's property also equals defrauding him. Since, however, the accusation of injustice comes after the manager had given his customers debt reductions, it is reasonable to assume that the accusation refers to this incident.

That the manager had the accounts in the promissory notes of the debtors altered could be explained in one of the three ways. One explanation is that this was an outright fraud. And the manager was a cheat. His action was tantamount to falsification of documents, therefore he was unjust (Jeremais: 46–47). The problem with this explanation is that it does not take into account the economic practices of the time. According to such practice, as shown above, the manager had powers to reduce debts and the story seems to indicate his exercise of such powers. To see him as acting fraudulently is therefore not convincing.

The second explanation takes into account the economic background of the story. According to this background, such a manager was generally a household slave and did not receive a salary. Custom permitted him to charge fees from his customers for his services. This was the interest that the customers had to pay on loans, and he could keep all or part of it, returning the rest to the master. Because the reductions he made to the customers represent the fees he had charged them, he was therefore not defrauding his master (Fitzmeyer, 1974:175–77). This explanation raises two problems. The first is that there is no way of knowing how much of what the customers had to pay represented the capital and how much represented the interest. Therefore, it seems arbitrary to say that the reductions represent the interest, that is, the manager's fees. The second problem is that the text consistently says that the amount owed belonged to the master of the estate (vv. 5,7). There is no indication that the part of what was owed belonged to the manager.

The third explanation takes the background of the text into consideration but also takes the text itself seriously. From the background of the text it is clear that the manager had powers to liquidate debts and give reduction. It is also clear from the text that, at the time he was dismissed, the loans had not matured, for he had to call in the borrowers, not to pay what they owed, but to issue fresh bonds for payment at maturity. The fact that the loans had not matured before he was dismissed means that he was no longer entitled to the interest; it would, when paid, revert to the master. This means that at the time he altered the bonds the amount owed by the debtors (principal plus interest) belonged to the master. Since the manager had power to reduce debts, it seems persuasive to interpret what he did as an exercise of power. It was not therefore a matter of foregoing his fees or a matter of fraud. Nor does the text describe him as falsifying the bonds. He was acting within his legitimate duties.

How then does one explain that at v.8a the rich man calls the manager unjust? The rich man calls the manager unjust in the very act of praising him. The manager's acuteness is praiseworthy, but his act of giving debt reductions to these exploited farmers, which he had powers to do, is seen by the rich man as "unjust." This depicts the exploitative economic system's concept of justice, which is giving to everyone their dues. Whatever a person has is their due, and nobody else's. There is no questioning how and where they got it. Thus, all the wealth and all the power which rich people have are due to them, and it should be given to them (no matter the extent of exploitation they engaged in to get rich). And to the poor who have nothing, nothing is their due; they are not entitled to anything, and so they deserve to be given nothing. To do otherwise, that is, to give some of what is due to the rich to the poor, is to be "unjust." In this sense the rich man called his employee "unjust" for reducing the debts of his customers. The concept of justice in the economic system of his time creates a system whereby the poor toil daily to create the wealth which the rich enjoy. Wherever it operates, the rich are kept rich, and the poor, poor.

Interpretation

From the textual analysis and the historical clarifications given above, I shall now reread the parable of the shrewd manager dynamically against the background of West African peasant farmers presented earlier.

The text presents a rich man who owns an estate but who is an absentee landlord. He has a manager looking after the affairs of the estate. He comes in occasionally to check on the manager and collect the proceeds of the estate. On one such occasion he gets information about the manager wasting his goods and decides to dismiss him. He orders the manager to turn in an account of the estate in preparation for dismissal.

The manager, the rich man's agent, bears the brunt of the work at the estate. He toils for the rich man, he is at his beck and call, and keeps the accounts of the estate. Even though he has wide powers, he is only an employee and can be unilaterally dismissed and stripped of these powers at any moment, with the shortest notice, and for any reason determined by the master. In other words, because he is only an employee, and he is poor, he has no rights. He is therefore an object of exploitation by the rich man and a victim of the vagaries of the economic system of his society.

The customers at the estate, who are mainly the local peasant farmers, know that the manager is not the master of the estate, but he works for a master and is responsible to the master, even though he is rarely seen at the estate. They know also that the debts they owe at the estate are owed to the master and not to the manager even though he does the transactions (vv. 5, 7). They may not know the master in person, but that does not matter. In their eyes, therefore, the master is the lender (not the manager who does the transactions) and they are the borrowers; he has economic power and occupies an economically strong position while they have no economic power and occupy a weak position. They borrow from him to be able to cultivate the land during the farming season. At harvest, what would have accrued to them as profit from their sweat and toil has to be paid out in kind in respect of the loan. The rich man sells the produce of the farmers for profit and thus gets richer. He remains the lender in the community while the farmers remain the borrowers. This is exploitation, an economic arrangement whereby the rich stay rich and the poor stay poor. It is also an economic situation that involves usury, which was forbidden by Jewish law.

It is clear from the above that the rich man is presented in the story as an exploiter and as the object of critique. As the rich man stands in contrast to the poor Lazarus (16:19–31), so too does the master in the parable of the shrewd manager stand in contrast in terms of economic power and position to his employee and the peasant farmers. And by extension, the economic system he represents—an economic system that favors exploitation—is also being critiqued.

Aware that he is to lose his job, the manager plans for the future. He first thinks of joining the band of peasant farmers in the locality, but discards the idea because he had not been trained for that sort of profession. Next, he thinks of begging. Having wielded some power in the economic status quo and having a high self image, he feels it is too shameful to beg. One has the impression then that he has decided to look for another "blue-collar" job. Meanwhile, until he gets another job, how does he live? He knows that as soon as he loses his job he is likely to lose the friendship of his former associates. Therefore, he decides on a public relations strategy to create a new circle of friends from his peasant farmer customers. He knows that he has powers to reduce their debts, and that as exploited people like himself, some debt reduction would bring some relief to them. Consequently, he decides to act in solidarity with them in the expectation that they would respond in solidarity with him when he is dismissed. He calls them in and gives them debt reductions of fifty percent and twenty percent.

In fact, what the farmers got is not so much a matter of charity, but a matter of justice. Charity supposes that a person has no right to what they get, but gets it purely out of the benevolence of the giver who is looked upon as a benefactor. Justice supposes that a person has a right to what they get. Did the farmers have a right to the debt reductions they got? Legally, they had. Here was a case of usury expressly forbidden by law, and in theory they could claim back interest they were charged in the law court. We have no way of knowing whether or not all of the reductions represent the interest they were to pay, but it remains that they had a legal right to get back what was charged interest. Morally, too, they had a right to the debt reduction. The estate was built upon their labor. They were the people generating wealth for the estate. They had a moral right to restitution for exploitation.

The manager's action is restitutive and is an action of self-criticism. To some extent, it parallels that of Zacchaeus (Luke 19:1–10) who, like the manager, had been an agent for an oppressive system. The debt reductions make up for the exploitation the farmers had suffered from the system through him. He therefore deserves to hear words similar to those spoken by Jesus to Zacchaeus: "Today has salvation come to you." Unlike Zaccheaus, he may not have been fully conscious of the restitutive nature of his action, yet that his action was such and had an eschatological effect is clear from the use of the expression φρονίμως ἐποίησεν (he acted wisely v. 8a) to describe it. As used in the Gospel, the adverb φρονίμως describes actions that have eschatological implications.

In its holistic sense, salvation involves forgiveness of sin and the continued living in harmonious peaceful fellowship with others (Ps 133:1) as a sign of eschatological reality. Salvation, in this conception, starts on earth but continues unto eternity (Ukpong, 1983:19). It is a reality that is both present and eschatological, material and spiritual. It is essential to the concept of the kingdom that Jesus inaugurated (Ukpong, 1993:150). Such is the salvation that Jesus imparted to Zaccheaus when he said: "Today has salvation come to this house" (Lk 19:9). He had brought his followers into Zacchaeus' house thereby integrating one who was regarded as an outcast into a fellowship and a community. Such integration and fellowship is what the dismissed manager sought with his former customers, when he gave them debt reductions (Lk 16:4). Hence, he is described as having acted wisely (φρονίμως ἐποίησεν).

Because of the exploitative nature of the economic system in which he operates, the rich man sees the manager's action of giving debt reduction to his customers as injustice (v. 8a). According to the concept of justice in this economic system, the poor have no right to anything; therefore it is unjust to give some of the rich man's property to them. However, there is another concept of justice whereby everyone is seen as having a right to the material goods of this world; where material wealth is regarded as God's own gift to humanity to be shared equitably in such a way that nobody is in want. According to this world-view, to exploit another human being is a crime. The poor are to be treated with dignity and love. Those who have more than others must use their wealth to benefit others. This was the authentic world-view of ancient Israel which the prophets constantly sought to sustain, which got gradually eroded. It is the world-view of African traditional society in which justice is a matter of sharing the earth's wealth in such a way that nobody is exploited and all have enough to live on.

Therefore, the manager's action of sharing the debts of his customers is in line with this latter concept of justice. It is a critique of the exploitative concept of justice operative in his society, of the rich man, his master, as an exploiter, and of his former self as an agent of the oppressive system. By calling the manager "unjust" in the very act of praising his ingenuity (v. 8a), the master acknowledges the manager's critique. His employee's action has challenged his sense of justice and that of his society. As a rich man, he already had more than enough and did not really need what the farmers owed him. Rather, these farmers stood in far greater need than himself.

Today, Two-Thirds World countries are groaning under the heavy weight of international debt and the International Monetary Fund's Economic Structural Adjustment Program (ESAP). The latter is borne out of desire to streamline the weak economies of the Two-Thirds World in relation to the economies of the West. Everywhere the immediate impact has been massive suffering for the ordinary people of Two-Thirds World countries, where the Program has been launched. The ultimate aim is not change or improvement, but to keep people where they "belong"; that is, the weak to continue being weak and the strong to remain strong. Both packages, the debt issue and the ESAP, are under the control of the rich countries of the West.

In the light of the parable of the shrewd manager one is prompted to ask: for whose benefit is the Two-Thirds World carrying debt and the burden of ESAP? And how did the poor countries become poor borrowers in the first place? Is it not through the exploitation of these countries by the rich ones? In the case of debt one often hears the argument: "Debt is debt and charity is charity, justice demands debt to be paid." This is of course the jargon of an exploitative system. The full argument is simple: the rich nations have, and so they must get back what they lent out so as to keep what is due to them; the poor countries have nothing and so nothing is due to them. Therefore, they must pay back what they got from the rich nations with interest lest they should have something for which they are not entitled. The same basic logic underlines the ESAP package. I, and other readers from Two-Thirds World countries, see the parable of the shrewd manager as a critique of this system and of the concept of justice that operates in this situation, including the current concept of justice that operates in the exploitative world economy of today. The parable thus challenges Christians to work toward the reversal of the situation.

The manager of the estate, as long as he was the agent of the rich man, belonged to the power structure of the exploitative economic system. As long as the system favored him, he was happy to maintain the status quo. But then the sharp axe of the system fell. This became the moment of crisis, leading him to turn against the system and critique it. His crisis became the catalyst for the inauguration of a new system of justice. To the peasant farmers he was a hero: he acted on their behalf. Here the Christian is being challenged to work for a new system of justice in order to bring about the historical and eschatological realization of the kingdom, which starts with human fellowship here on this earth and continues into eternity.

Moments of life crisis are to be converted into opportunities to take up such challenges. Like the dismissed manager, Christians do not engage in self-pity nor do they despair or bemoan their fate when faced with a crisis. Rather they take the situation as a challenge to rise to new heights in response to the demands of the values of the kingdom within their community.

In sum, therefore, this parable challenges Christians to be committed to work towards the *reversal* of oppressive structures of contemporary economic systems; and to take life crises as challenges to rise to new heights in response to the demands of the kingdom.

Conclusion

As I pointed out at the beginning, my interpretation of the parable of the shrewd manager is offered not as *the meaning* of the parable, but as one of the many possible valid interpretations. The background which informed the interpretation is that of rural West African peasant farmers, especially their experience of exploitation by the middlemen agricultural traders. This reading identifies with the peasant farmers in the story and views the situation described in the parable from their perspective. Consequently, the parable is seen as a critique of the exploitative economic system of the society for that time and for today. It challenges Christians today to be a catalyst for bringing about a new order of justice in the world.

This perspective of reading has led to the conclusion that the rich man in the story is not the benevolent grand personage he is often thought to be, but an exploiter. The reading has also concluded that the manager of the estate is not the villain he is often thought to be, but the hero of the story, for having acted on behalf of the exploited peasant farmers. This approach has brought to life the image of the peasant farmers in the story, an image not generally evident when other exegetical approaches are used.

WORKS CONSULTED

Bartdorf, I.
    1984   "Interpreting Jesus Since Bultmann: Selected Paradigms and their Hermeneutical Matrix." Pp. 210–20 in *SBL Seminar Papers 23*. Ed. Kent H. Richards. Chico, CA: Scholars.

Bultmann, Rudolf
    1963   *History of the Synoptic Tradition*. Oxford: Blackwell.

Croatto, J. S.
    1987   *Biblical Hermeneutics: Towards a Theory of Reading as the Production of Meaning*. Maryknoll, NY: Orbis.

Culbertson, P.
    1988   "Reclaiming the Matthean Vineyard Parables." *Encounter* 49:257–83.

Derrett, J. D. M.
    1960–61   "Fresh Light on St. Luke XVI. I. The Parable of the Unjust Servant." *NTS* 7:198–219.

Dickson, K. A.
    1973   "The Old Testament and African Theology." *Ghana Bulletin of Theology* 4:31–40.

Ellingworth, P., ed.
    1969   *Biblical Revelation and African Beliefs*. London: Lutterworth.

Fitzmyer, Joseph A.
    1974   "The Story of the Dishonest Manager (LK. 16:1–13)." Pp. 161–84 in *Essays on the Semitic Background of the New Testament*. Ed. Joseph A. Fitzmyer. Atlanta: Scholars.
    1985   "The Parable of the Dishonest Manager (Lk 16:1–8a)." Pp. 1094–111 in *The Gospel According to Luke x–xxiv*. The Anchor Bible. New York: Doubleday.

Gibson, M. D.
    1902–3   "On the Parable of the Unjust Steward." *ExpT* 14:334.

Hiers, P. H.
    1970   "Friends By Unrighteous Mammon. The Eschatological Proletariat (Lk 16:9)." *JAAR* 38:30–37.

Jeffre, C.
    1972   *A New Age in Theology*. New York: Paulist.

Jeremais, Joachim
    1963   *The Parables of Jesus*. London: SCM.

Manson, T. W.
 1971 *The Sayings of Jesus As Recorded in the Gospel According to St. Matthew and St. Luke Arranged With Introduction and Commentary.* London: SCM.

McDonald, J. I. H.
 1989 "Romans 13:1-7: A Test Case for New Testament Interpretation." *NTS* 35:540-49.

Mveng, E. and Werblowsky, R. J. Z., eds.
 1972 *Proceedings of the Jerusalem Congress on Black Africa and the Bible.* Jerusalem.

Prewisker, H.
 1949 "Luke 16:1-7." *Theologische Literatur Zeitung* 74:85-92.

Schreiter, R.
 1985 *Constructing Local Theologies.* Maryknoll, NY: Orbis.

Stuhlmacher, Peter
 1979 *Historical Criticism and Theological Interpretation of Scripture.* London: SPCK.

Topel, L. John
 1975 "On the Injustice of the Unjust Steward: Lk. 16:1-13." *CBQ* 37:216-27.

Ukpong, Justin S.
 1983 "Redemption: A Biblical Hermeneutic." *Catholic Witness* 3:14-26.
 1987 *Sacrifice: African and Biblical.* Rome: Urbaniana University Press.
 1993 "Proclaiming The Kingdom of God in Africa Today." Pp. 149-58 in *Proclaiming the Kingdom. Essays in Contextual New Testament Studies.* Ed. Justin S. Ukpong. Port Harcourt: CIWA.
 1994 "Towards a Renewed Approach to Inculturation Theology." *Journal of Inculturation Theology* 1:8-24.

Williams, F. E.
 1970 "Is Almsgiving the Point of the 'Unjust Steward'?" *JBL* 83:293-97.

V
DOING THEOLOGY WITH ORDINARY READERS

WORK, THE BIBLE, WORKERS, AND THEOLOGIANS: ELEMENTS OF A WORKERS' THEOLOGY[1]

Albert Nolan
Institute for Contextual Theology
Johannesburg, South Africa

ABSTRACT

What does it mean to construct a genuine theology of work? This essay discusses the elements involved in developing a theology of work that is the product of workers themselves. The usual role of the professional theologian as the expert who uses the insights of others is analyzed and critiqued. A rather different role for the theologian emerges within a process in which the experience, faith, biblical interpretations, and interests of workers are fundamental.

INTRODUCTION

It seems to me that many people concerned with a theology of work have been moving gradually towards at least one very important conclusion. The conclusion is this: a genuine theology of work will have to be a worker's theology, that is to say, a theology constructed by workers and for workers—a theological reflection of workers upon their experience of work and their experience of struggle. This does not mean that the professional theologian, biblical scholar, or pastor will have no role to play in the construction of a theology of work but that they will have a subordinate role to play. To say that a genuine theology of work must be constructed by Christian workers and not expert theologians raises a host of questions. These are the questions I would like to deal with in this article, but first I must try to explain why workers themselves will have to do this theology.

---

[1] An earlier version of this essay can be found in James R. Cochrane and Gerald O. West, *The Threefold Cord: Theology, Work and Labour* (Pietermaritzburg: Cluster, 1991).

Workers' Experience

I think I can safely say that the reason why theologians have had so little success in the construction of a theology of work is that professional theologians today are not workers, are not members of the working class, and therefore do not have first hand experience of work—at least not in the sense of labour or manual work.

As theologians and academics, our experience of work, intellectual work, can be of value in constructing a theology of work; but it is not the primary experience. The primary experience is that of the worker or labourer, the experience of the working class. It is the experience of working for a wage, working for a boss, working with one's hands. It is the experience of being used as a unit of labour, a machine, of being exploited for profit. It is the experience of alienation from one's work, from the product of one's labour, and therefore of alienation from oneself and from other workers. It is the experience of struggle for better wages, for better working conditions, for another system of work and ownership. It is a struggle for security, for full employment, and so forth.

We know about this. We have heard about it and read about it. We have talked about it, *but it is not our experience*. We deal with it and speculate about it *secondhand*. In the task of constructing a theology of work, this is a distinct disadvantage. Whatever we produce, no matter how scholarly and scientific it may be, will remain secondhand and therefore second-best. As such, in practice our theology of work will be of minimal interest and value to Christian workers.

The Bible and Work

But the problem is even more serious than that. If we ourselves do not have the experience of work that we are reflecting upon in a theology of work, then no matter how well we know the Bible and Christian tradition, we will simply never be able to see in God's word what the workers see in God's word. No matter how well we know the Hebrew and Greek words of the Bible, no matter how thoroughly and critically we study the Bible, we will always miss some of the things that a worker will notice about what is said in the Bible.

A recent example of this, though it does not refer primarily or exclusively to workers, is the discovery of the theme of oppression in the Bible. Biblical scholars, because they are generally not oppressed people themselves, had missed the extensive description of oppression in the Bible. Because biblical scholars live in a middle class environment, share the experience of bourgeois individualism, and think of suffering, affliction, and problems in personal terms, they did not notice what the Bible was saying about national, political, and economic oppression.

In contrast, when oppressed people began to re-read the Bible, confident that they themselves were capable of interpreting it, they noticed a consistent theme of oppression. Because of this Thomas Hanks and Elsa Tamez began to study the Hebrew and Greek words for oppression in the Bible. Their studies were enormously revealing. Walter Wink says of Tamez' book:

> Why haven't we North American Biblical scholars done such a systematic study of the words for oppression in the Bible? If the answer is that we who possess the critical skills are not ourselves oppressed, then it becomes imperative that we listen all the more carefully to these voices from the South (meaning the Third World).

That is true, but from discussion with Wink, I would say that he has not yet understood the full implications of this discovery. It is not just a matter of *listening* to the oppressed; it is a matter of recognizing that the oppressed themselves will have to construct a theology of oppression, albeit sometimes with technical assistance from the experts who are not themselves oppressed.

If we now return to our subject of a theology of work, I am proposing that it is workers who must re-read the Bible from the point of view of their experience of work. I am not suggesting that they will merely notice the frequent references to work or labour in the Bible which we the experts might overlook because we are not workers. That is one possibility, and that might lead to a systematic study of the use of words for work in the Bible. But more than that, I think workers would notice something of their own experience in texts that do not make use of the word "work" at all. And that indeed is something that we might easily overlook.

For example, something that we *might* overlook and a worker *might* notice (of course, I am now guessing just to illustrate my point) is that in the story of creation there are two interwoven strands characterizing God, and they do not correspond to the scholarly strands of the priestly tradition (P) and Yahwistic tradition (J). The two strands I am talking about appear in both P and J traditions. In the one strand God acts like a "boss," a manager, a Lord, or king. God issues commands: "Let the earth produce vegetation," etc. And this is followed each time by the statement: "And it was so."

The second strand follows immediately after the first on almost all the days of creation. God acts like a *worker* and not like a *boss*. Here God is said to have made or created or fashioned the vault, the two great lights, the great sea-monsters, the animals, and the first human beings. The vault or firmament, the sky, is pictured as a huge inverted bowl of hammered metal. In verse 7 God is *not* said to have created this, but to have made it or manufactured it, which suggests a picture of God hammering out the sky like a metalworker. Also like a worker, God can stand back from the product of his/her hands and show appreciation and satisfaction by seeing it as good. And finally, like a worker, God rests on the seventh day because God is tired: "God rested on the seventh day after all the work God had been doing." This strand in the story of creation provides us with an image of God that must have come orginally and immediately from workers of some kind. It is an image of God as the great worker.

This is but one example. Who knows what other perspectives might become visible when the Bible is viewed through the eyes of the working class? What of perspectives on God, on Jesus, on the Holy Spirit, on the oppression of workers in the story of Exodus, on the Kingdom or Reign of God that Jesus describes as like farm work: sowing, ploughing, planting, watering, weeding, and harvesting? How would someone whose work is prostitution interpret Jesus' attitude to prostitutes and his saying that they will enter the Kingdom before the theologians of that time, the scribes and Pharisees? There are numerous possibilities here for biblical interpretation.

Workers and Their Interests

But there is yet another reason why a theology of work would have to be a worker's theology: because only they can determine whether their interests are being addressed. It is always important to raise the question of *interests*. In whose interests would a theology of work be? Would it serve the interests of the workers or the managers and owners or the theologians themselves?

Now it would not be impossible for professional theologians to construct a theology of work that served the interests of workers, but it is unlikely and hazardous. There have been theologies of work before in the history of the Church, and generally they have not served the interests of workers. An example would be the theology that came to be known as "the work ethic." That theology certainly served the interests of the "bosses" who got more out of their workers by promoting hard work as a Christian ethical demand. If one wants to be quite sure that a theology of work in South Africa today serves the interests of the worker, it must be a theology that is constructed by workers and for workers.

This question of interests can be put in another way: who benefits theologically from a particular theology of work? A theology, according to Augustine, is supposed to nourish, strengthen, and confirm the faith of Christians. So the question becomes *whose faith* is being nourished, strengthened, and confirmed by this envisaged theology of work? The faith of the worker or the faith of the professional theologian?

If the purpose of a South African theology of work is to nourish and strengthen the faith and commitment of workers in South Africa, then it must be constructed by workers. This kind of theology would also be of value to others, including professional theologians and the middle classes—mostly because it would challenge us and open our eyes to dimensions of faith that would probably not otherwise be available to us. But the primary purpose of a theology of work must be to deepen and clarify the faith of workers. Hence my argument that it is the workers themselves who must construct a theology of work.

Being Made Use Of

At first sight this claim that workers themselves may seem to be impractical, and various problems may be raised against such an argument.

It might be argued that the Christian worker does not have the theological and biblical expertise to do the job properly, that he or she also does not have the time or leisure to do it, and finally, that the average Christian worker will simply not have the inclination, the desire, or the motivation to do it. These indeed are the practical problems that we shall have to look into. Let us take them one by one.

It is clear that the average worker does not have the theological and biblical expertise required to construct a theology of work. What the worker does have is the *experience* of work, and what the Christian worker also has is *faith*. Out of this, and by simply hearing the stories of the Bible, an elementary, perhaps somewhat superficial theology, can be constructed. But if it is to have any real depth and consistency, it must then make use of the experts. Note that I say *make use of*.

The ideal situation for constructing a theology of work is not that the professional theology *makes use of* the insights of workers, but that workers *make use of* the expertise and technical knowledge of academics, so that it is, and remains, in fact, a worker's theology. In practice this means that we, the trained theologians and clergy, have to learn the skill of being used, of putting our expertise into the hands of the working class as a service to them, what Jesus called "learning to serve rather than to be served."

This is much more difficult to do than it might appear to be. As academics, intellectuals, or biblical scholars we are more accustomed to making use of the insights of others than allowing ourselves to be made use of. It requires a conscious and concerted effort to do more than just listen to what workers have to say. In fact it requires a confident and militant group of workers who will dictate their needs and interests to us and correct us whenever we begin to determine the pace and the requirements. In other words, it requires on our part a good dose of old fashioned *humility*: the humility to hand over our knowledge, skills, and resources to the working class for them to use as they wish.

Allowing ourselves to be used in this way also requires of us an enormous act of *trust*, an act of confidence in the truth and the value of the interests of the working class. This will often mean working in groups instead of working alone at our desks, developing an oral theology instead of a book theology, collecting opinions and expressions of faith that we cannot fully identify with and sacrificing any personal prestige associated with the fact that what we write are not our original ideas. That requires more than humility; it requires a kind of theological *kenosis*.

The second practical problem is that workers on the whole do not have the time or the leisure to indulge in such pursuits as constructing a theology of work. Of course it need not take a great deal of time, but it would certainly have to be done where and when workers do have time, for example, on Sundays, as part of the rest or leisurely reflection that a Christian might associate with going to church on a Sunday. It would not be possible to do it at conferences or meetings during the week, when workers have to earn their living. Moreover it would have to be done at the *pace* that Christian workers themselves set for it, slowly and over the years according to the available time. This requires patience on our part, not as a condescending practice, but a realization that it is better to go slowly and carefully.

However, whether workers set aside time for this at all and how much time they set aside for it will depend upon whether they see the exercise of constructing a theology as in their interests or not. And that brings us to the third practical problem: whether the average Christian worker has any inclination, desire, or perceived need to do theology.

The working class will want to know what earthly use a theology of work might be to them in their struggle for liberation as workers, and we would have to give them some initial indication of what use it might have. It is here that the professional theologian might have to take the initiative, but only in order to get the process started, in order to get the initial interest of the worker. What will have to be shown is that a theology of work might be useful not only for theology or for the Church, but also, and much more importantly, for the worker and for his and her struggles.

Workers and a Framework for a Theology of Work

To this end I want to suggest a framework that may provide this initial interest or motivation. The framework takes the form of a series of questions that might look into the interests of the working class.

An initial question might be: Is work a blessing or a curse? This would enable a worker who has perhaps not given the matter too much thought to examine his/her own experience of work. Perhaps they will find that work is sometimes a curse and sometimes a blessing. I would guess that they would experience work as a curse when they have to work long hours, travel long distances, earn starvation wages, work in unsafe conditions, live in hostels, work for a boss, and so forth. Other experiences of work as a curse might also emerge, like women's unpaid and unrecognized work, or their double shift, or their being forced by circumstances to sell their bodies. And who knows what other aspects of work might be experienced as a curse.

Then there would be the experience of work as a blessing, like having a job at all, or having a good job, a well-paid job. Perhaps workers could dream of work possibilities that would be a blessing, like not working for a boss, or working for workers as a trade unionist, or political work, or some kind of work that would be creative and rewarding in itself. This would then serve as the beginning of an analysis of the experience of work, especially if the workers went on to discuss what makes work a curse and what would make it a blessing.

The second question, I suggest, might be something like this: does the Bible see work as a blessing or as a curse? It would soon be recognized that the Bible has the same ambiguous attitude to work. Sometimes it is seen as a curse, and sometimes it is seen as a blessing. God is in a way a worker who constructed the world and enjoyed it. God made human beings in his/her image and likeness to be workers, cultivators of the earth, like God, and to enjoy it. But something went wrong and now work has become a curse: "by the sweat of your brow...."

One might then speculate about what went wrong, but that is a difficult question, and I suggest we first try a question like this: how can work be redeemed? This question really asks how work can be changed from a curse into a blessing. The worker, and especially the trade unionist, will then have their own answers, like the organization of workers into trade unions, strikes and negotiations, support from the Church, the struggle for political change, working class power and leadership, etc.

How does the redemption of work fit into God's redemption? The final question would be about what redemption of work has to do with God, with God's redemption, with the redemption or salvation that is preached by the Church. This would open up the possibility of re-reading the Bible as a book about the redemption of work or the redemption of workers from the slavery or bondage of forced labour. But then what does this have to do with sin? And whose sin turns works into a curse?

Conclusion

My suggestion is that these, or some such other initial questions, might develop an interest in a re-reading of the Bible and the constructing of a theology of work among Christian workers. Given that research by the Institute for Contextual Theology has shown that 80% of workers already have a siginificant interest in the Bible, such questions would not be inappropriate. The Bible does not belong only to the bosses; workers can resist and re-read the Bible, discovering resources that favour the workers as victims of oppression and sin. This means the Bible can indeed become "a weapon" in the struggle for liberation and life.

Would this provide the motivation for participating in the construction of a theology of work or a worker's theology? Would such questions not enable the process to begin? Would they not enable Christian workers to discover they already have the beginnings of a theology?

Works Consulted

ICT Church and Labour Research Group
    1991   "Workers, the Church and the Alienation of Religious Life." In *The Threefold Cord: Theology, Work and Labour.* Ed. James R. Cochrane and Gerald O. West. Pietermaritzburg: Cluster.

OLD TESTAMENT THEOLOGY, FOR WHOM?

Gunther H. Wittenberg
University of Natal
South Africa

ABSTRACT

Old Testament Theology as a discipline is generally considered to have been initiated by Johann Philip Gabler. Most of the issues which have dominated scholarly debate are already present in his inaugural lecture: the quest for certainty, emphasis on methodology, the systematic presentation of religious ideas as the task of the Old Testament Theology, the rejection of the individual and specific in favor of the generalized and timeless, and the use of historical criticism as a preliminary tool while at the same time denying the validity of history for theology. This dominant paradigm belongs to the "knowledge system" which the economist Marglin terms *episteme*. It is no longer adequate for an Old Testament Theology relevant to our context. We need to develop a new approach belonging to a different "knowledge system," *da'at*, in which not religious ideas but context and commitment to the poor and the oppressed would be fundamental and in which insights of social scientists (Geertz and Weber) make important contributions. Such an Old Testament Theology needs to tell the story (taking up a suggestion by von Rad) how Israel obtained its deepest theological insights within the context of historical struggles and conflicts.

INTRODUCTION

At annual congresses of the Old Testament Society of Southern Africa it has often been observed that participation in the Society is an almost totally white affair with little black participation. Although the point has often been made that blacks have a natural affinity to the Old Testament, there are almost no black Old Testament scholars in South Africa and few have chosen the Old Testament as a discipline of study.

Nonetheless we see that the Bible still plays a significant role in black communities. There is general agreement that the Bible is of fundamental importance for their life and faith; indeed, that the Bible can and does play an important role in the empowerment of communities for liberation. But ordinary black parishioners have little biblical knowledge, and there is little material which could make the insights of biblical scholarship available to ordinary members of congregations.

It is obvious that theological education, especially as far as biblical scholarship is concerned, has to play a crucial role in bridging the gap. Black students will one day be the leaders of their communities and will have to perform the function of bridge-building. But experience shows that this is seldom achieved. As presented in most textbooks, Old Testament Theology seems inaccessible to black students.

The question needs to be asked: Old Testament Theology for whom? Who is the dialogue partner? Is it the international academic community, or is it the ordinary people in the grassroots communities, particularly the poor and oppressed?

In trying to answer this question I want to highlight some of the issues with special reference to Johann Philipp Gabler (1753–1826), who is generally considered the founder of the discipline.

The Paradigm of Old Testament Theology Initiated by Gabler

A major "paradigm shift" in Old Testament Theology happened in the time of the Enlightenment. This is obvious when we compare Gabler's inaugural address to the theological faculty of the University of Altdorf (1787), "On the Proper Distinction Between Biblical and Dogmatic Theology and the Specific Objectives of Each,"[1] and the *Collegium biblicum*,"A Biblical Collection of Old Testament and New Testament Texts Explicated in Relation to the Series of Standard Theological Topics," of Sebastian Schmidt, a Lutheran orthodox theologian from Strassburg (1617–96) (cf. Hayes and Prussner: 5–7).

Schmidt's *Collegium biblicum* was designed as a textbook to teach students the proof texts that supported and demonstrated the correctness of Protestant church dogma. Schmidt's treatment was arranged in two sections, one for the Old Testament and one for the New Testament. Each in turn was subdivided according to the various doctrines of the Lutheran churches. In the organization of his subject matter Schmidt followed the standard outline of the orthodox system of Church doctrine. This provided a set pattern: first an exposition of the dogmas was given, then supporting biblical passages were selected, and finally those passages were expounded.

Dicta probantia volumes performed both a pedagogical and a theological function (Hayes and Prussner: 7). In their support of the dogmatic system they reflected the orthodox assumption that Christian thought and life had to be based on the Bible. But a methodology of "proof text" theology has serious shortcomings. First, according to the Orthodox scholastics church dogma contained the correct interpretation of the Christian religion. This was deemed to be sacrosanct, true for all time, and unchangeable. Scripture was considered to give it supernatural approval. Accordingly, the Bible's own inerrancy became a fundamental necessity. Yet, despite the prestige attached to Scripture, the infallible doctrines actually outweighed the infallible Bible whose role was reduced to one of providing proofs for the truth of the dogmas (Hayes and Prussner: 18).

Second, biblical theology could be only a very limited undertaking. Because Old Testament Theology was ancillary to Church dogmatics, it was restricted to the selection and exposition of those texts which were deemed suitable for elucidating and supporting the individual doctrines (Jacob: 13). The Old Testament was not allowed to speak for itself. Instead, it was compressed within the narrow confines of a dogmatic system. By limiting the attention to a few isolated passages, it could hardly do justice to the wealth of Old Testament literature.

Comparing J. P. Gabler's Altdorf lecture with Schmidt's *Collegium* the difference is striking. Gabler initiated a new paradigm of Old Testament theology based on a completely different approach. It has had far-reaching implications on Old Testament Theology as a discipline. I want to highlight a few basic points which need to be developed in greater detail.

Certainty

The basis of Gabler's project was the quest for certainty. Gabler wanted to get away from the divergent and conflicting church opinions reflected in the different church doctrines and to place the science of Old Testament Theology on a sure foundation (Sandys-Wunsch and Eldredge: 134). The quest for certainty is also at the foundation of the orthodox doctrine of the inerrancy of Scripture, but the method of arriving at certainty differs fundamentally. In Orthodoxy certainty is based on authority, while in the Enlightenment certainty is obtained through the scientific character of the methods of investigation.

Methodology

Gabler's inaugural lecture concerns methodology. He argues for drawing a clear distinction between biblical religion or biblical theology, and theology proper—dogmatics. Biblical theology, so far only an ancillary to dogmatics, needed to become an independent discipline with clearly defined goals. Gabler proposed the following method for arriving at such a biblical theology. Using the tools of historical critical exegesis, the sacred ideas of the biblical materials must be collected and arranged according to the historical periods from which they come (Sandys-Wunsch and Eldredge: 139). Then, those words and ideas which are historically conditioned and therefore no longer relevant have to be placed in a different category from "the true sacred ideas" the *"notiones universae"* or *"notiones purae"* of the relevant biblical authors (Sandys-Wunsch and Eldredge: 141, Merk: 40). This sifting would have to be done from a historical perspective as a purely descriptive task, as a true and accurate description of the Bible in its various periods and contexts. Finally, those ideas have to be chosen from among the *"dicta classica"* which are not restricted to a particular time and place but are truly universal. They must be carefully arranged in a system in order to serve as a sure foundation for dogmatic theology. This is biblical theology in the strict sense of the word (Sandys-Wunsch and Eldredge: 142).

The emphasis on method has been the hallmark of Biblical scholarship up to the present day. The discipline of source criticism, which has had such a profound effect on the development of Old Testament scholarship during the 19th century, was considered to present the necessary precondition for historical studies and the reaching of "assured results" in biblical scholarship.

Religious Ideas

The paradigm shift from Schmidt to Gabler is particularly striking in the new emphasis on sacred or religious ideas as the subject matter for Old Testament Theology.

How much Gabler's definition of the task of biblical theology, soon after to be split up into Old Testament theology and New Testament theology, has determined the development of the discipline of Old Testament theology may be gathered from the following three quotations. The first is taken from Edmond Jacob's "Theology of the Old Testament" (1958). "The theology of the Old Testament may be defined as the systematic account of the specific religious ideas which can be found throughout the Old Testament and which form its profound unity" (Jacob: 11). The second is taken from R. E. Clements, "Old Testament Theology: A Fresh Approach" (1978). Coming from Gabler, Clements' approach does not seem to be so fresh after all.

> We may conclude from these preliminary remarks that a theology of the Old Testament must be about the religious ideas contained in this literature. How these ideas are to be systematized, and to what extent they constitute a unifying factor in the literature, are questions that must be considered in relation to these writings, and, in turn, to the nature of the religion out of which these writings emerged. (3f.)

Finally, we turn to Jesper Høgenhaven's "Problems and Prospects of Old Testament Theology" (1988). The issues raised by Gabler still determine how the theological task is defined.

> The task of biblical theology may be described as the completing and summarizing of exegetical results. Whilst biblical exegesis is concerned with analyzing individual texts or books of the Bible, biblical theology attempts to establish the main lines within each book, and to explain how the concepts and ideas of the various parts of the Bible are interrelated. Biblical theology, in other words, is a historical and descriptive discipline rather than a normative and prescriptive one. It belongs to the realm of historical theology, not to that of systematic theology. (93)

During the 19th century biblical theology took up Gabler's task not only by collecting and systematizing the sacred ideas, usually according to the basic subdivisions from dogmatics, into Theology-Anthropology-Soteriology, but also, which was more important, by searching for a basic principle, the "basic idea" (*Grundidee*) of Israelite religion on which everything else was dependent. Under the influence of Hegel's philosophy the history of Old Testament religion was understood as a development of this basic idea (Cf. Smend: 8–16). In our century Hegel's philophy is no longer the dominant influence in Old Testament scholarship, but the problem of a centre is still one of the most hotly debated issues in Old Testament theology (Cf. Fohrer, Smend; Hasel; Reventlow: 125–33; Hasel: 139–71).

Let me quote some well-known Old Testament theologies to illustrate how the basic framework set by Gabler determines the work of Old Testament theologians even today. In his massive Old Testament Theology (1933), Eichrodt took "covenant" as the central concept. He emphasized that this concept was taken from the Old Testament itself and not imposed from the outside. Vriezen, in the first edition of his *An Outline of Old Testament Theology* (1949) follows the tripartite division into Theology, Anthropology, and Eschatology. In the second edition he establishes the "communion" concept as the central organizing element for his structure of Old Testament Theology (1970:8). Fohrer disagrees and claims

> that we discover a great number of religious and theological views in the Old Testament and great differences between the various tendencies and opinions. But the rule of God and man [sic] form the coherent and uniting elements in this plurality. They are connected with one another and belong together like the two focuses of an ellipse. (200)

W. H. Schmidt wants to develop an Old Testament theology from the center of the exclusiveness of God as expressed in the first commandment, and Zimmerli (14) states that the "central focus" of the theology of the Old Testament which has to be the point of departure is "where the faith of the Old Testament specifically confesses the God of Israel under the name of Yahweh." The revelation of the name Yahweh (Exod 20:2-3) is the actual foundation of everything which follows (Zimmerli: 17).

It would serve no purpose to expand on this list. The point I wanted to make is, I hope, clear. With his emphasis on the religious or sacred ideas Gabler set the framework for the basic approaches to Old Testament theology as a discipline. There are great variations in the arrangement of subject matter and emphasis, but the framework remains basically fixed.

Theologians of the Old Testament

Gabler realizes that there are different authors and different theologies in the Old Testament. Only a careful comparison among them will show which of their ideas are of universal significance and which are only their own opinions. "It is of great interest whether the Apostle proposes some opinion as a part of Christian doctrine or some opinion that is shaped to the needs of the time, which must be considered merely premises, as the logicians call them" (Sandys-Wunsch and Eldredge: 141). For the development of an Old Testament theology Gabler therefore suggests that everything personal, individual, and time-bound should be discarded in favour of the timeless, the abstract, the universal. Old Testament theologies in this tradition therefore do no concentrate on the individual authors. Profiles of individual authors, say Old Testament prophets, with their sharply differing and possibly conflicting viewpoints, are discarded in favour of impersonal generalized statements.

History

Gabler's biblical theology is a historical discipline. He demands the consistent use of the historical critical method, the interpretation of biblical texts with the methods used for any other type of literature (Merk: 41). At the same time the method of historical critical exegesis provides the basis for the critical elimination of those elements which are only historical and of no use to dogmatics. Only religious ideas of universal validity are important; they are the kernel; history is merely a husk to be discarded. Gabler believes that there are eternal ideas somehow hidden within historical material. He does not realize that religious ideas themselves are historically conditioned (Merk: 43).

The development of Old Testament scholarship during the 19th century led to a progressive disintegration of the distinction between the timeless and universally valid truths and historically conditioned relative opinions. History was undermining dogmatics (Smend: 12). Biblical theology split into the two sub-disciplines Old Testament and New Testament Theology, and then separated from History of Israelite Religion. As the century progressed, with the discovery of many new sources opening up the world of ancient Near Eastern cultures, there seemed less and less scope for a biblical theology as Gabler had conceived it. History of Israelite Religion seemed to be a much more appropriate approach than Old Testament Theology to deal with the historical nature of the Old Testament (Eissfeldt: 1; Sandys-Wunsch and Eldredge: 157f.).

In comparison with most Old Testament theologies von Rad's *Old Testament Theology* is a new departure. Von Rad (1962:105–28) also attempts to establish a proper distinction between History of Religion and Theology. He believes that it would be possible to draw a tolerably complete and objective picture of Israelite religion, but that this is not the task of theology. Old Testament theology has to deal with the testimonies or the "confessions" of Israel. The subject of Old Testament theology is the "world made up of testimonies" and not "a systematically ordered 'world of the faith' of Israel" (111). According to von Rad, it is a feature common to the Old Testament documents that they "confine themselves to representing Jahweh's relationship to Israel and the world in one aspect only, namely as a continuing divine activity in history" (1962:106). The Old Testament is not a systematic survey; it has no centre. Von Rad vigorously denied this (1962:115), arguing that the Old Testament tells a story. It tells of Yahweh's revelation in a number of separate historical acts without exhibiting a "centre" which would render possible a theological systematization of these narratives. Von Rad emphasized the priority in theology of event over *"logos"* (1962:116). The "theological" achievement of Israel consists mainly in the reworking, rearrangement, and continual reinterpretation of its historical traditions.

Although von Rad's approach goes beyond the framework set by Gabler, he does not go far enough, and in the following two respects is still determined by the dominant paradigm.

Von Rad no longer talks of religious ideas; he speaks of Israel's traditions. But even with the emphasis on traditions von Rad does not yet move beyond the ideological, the realm of ideas. He firmly believed that only what Israel thought and said about God was the subject matter of Old Testament theology. In the sixties there was a heated debate between von Rad and some of his critics, such as Franz Hesse (1960, 1969), about the role of "actual" history as reconstructed by the historians. Von Rad (1963) denied that it had any theological validity whatsoever. Of theological significance could be only the picture which Israel itself drew of its history, even if that differed substantially from the actual historical events as established by historians. This position does not really take us beyond the original framework laid down by Gabler with respect to the meaning and significance of history.

The pillars on which von Rad's whole conception rests, the small historical creed, the basic formative role of Israel's cult in the post-settlement period for the canonical form of Israel's saving history and its setting in the all-Israelite amphictyony, a view von Rad shared with Noth—all have been subjected to fundamental critique in recent years. It is therefore perhaps not without reason that von Rad's approach has not found any successor, and that the most recent works of Old Testament Theology, such as the one by R. E. Clements or H. D. Preuss have reverted to earlier approaches.

In recent years there has been an extensive debate about the question of methodology in Old Testament theology (see Hasel, 1991:28–114). The established paradigm in Old Testament theology has come under increasing attack. But really new approaches have not yet emerged. On the whole, Old Testament theology still follows the paradigm established by Gabler, although there is a recognition that it is no longer adequate. Brueggemann (1984:1) therefore remarks in this connection: "The only two things sure about Old Testament Theology are: 1. The ways of Eichrodt and von Rad are no longer adequate. 2. There is no consensus among us what comes next." And Gerhard Hasel (1985:34) comments: "There is today a greater variety than ever before in Old Testament Theologies. There is still no consensus on methodology for Old Testament Theology and none seems to be emerging."

Knowledge Systems

What would be the essential ingredients of a new approach to Old Testament Theology? Perhaps basic considerations in liberation theology can point the way. Per Frostin (3) has drawn attention to the fact that liberation theology starts with an epistemological break from the established methodology of First World theology. Third World theologians have argued persistently for a new *method* of doing theology which differs from the academic theology practiced in the West.

> We reject as irrelevant an academic type of theology that is divorced from action. We are prepared for a radical break in epistemology which makes commitment the first act of theology and engages in critical reflection on the praxis of reality of the Third World. (3)

Frostin notes that epistemological issues are continuously stressed at Ecumencial Association of Third World Theologians (EATWOT) conferences, because epistemology is related to the most fundamental aspect of scientific work, defining the ground rules of the quest for truth. There is no single epistemology, but specific epistemologies which belong to distinct ways of knowing. The economist Marglin (232) therefore speaks of *systems of knowledge*, each with its own epistemology, that is, its own theory of what counts as knowledge, and its mode of transmission dealing with the manner of receiving and distributing knowledge.

The comparison between Schmidt and Gabler has shown that theology is also governed by respective systems of knowledge. Drawing mainly on Marglin's work, I therefore want to look at Gabler's work from the perspective of its basic system of knowledge, and then to contrast it with a system of knowledge in which commitment to the poor and oppressed is fundamental. Following Marglin I will call the knowledge system which determines Gabler's approach, and which has dominated the approaches to Old Testament Theology up to the present day, *episteme*, the Greek term for "knowledge." This term is particularly appropriate because the study of ideas in theology is a heritage of Greek philosophy. The five points which we listed as being characteristic of Gabler's approach are also characteristics of *episteme* according to Marglin.

Dominating Knowledge—episteme

Gabler was looking for certainty. His ideal for the development of biblical theology was therefore the systematic presentation of God's eternal truths or the unchanging ideas found in the Bible. This is characteristic also of *episteme*. "*Episteme* lays claim to *universality*, to being applicable at all times and places to all questions. Indeed adherents of *episteme* do not in general see it as one system of knowledge among many, but as knowledge pure and simple" (233).

Gabler emphasized sound method for developing an Old Testament theology. Method is also essential for *episteme*. It is knowledge based on *logical deduction from self-evident first principles*. The best model is perhaps Euclidean geometry (Marglin: 233). The rationalist theologians of the Enlightenment aimed at a theology which would be equally sure and axiomatic. Gabler advocated a "true biblical theology" which would ensure a sound basis for the work of dogmatic theology. "Logical deduction" implies a method according to which one proceeds by small steps with nothing left out, nothing left to chance or to the imagination (Marglin: 233). Gabler, and the historical critics after him, advocated a method prescribing each step by which they hoped to achieve assured results.

Gabler's interest was in religious ideas. Epistemic knowledge, accordingly, is purely *cerebral*. Since Descartes mind is separate from body, and *episteme* pertains to the mind alone (Marglin: 233). *Episteme* is theoretical knowledge generally acquired through formal schooling based on books. Indeed, knowledge in the West has more and more come to be equated with what is taught in the schools. This applies equally to theological education.

Gabler realised that the Old Testament contains the work of many theologians. But his concern was to extract from their works those ideas which had eternal validity. *Episteme* is therefore *impersonal* knowledge (Marglin: 234). Eternally valid theological ideas cannot be personal. They have to be abstract if they are to be applicable in all places and at all times. The impression that Old Testament theologies are often abstract is entirely in accordance with this basic characteristic of *episteme*.

"Epistemic knowledge is *analytic*. It decomposes, breaks down, a body of knowlegde into its components. It is thus directly and immediately reproducible. It is fully *articulate*, and within *episteme* it may be said that what cannot be articulated does not even count as knowledge" (Marglin: 233). Historical criticism, especially the method of source criticism, which has had such a profound effect on the development of Old Testament theology, belongs to this category of analytic knowledge, often breaking down texts into a number of sub-units which are critically analysed. It determined Gabler's view of history as being something to be discarded without direct relevance for Old Testament Theology proper.

Episteme is the dominant knowledge system of the West. It is also the established, hegemonic paradigm (Frostin) of the theological disciplines taught in the academy. Since Gabler, Old Testament Theology developed as a discipline in accordance with the methods and basic criteria of the dominant paradigm.

Knowlege "From Below"—da'at

In an illuminating passage Gustavo Gutierrez has identified the difference between the dominant theology of the West and the new theological project of liberation theology developed in Latin America. He states that the challenge to Western theology is posed by non-believers whereas the challenge in Latin America "does not come pricipally from the non-believer, but from the non-person, i.e. the person who is not recognized as human by the dominant social order: the poor, the exploited, the one who is systematically and legally despoiled of his human nature, the one who hardly feels human" (Gutierrez: 69; cf. Gibellini: 13). In order to speak meaningfully of God to the poor in an inhuman world Gutierrez demands a theology "from the underside of history" (169).

Graham Philpott, working in the informal settlement of Amawoti, near Durban, South Africa, makes a similar point when he notes that

> members of the oppressed community are often the invisible participants of society, the superfluous unknown people, marginalised by the dominant sectors of society....They have no access to the institutions that are responsi-

ble for the production of knowledge, and have no way of influencing the development of appropriate and useful knowledge, let alone determining which questions and issues are researched. (17)

He emphasizes that the theologian should

> hear, understand, and learn from those who are usually excluded from the enterprise of the production of theological knowledge, and to allow this "invisible" knowledge and experience to challenge and reshape traditional theological formulations which were generated from within the context of the dominant. (17)

This "knowledge from below" arises from the reflection on the Christian praxis in confrontation with the Bible. The outcome of this communal reflection on the Bible in which the concerns of the poor are taken seriously is recorded in Philpott's book. Cochrane observes:

> ...we have here a prime example of the new paradigm for doing theology at local base ecclesial community level....Theology, properly understood, is not mere theory, but the reflection of Christians on their faith in the world. Theology cannot therefore be ripped out of a practice of ministry in the world without in the long run self-destructing, or without losing its reason for being. (8)

A project with a similar aim is the Institute for the Study of the Bible (ISB), linked to the School of Theology at the University of Natal, Pietermaritzburg. It seeks to establish an interface between biblical studies and ordinary readers of the Bible in the church and community in order to facilitate social transformation. Through the input from grassroots communities the process of Bible studies not only aims at empowering the poor and oppressed who take part in this process, but also seeks to transform the teaching of Biblical Studies at the School of Theology. In this process a new approach to the discipline of Old Testament Theology is emerging. It belongs to a different knowledge system which I term *da`at* to distinguish it from *episteme*.

Drawing again on Marglin's work, I want to concretize the discussion by contrasting "dominating knowledge" (*episteme*) with "knowledge from below" (*da`at*).[2]

While dominating knowledge (*episteme*) makes universalist claims and "disenfranchises those outside," knowledge "from below" makes no such claim (Marglin: 234). It is "local knowledge";[3] it is the knowledge about "the kin-dom of God in Amawoti" (Philpott). Only in its particu-

---

[2] Marglin contrasts the two different types of knowledge using the two different Greek terms *episteme* and *techne*.

[3] Cf. the title of the book by Clifford Geertz: *Local Knowledge: Further Esssays in Interpretive Anthropology.*

larity and specificity does it have any significance. The same applies to *da'at*. Knowledge of God according to Hebrew conceptions changes according to historical circumstances. God's Word is always directed at a particular historical situation, *da'at* is *contextual*.[4]

Knowledge "from below" "belies the mind/body dualism which is basic to *episteme*" (Marglin: 234). In the contextual Bible studies in Amawoti and in the ISB one knows with and through one's hands and eyes and heart as well as with one's head, because the biblical knowledge of God, *da'at*, is not "objective" and abstract, removed from the whole realm of emotions. "Taste and see that the Lord is good" (Ps 34:8).

Knowledge of God, *da'at 'elohim*, involves commitment. That is as true for the knowledge "from below" among the community in Amawoti or ISB Bible study groups, as it is for the Hebrews according to the Old Testament witness: "Know that the Lord is God!" (Ps 100:3). This is no theoretical knowledge, but it demands a decision for God and against the idols. This is one of the most fundamental themes of Old Testament theology.[5] Knowledge of God—theology—therefore does not arise out of a collection of abstract ideas which are brought into a system, but it arises in *conflict*, in struggle. Therefore *da'at* is intensely *practical*, to the point that, one could almost say, it reveals itself only through practice (Marglin: 235).

Where *episteme* is impersonal, knowledge "from below," *da'at*, is intensely personal and communal. It depends on networks of relationships and cannot be transmitted or even maintained apart from these relationships. This is certainly the experience of grassroots communities studying the Bible together, but it can easily be demonstrated from the Old Testament as well. *da'at* is therefore community-based and cannot be understood apart from the communicative process within that community.

In contrast with the basis of *episteme* in logical deduction from self-evident axioms, the basis of *da'at* is varied (Marglin: 234). Knowledge "from below" needs its "organic intellectuals" charged with understanding the faith of the poor and oppressed people (Segundo: 23), just as knowledge of God in Hebrew thinking is based on the instruction of the priest or the revelation of Yahweh's word to the prophet.[6] Not only the content but also the bearers of the Word are important.

---

[4] According to Exod 7:7 Israel will know that Yahweh is God through his historical act of liberation. The prophet Ezekiel also emphasizes Yahweh's acts in history as the basis of "knowledge of God." Cf. Zimmerli.

[5] Cf. the struggle of Elijah against Baal worship and the challenge he posed for or against Yahweh.

[6] Hosea attacks the priests for having rejected the *da'at 'elohim* (Hos 4:6, see also 4:1; 10:12). Cf. Wolff: 182–205.

In contrast with the analytic nature of *episteme*, which breaks down knowledge into parts, *da`at* is concerned with the whole. Its preferred means of transmission is the story, not the theological treatise. Bible studies in communities live from stories just as Israel again and again retold its own story to obtain a view of the whole, of what God had done and was planning to do with the people of God.

Towards a New Approach in Old Testament Theology

I do not believe that it is possible to get rid of *episteme* in theology. But we need to retrieve some of the basic characteristics of *da`at* if we want develop an Old Testament theology which is truly contextual and relevant not only for the academy but also, most importantly, for poor and oppressed communities. Von Rad has pointed the way in some respects. In his *Old Testament Theology* he has shown that theological knowledge in the Old Testament is not rational, based on concepts (1962:116). In short it is not *episteme* but *da`at*. Theology in the Old Testament is not an abstract body of knowledge which one can learn by heart and pass on, but a process in which one has to be involved, a way in which ever new decisions have to be taken, a response to the concrete challenges of history which cannot be divorced and abstracted from them.

How do we arrive at such a new approach? In developing a new approach to Old Testament theology we need to draw on the basic characteristics of *da`at* which we have outlined above.

The Contextual Nature of Old Testament Theology

Whereas Gabler emphasized religious ideas to the detriment of history, a new approach towards Old Testament theology shaped by the poor and marginalized as dialogue partners needs to understand it within the context of the social, economic, and political history of Israel. Following Geertz, we need "thick description" (1973:6f.) in which the study of inscription is no longer "severed from the study of inscribing, the study of fixed meaning" no longer severed "from the study of social processes that fix it" (1983:32). Thereby the social sciences become important not only for History of Israel and History of Israelite Religion but also for Old Testament Theology. The watertight compartments which developed between the disciplines after the First World War, especially through the influence of Dialectical Theology (cf. esp. Eissfeldt), need to be broken up. Theology, too, not only Israelite Religion, needs to be seen as embedded in the socio-economic and cultural history of the people of Israel. This refiguration would certainly represent a "sea change" (Geertz, 1983:34) in our notion of what Old Testament theology means and of what we need to know in order to be relevant for our own context.

The Conflictual Nature of Old Testament Theology

Walter Brueggemann (1983) is possibly the first to have introduced sociological categories into the discipline of Old Testmanent Theology. Brueggemann draws on an insight by Claus Westermann (9–34) that the Old Testament does not speak about God uniformly, but in at least two different ways, namely the saving God in the context of history and the blessing God in the context of creation. He links these two different modes of speaking of God to two different trajectories, the one derived from Moses, the other from the Davidic monarchy. The theology in the royal trajectory supports the monarchy and the privileged upper class, while in the Mosaic trajectory, which Brueggemann also calls the "liberation trajectory," the focus is on God's justice and the concern for the poor.

By linking different modes of theologizing in the Old Testament to different social groups, Brueggemann has contributed significantly to the Old Testament theology debate, but his own proposal is not satisfactory. By using the term trajectory he remains within the paradigm initiated by Gabler. One gets the impression that the two trajectories run alongside each other without interaction. The concept trajectory does not yet take us into the actual struggles and conflicts out of which ideas and traditions ultimately derive. We have to go a step further and ask how theologies interact, how they function in the communicative process of ancient Israelite society.

The Role of Theology in the Communicative Process

What is being communicated by the theology which has found expression in the Old Testament? One answer is: power. Robert B. Coote and Mary P. Coote try to demonstrate that the Bible is the product of ruling classes. They argue that there is an inextricable link between the biblical text and political power. "The history of scripture is a history of power, and of powerful organizations" (3). Ruling elites have always used religion to support and legitimate their own interests. It was no different in Israel. Those who wrote did so to satisfy the needs for legitimation of the Judahite kings and the ruling class.

There are, of course, many Old Testament texts which seem to support Cootes and Cootes' view. Old Testament scholarship has done particularly fruitful research into the Jerusalem cult traditions and the role of Israelite royal ideology. Drawing on Durkheim's theory of ritual, Lukes has suggested that many rituals can be seen as modes of exercising, or seeking to exercise, power along the cognitive dimension as crucial elements in the "mobilization of bias" (289, 301). This could be seen as an apt description of the ritual of the temple of Jerusalem considering the theology of the royal psalms and role of the king in the state cult (cf. von Rad, 1966).

Nevertheless, Cootes and Cootes' view is highly one-sided and simplistic. Without going into details I want to highlight three areas in which serious questions have to be raised about this whole conception. There is first of all the negative evaluation of the Israelite monarchy in many of the Old Testament sources, especially the Deuteronomistic History. To explain this with reference to the frequent change in dynasties and the antagonisms between those in power begs more questions than it answers.

Secondly, Cootes and Cootes always refer to the Old Testament laws as royal laws, David's laws (28), Hezekiah's laws (55), Josia's laws (61), written down in the royal scriptorium at the king's command. But they do not answer the question, why it is that the monarchy plays no role in the Old Testament law codes apart from Deut 17:14-17, which severely restricts the king's power. Why is it that, unlike all other ancient Near Eastern law codes which were promulgated by kings, the Old Testament resolutely affirms that Moses alone is the lawgiver of all the law codes? All law ultimately derives from the revelation of the Law on Mount Sinai. The information that Moses' name is given to the author of David's law in order to give absolute authority to David's rule; that David is identified with Moses (30) is speculation not borne out by an exegesis of the texts.

The third area where serious questions need to be asked is Cootes and Cootes' view of prophecy. In order to give plausibility to their thesis that all of the Old Testament literary works have been written by scribes reflecting the views of the ruling class, they have to downplay the role of the prophets. It is important to note their use of terminology. They consistently refrain from using the accepted term "prophet" and, instead, use the term "saint" possibly accompanied by an epithet, eg. "eccentric" of Elijah (44), to emphasize their marginal role. This is to ignore the textual evidence in favour of an unnuanced schema of a hegemonic Bible.

The three contentious areas, the role of monarchy, the significance of Law, and the importance of prophecy, seem rather to point in a different direction than Cootes and Cootes want us to take. They are indications that we do not have in the Old Testament a uniform theology supporting state power, but rather, as Brueggemann has affirmed, a complex picture of contending theologies, including a theology that challenges and resists state power, a resistance theology.

The Role of the Theologians

In order to understand the dynamics of this resistance theology in the social conflicts of ancient Israel, we have to consider the social groups which have been the bearers of resistance theology. In this context Max Weber's theory of rationalisation can provide a useful model.

Weber investigated the role of ethics and rationalization as the basis of social action. According to Weber, rational reflection, and this means in our context theological reflection, can involve on the one hand "the intellectual elaboration and deliberate sublimation of cultured man's 'inner compulsion' not only to understand the world as a 'meaningful cosmos' but also to take a consistent and unified stance toward it." According to Roth and Schluchter (15), "this type of rationalism may be called *metaphysical-ethical rationalism.*" It can also refer "to the achievement of a methodical way of life. Here rationalism is the consequence of the institutionalization of configurations of meaning and interest." Roth and Schluchter call this rationalism a *practical rationalism*. Weber was especially interested in the way both interact to lead to social action.

In his *Ancient Judaism* (169–74; 205–18; 223–25; 235) Weber advanced the thesis that Israelite intellectuals were responsible for developing an alternative form of theology which could oppose and challenge the dominant theology communicated by state ritual. Although the term "intellectual" is really a modern concept (cf. Kippenberg: 70), Weber uses it to characterize a certain group in ancient Israel which were educated enough to be considered part of the ruling class, but who specifically took up the cause of the uneducated, the poor and oppressed. They became the educators of the lower classes and gave expression to an ideology which served their basic interests. In this connection Weber mentions three groups which provided an alternative theology: Levites, prophets, and lay intellectuals. An Old Testament Theology will not only have to consider the content of their theology, but also the conflicts and problems to which their theology responded.

Old Testament Theology as Story Telling

The Old Testament tells a story. Von Rad was right when he emphasized this point over against those who felt that the task of Old Testament theology was the systematic presentation of Israel's religious ideas. It seems to me that we need to tell the story of how Israel obtained its deepest theological insights, how its theology was formed in the context of conflict and opposition. I do not believe that we should only tell the story which Israel itself told, as von Rad suggested, because that story is but the end product of a much more dramatic story (including contending stories). The confessional formulae which von Rad believed to have stood at the beginning of Israel's tradition history are the culmination of long process of struggle, conflict, and theological reflection. We need to look at the historical context, at the groups involved in the process, and to employ the tools supplied by the social sciences to understand that process. And we need ourselves to be involved, seeking to understand God's will and purpose for us in our own context if we wish to gain *da`at*, a knowledge of God, based on the biblical witness, which is helpful and dynamic for the manifold challenges in our time.

The task of writing a theology of the Old Testament, then, cannot simply consist in gathering the religious ideas of the Old Testament and bringing them into a systematic order, but in treating the theology of the Old Testament we have to take cognizance of the context in which these insights were formulated. To attempt such a task for the whole of the Old Testament would be a massive undertaking. The objective should therefore be much more modest. We should concentrate on one central issue which proved of decisive significance for the development of Israel's theology, even if we have to recognize that not everything in the Old Testament will be covered. That issue, in my opinion, is the establishment of royal-imperial power and the resistance to that power, the establishment of a hegemonic theology, on the one hand, which is challenged by a new type of theology, on the other.

This theology is not ready at hand, but is only formulated and developed in the process of resistance and opposition. In order to make that theology relevant for our own situation, we would have to retell the story of this theology, concentrating not only on theological ideas or theological traditions, but taking into consideration the historical context and the various social groups and their struggles which gave rise to those traditions. Such a theology could serve as a model for struggles of resistance and theological reflection arising out of struggles in our own South African context.

WORKS CONSULTED

Brueggemann, Walter
    1983   "Trajectories in Old Testament Literature and the Sociology of Ancient Israel." Pp. 306–33 in *The Bible and Liberation: Biblical and Social Hermeneutics*. Ed. Norman K. Gottwald. Maryknoll: Orbis.
    1984   "Futures in Old Testament Theology." *Horizons in Biblical Theology* 6:1–11.

Clements, Ronald E.
1978   *Old Testament Theology: A Fresh Approach.* Marshalls Theological Library. London: Marshall, Morgan and Scott.

Cochrane, James R.
1993   "Foreword." Pp. 7–10 in *Jesus is Tricky and God is Undemocratic: The Kindom of God in Amawoti* by Graham Philpott. Pietermaritzburg: Cluster.

Coote, Robert B. and Mary P. Coote
1990   *Power, Politics and the Making of the Bible: An Introduction.* Minneapolis: Fortress.

Eichrodt, Walther
1961   *Theology of the Old Testament. Volume 1.* Trans. J. A. Baker. The Old Testament Library. London: SCM.

Eissfeldt, Otto
1926   "Israelitisch-jüdische Religionsgeschichte und alttestamentliche Theologie." *Zeitschrift für die alttestamentliche Wissenschaft* 44:1–12.

Fohrer, Georg
1966   "The Centre of a Theology of the Old Testament." *Nederduitse Gereformeerde Teologiese Tydskrif* 7:198–206.

Frostin, Per
1988   *Liberation Theology in Tanzania and South Africa. A First World Interpretation.* Studia Theologica Lundensis 42. Lund: Lund University Press.

Geertz, Clifford
1973   *The Interpretation of Cultures: Selected Essays.* New York: Basic.
1983   *Local Knowledge: Further Essays in Interpretive Anthropology.* New York: Basic.

Gibellini, Rosino
1987   *The Liberation Theology Debate.* Trans. John Bowden. London: SCM.

Gutiérrez, Gustavo
1983   *The Power of the Poor in History.* London: SCM.

Hasel, Gerhard F.
1974   "The Problem of the Center in the Old Testament Theology Debate." *Zeitschrift für die alttestamentliche Wissenschaft* 86:65–82.
1985   "Major Recent Issues in Old Testament Theology." *JSOT* 31:31–53.
1991   *Old Testament Theology: Basic Issues in the Current Debate.* Revised and expanded fourth edition. Grand Rapids: William B. Eerdmans.

Hayes, John H. and Frederick C. Prussner
1985   *Old Testament Theology: Its History and Development.* London: SCM.

Hesse, Franz
1960   "Kerygma oder geschichtliche Wirklichkeit?" *Zeitschrift für Theologie und Kirche* 57:17–26.
1969   "Bewährt sich eine 'Theologie der Heilstatsachen' am Alten Testament?" *Zeitschrift für die alttestamentliche Wissenschaft* 81:1–17.

Høgenhaven, Jesper
1987   *Problems and Prospects of Old Testament Theology.* The Biblical Seminar. Sheffield: JSOT.

Jacob, Edmond
1958   *Theology of the Old Testament.* London: Hodder & Stoughton.

Kippenberg, Hans G.
1991   *Die vorderasiatischen Erlösungsreligionen in ihrem Zusammenhang mit der antiken Stadtherrschaft: Max-Weber-Vorlesungen 1988.* Suhrkamp Taschenbuch Wissenschaft 917. Frankfurt: Suhrkamp.

Lukes, Steven
1975   "Political Ritual and Social Integration." *Sociology* 9: 289–308.

Marglin, Stephen
1990   "Losing Touch: The Cultural Conditions of Worker Accommodation and Resistance." Pp. 217–82 in *Dominating Knowledge: Development, Culture, and Resistance.* Ed. Frédérique Apffel Marglin and Stephen A. Marglin. WIDER Studies in Development Economics. Oxford: Clarendon.

Merk, Otto
1972   *Biblische Theologie des Neuen Testaments in ihrer Anfangszeit. Ihre methodischen Probleme bei Johann Philipp Gabler und Georg Lorenz Bauer und deren Nachwirkungen.* Marburger Theologische Studien 9. Marburg: N. G. Elwert Verlag.

Philpott, Graham
1993   *Jesus is Tricky and God is Undemocratic: the Kin-dom of God in Amawoti.* Pietermaritzburg: Cluster.

Preuss, Horst Dietrich
1991   *Theologie des Alten Testaments. Band 1 JHWHs erwählendes und verpflichtendes Handeln.* Stuttgart: Kohlhammer.

Reventlow, Henning Graf
1985   *Problems of Old Testament Theology in the Twentieth Century.* London: SCM.

Roth, Guenther and Wolfgang Schluchter
1979   *Max Weber's Vision of History: Ethics and Methods.* Berkeley: University of California Press.

Sandys-Wunsch, John and Laurence Eldredge
1980   "J. P. Gabler and the Distinction between Biblical and Dogmatic Theology: Translation, Commentary, and Discussion of His Originality." *SJT* 33:133–58.

Schmidt, Werner H.
1969   *Das erste Gebot. Seine Bedeutung für das Alte Testament.* Theologische Existenz heute 165. München: Kaiser.

Segundo, J. L.
  1985 "The Shift within Latin American Theology." *Journal of Theology for Southern Africa* 52:17–29.

Smend, Rudolf
  1970 *Die Mitte des Alten Testaments*. Theologische Studien 101. Zurich: EVZ-Verlag.

Von Rad, Gerhard
  1962 *Old Testament Theology. Vol. I: The Theology of Israel's Historical Traditions*. New York: Harper & Row.
  1963 "Offene Fragen im Umkreis einer Theologie des Alten Testaments." *Theologische Literaturzeitung* 88. Col. 401–416.
  1966 "The Royal Ritual in Judah." Pp. 222–31 in *The Problem of the Hexateuch and Other Essays*. Edinburgh: Oliver & Boyd.

Vriezen, Th. C.
  1970 *An Outline of Old Testament Theology*. 2nd edition. Oxford: Basil Blackwell.

Weber, Max
  1952 *Ancient Judaism*. Trans. H. H. Gerth and D. Martindale. London: George Allen & Unwin.

Westermann, Claus
  1982 *Elements of Old Testament Theology*. Atlanta: John Knox.

Wolff, Hans Walter
  1964 "'Wissen um Gott' bei Hosea als Urform der Theologie." Pp. 182–205 in *Gesammelte Studien zum Alten Testament*. Theologische Bücherei 22. München: Chr. Kaiser.

Zimmerli, Walther
  1969 "Erkenntnis Gottes nach dem Buche Ezekiel." Pp. 41–119 in *Gottes Offenbarung. Gesammelte Aufsätze zum Alten Testament*. Theologische Bücherei 19. 2nd ed. München: Chr. Kaiser
  1978 *Old Testament Theology in Outline*. Edinburgh: T. & T. Clark.

VI
RESPONDENTS

SCHOLAR AND ORDINARY READER
—MORE THAN A SIMPLE INTERFACE

Bernard C. Lategan
University of Stellenbosch
South Africa

ABSTRACT

As a response to the essays collected in this volume, the scholar/ordinary reader interface is explored further. It is argued that this interface is the meeting point of a further series of contrasts: "dominant/dominated," "theoretical/empirical," "male/female," "text-centered/oral culture," "exegesis/theology," "North/South." These contrasts are briefly discussed, in order to indicate the potential of and problems related to the focus on the role of the ordinary reader.

For many in the field of biblical scholarship, the world of the reader is still a strange environment, regarded with apprehension and misgivings. But for those who dare to explore this terrain, there are also surprises in store. The shift of attention to the interaction between text and reader, away from the relationship between author and text, or from a preoccupation with the text as such, is not as innocent as it may seem. For many, it is the opening of a Pandora's box of uncontrollable responses and subjective opinions. For others, it is a way in which the potential of the text is unlocked. Fowler (3) refers to the gulf which still exists between biblical scholarship and literary theory and criticism; two guilds separated by different cultures, histories, languages, and concerns. His own book on Mark is an attempt at bridge-building, but he is realistic enough to know that it will not be an easy task. However, in his concern to initiate a dialogue between the two parties, Fowler makes an important point. "The philological-historical critic who seeks the world behind the Gospels, the world that produced the Gospels, dwells in the world in front of the Gospels and is actively contributing to an ongoing reception history" (2). The world of the reader forms the inescapable context—also for the historical critic. He or she is already part of it. The very critical activity which is the core business of the critic depends on an (ongoing) act of reading, and everything said about the text, its origin, background, and history, is reader- and reading-mediated. The advantage of facing up to this reality, is that it enables critics to take distance from their own work, from the way they treat their sources, and how they themselves create a text in the process of their critical activities. The result could only benefit the quality of criticism itself.

The present volume wants to be more than just another collection of readers reading or just a further attempt to initiate a dialogue between reader- and non-reader-oriented members of the guild. The focus is on two types of reading—"critical" and "ordinary"—and on the interface between them.

The contrast between critical and ordinary reading echoes the distinction introduced by George Steiner in his seminal 1979 essay "'Critic'/'Reader.'" For Steiner, the pure (hypothetical) critic and the pure (hypothetical) reader represent the two extremes of a continuum. He ascribes specific roles to each and to the authority they have or do not have. The qualification "ordinary" in the title of the present volume is not without reason, as will be indicated below. What Steiner is talking about, are *functions*, not so much *persons*. The same person may chose to fulfill both roles, as Fowler consciously does (30–31). But is the hypothetical reader then becoming a real reader? The interface between critical and ordinary readings is much more complex than what would appear at first sight and needs to be explored further.

Although the present volume is a sustained attempt to explore facets of the interchange between critical and ordinary readings, it masks the fact that this interface is in fact the meeting place of a series of other contrasts. When one reads through the material, with its variations in topics and quality, it becomes clear that the node "critical/ordinary" is also the cross-over point of at least the following contrasts: "dominant/dominated," "theoretical/empirical," "male/female," "text-centered/oral culture," "exegesis/theology," "North/South." There are other, more subtle contrasts, but this list may serve as the basis for a brief response to the collection as a whole.

Dominant/Dominated

At the heart of West's contribution and the work of the Institute for the Study of the Bible as a whole is the desire to lend a voice to the dominated, or rather, to facilitate a process through which the discourses of the dominated can be shaped and heard. It is at the same time a recognition of how strongly power and power relationships affect the reading of the Bible. There are many subtle and less subtle ways in which dominance can be achieved (Scott's "thin" and "thick" versions of ideological hegemony), including convincing the dominated that their aspirations, although justified in themselves, can never be achieved in reality and that the only way to survive is to accept the conditions in which they find themselves. In this case, the language of the dominated remains intact and the dominated accommodate themselves to it. But it can also happen, in terms of Scott's concept of the "hidden transcript," that a discourse of the dominated does exist, but is driven underground. West and his colleagues would like to be instrumental in bringing this discourse to the surface. For this reason the interaction between *committed* or *socially engaged* biblical scholars and *ordinary* readers from poor and marginalized communities forms the focus of their work.

But it is exactly the choice of the terms "scholar" and "ordinary" which creates a problem for the intended servant role of acting as midwife for discourses of the dominated, as West well knows. According to Steiner's original distinction between critic (or scholar) and (ordinary reader), the role of the critic is *inherently* that of a master, and the reader that of a servant. "The critic is judge and master of the text", while "the reader is servant to the text" (449). As Fowler (27) aptly explains: "...the critic steps back from the text to strike a magisterial pose of critical, objectifying distance, whereas the reader tries to eliminate the distance between himself (*sic*) and the text to allow the merging of his being with that of the text."

Is the choice of Steiner's distinction between "critic" and "reader" ("scholar" and "ordinary reader" in West's terms) the right one for West's purpose? Is it at all possible to rectify the power imbalance inherent in the terminology and in the roles of critic and reader? West is acutely aware of the problem and takes all kinds of precautionary measures. The playing fields must be leveled. The process must be an exchange between equals, without the scholars dominating right from the outset. As he points out, the initial request for assistance from scholars came *after* the poor and marginalized have spoken out in some form or another, *inter alia* through *The Kairos Document*. It is for this reason that the ISB adopted the policy to become involved with communities only at their specific request and on condition that these communities drive the process. The basic assumption is that resources for a contextual reading of the Bible are to be found *both* in biblical studies *and* in the communities themselves. Hard experience has shown that scholars either idealize or minimize the contribution of communities in this respect. Therefore the explicit choice for *"Reading With"* as the title for this volume to indicate the mood and mode in which the readings were conducted. Not "listening to," presupposing the voice of a wholly self-knowing subject free from ideology, nor a "speaking for," denying the subject status of the community. "Speaking with" intends to take seriously the subjectivity of both the biblical scholar and the ordinary poor and marginalized reader of the Bible. Special care is taken to ensure that the community retains the initiative in setting the agenda and determining the programme.

This attempt at democratizing the reading process is laudable, but is it sustainable? It requires extraordinary self-discipline from scholars *not* to pontificate on the basis of their supposed superior knowledge. But their very presence can be intimidating or raise the expectation of authoritative information. Dube admits to problems which this factor has caused in her research. The challenge remains to create space for an independent and even contra- or critical reading and to develop it into a liberating tool for reader and community alike.

Theoretical/Empirical

"Ordinary" in this volume also stands for "real" reader. All the contributions deal with actual readings of biblical texts in some form or another and the interface "critical" and "ordinary" is at the same time the meeting point of theory and practice. The distinction between theoretical and empirical reader research (cf. Groeben, Schmidt, Steinberg) does indeed represent two different areas of research. The latter is sometimes divided further into historical and contemporary empirical research (cf. Van Gorp, Ghesquiere and Segers). Empirical investigations of actual readings of biblical material are relatively scarce and the present contributions are to be welcomed. As can be expected, the focus is on contemporary, rather than on historical readers. But these studies also demonstrate some of the problems inherent in this type of research.

Critical for the theoretical/empirical interface is of course the relationship between the two. How is the one aspect determined or informed by the other? From the side of the scholar, theory obviously tends to dominate, while on the other hand, the real reader is (interestingly enough) not so easy to manipulate and often goes his or her own way. For a meaningful interaction, a sufficient body of empirical evidence is needed as counterfoil. In Mosala's contribution, a very persuasive theoretical framework is offered for the understanding of the African Independent Churches' remarkable growth and resilience. To interpret these churches as a subculture within the wider black working class, as a response to the dominant culture and as religious solidarity networks, which in rural areas can even serve an ideological function in filling the material gap left by the absence of the migrant worker from these households, offers a much more holistic and convincing way to understand the AICs. A further advantage is the way in which the interaction between theory and practice is conceptualized, whereby the initial (and necessary) theoretical framework remains open and whereby data is interpreted in terms of historical and cultural mediations, which may result in the formation of new theory.

Even so, the empirical results are just not substantial enough to uphold the heavy theoretical superstructure. They also do not seem to rise to the expectations created by this approach. The preliminary finding is that these churches do *not* have a special biblical hermeneutics and that they do not act in accordance with what could be expected from the theoretical framework. Hermeneutical weapons are not drawn from the concrete experiences of the work place and the social life of members. Furthermore, there is "neither a social nor a theological deliberateness in the movement's manner of appropriating the Bible form the perspective of a dominated race" (Mosala: 56). This discrepancy between theory and practice begs for more thorough and on-going empirical research.

Dube studies the same denomination, but in a different location (Botswana). In comparison to Mosala, the theoretical framework is less pronounced and not explicitly ideological-critically motivated, but it does contain similar notions. She understands the AICs approach as a quest for belonging: "A resistance and a demonstrated will to map their own identity in a world where discrimination against race, gender and sexual and religious orientation are too often justified at the expense of nurturing difference in life" (114). The results of her empirical research, based on both structured interviews and the analysis of sermons, are presented more extensively. It would be very interesting if Dube and Mosala could join forces to explore further the AICs.

The contribution of Draper illustrates challenges of a different kind. Quite apart from the literacy/orality difference (to which we shall return), just getting to the reader, whether a "participating" or "listening" reader in Mazamisa's terms, is wrought with difficulties. In this case, results were obtained in an indirect way by employing student interns as intermediaries. The real reader appears to be a resistant reader, that is, a reader resisting the theoretical key in which the proposed Bible studies were prepared. This design was based on the current way in which students are trained in an academic context, with emphasis on literary, historical, and socio-economic issues. The real readers preferred a "spiritual" key, and, despite having being trained in the "academic" paradigm, the student facilitators found the pull of the "spiritual" approach irresistible. Eventually, they returned to the tradition of the interpretive community from which they originally came. Draper raises the real question: Is our current theological curriculum and training methods meeting the needs of our students?

An interesting example of how the interaction with actual readers reshapes theoretical frameworks is the study of Wittenberg. The impetus to re-think theory is the direct result of exposure to the praxis of doing theology. Because the poor and marginalized have consciously been chosen as dialogue partners in the project of the ISB, the unsuitability of certain theological categories and the inaccessibility of certain concepts became very clear. This leads Wittenberg to revisit Gabler's seminal ideas on Old Testament theology as an independent discipline. In his quest for certainty, Gabler favored *episteme* (dominating knowledge) at the expense of *da'at* (knowledge from below). Wittenberg therefore argues for a theoretical revision, which would re-unite the reflective process of "doing" Old Testament theology with the social, economic, and political context which gave shape to the text of the Old Testament. Following Geertz, he proposes that the study of *inscription* no longer be severed from the study of *inscribing* and that the study of fixed meaning no longer be separated from the study of the social processes that fix it.

Less convincing with regard to the interaction between theory and practice is the study of Long. His very perceptive and competent analysis of relevant ideas of Gadamer, Derrida, Ricoeur, and especially the notion of "subjective criticism" of the post-structuralist David Bleich, provides the philosophical and hermeneutical framework for a reader-response approach to the biblical text. He concurs with Temma Berg's critique of a text-centered "reader-response" criticism and argues convincingly for a *"real-reader*-response criticism." However, when he comes to the actual reading of Revelation 2.1–7, it is not clear—apart from an increased awareness of the presence of the reader—how the reading differs fundamentally from paying close attention to the reader instructions of the text. The theoretical difference between a text-centered and a real reader-centered reading will have to be demonstrated more convincingly to persuade skeptical colleagues that this approach does bring something more than a close reading of the text.

Male/Female

The prominence of women readers in these studies is a clear indication to what extent the scholar/ordinary interface coincides with a male/female contrast. As Dube explains, women have always played a central role in the AICs as founders, bishops, archbishops, prophets, healers, and preachers. But also in other African religious communities, especially among the poor and marginalized, the importance of women is evident. Mosala shows how the system of migrant labor forced new responsibilities and duties on women, because of the long periods of absence of male members from rural households.

These historical circumstances have resulted in many hardships, but it has also contributed to the development of a strategy of resistance and a liberating way of reading the Bible and history. Recognizing the ordinary reader not only as a receptor or object, but as a subject in her own right, opens the way for women to co-determine the content and structure of theology. A lot of lip service is paid to the importance of women, but few effective strategies have been developed to give content and substance to pious assertions about the role of women. Taking the (ordinary) reader seriously is one such strategy. As Walker explains, it enables the reader to go beyond the world behind the text or the dominance of the text itself in order to explore the world in front of the text. By opting (following Ricoeur and Schneiders) for a hermeneutic that locates the meaning of the text in the world that it opens up for those who receive it, Walker is able on the one hand to claim continuity with the tradition represented by the text and on the other to deal with an intrinsically oppressive text in a way that is liberating for those who receive it.

Dube emphasizes the central role of the Spirit or *Moya* in the selfunderstanding of AICs. It becomes a way for readers in this tradition to integrate African and Christian spirituality. Their hermeneutic thus functions as both a model of resistance and of healing from imperial forces of imposition, which depends on devaluating difference and imposing a few universal standards. But especially for women this approach has powerful liberating potential. By claiming direct access to the Spirit, women can circumvent a male-dominated tradition. It enables them to break free "from the patriarchal and canonical constraints of biblical traditions. It allows them to claim divine empowerment and leadership despite their gender" (126).

In the ministry of liberation, healing plays a central role. It is inclusive, open to members and non-members, and related to all aspects of life, not only physical illness. It becomes "an act of restoring and maintaining God's creation against all forces that inhibit the fulfillment of individuals in society" (126). It thus assumes the dimension of a political struggle against institutional oppression and all social ills. This is the promise and solution offered by AICs and the main reason for their amazing growth and influence. "This space of healing becomes their political discourse of confronting social ills, not as helpless beings who are neglected by God, but as those who are in control and capable of changing their social conditions" (127). A reading in the Spirit empowers not only women in a special way, but all people of different religions, cultures, classes, races and gender. "This framework refuses to accept defeat, rejection, imperialism, unemployment, breakdown of relationships or any form of incapacity; that is, *even dogs can pick up the crumbs*" (127). The readings of ordinary people in this way form part of a process to restore God's diverse creation and to bring it to fulfillment.

Text-Centered/Oral Culture

It is ironic that the concentration on the reader should lead to the discovery of the importance of the hearer or listener. But this is exactly one of the results of Draper's study. It led to the discovery of two distinct groups within ranks of "ordinary" readers, namely those operating in a context of textuality and those living in the context of either primary orality or residual orality. This is a further dichotomy linked to the interface of scholarly and ordinary readers. For the present study, this is of paramount importance, because so many of the intented readers are actually listeners or hearers. The interrelationship between literacy and orality is more complex than usually assumed, as Draper reminds us. Furthermore, is effective communication possible between the two cultures? Most lecturers and critical readers trained at universities or seminaries operate in terms of a textually constructed universe. But, as the results of the study clearly show, the vast majority of "ordinary" readers lives in an oral culture. Are students effectively prepared to minister to such members? Is the preoccupation with print culture a help or a stumbling block in this regard? A remarkable finding was that students trained in historical methods and textual analysis apparently were able to revert back to oral culture quite easily. If this is the case, will they really be able to facilitate a paradigm switch from orality to textuality? Is it wise to strive for such a change? Draper raises further questions: "Is the text the same text for those whose thought processes are shaped by literacy as for those still living in a residually oral culture? Further, if they do read or use the text of the Bible, do they read or interpret in the same way?" (63). And how do those in living in primary orality appropriate the Bible and what is the power dynamic at work here? As Draper indicates, these questions merit further attention.

Exegesis/Theology

One of the sad side effects of recent developments in the field of theological scholarship is the growing alienation between biblical scholars and systematic theologians. As Wittenberg reminds us, the tension between "biblical theology" and "dogma" has a long history, going back to the eighteenth century. Recently, the tension is not so much between theology and dogma, but between Old and New Testament exegesis and systematic theology. The analytical, dissecting, and dispersing mode of contemporary exegesis, celebrating plurality of interpretation, seems to yield disappointing results for systematic theologians and quite unsuitable for their enterprise with its emphasis on synthesis, generalization, and concentration (cf. Smit). It is in the interest of both "parties" that a constructive dialogue gets underway again. It is therefore very encouraging to see that the concentration on the ordinary reader raises not only exegetical issues, but has clear theological implications, as the studies of Walker, Ukpong, Nolan, and Wittenberg show. The scholar/reader interface reveals a further complexity; it is not content with understanding how readers read, but also how these insights affect the whole of the theological enterprise.

What strategies are developed to achieve this goal?

Walker presents a comprehensive attempt (although provisional by her own admission) of a redefined theology of Mary. Here is a deliberate move from reading a text in its biblical form (Old and New Testament) to reading the text of church tradition and dogma. Choosing a *topos* firmly entrenched in dogma has both advantages and disadvantages. It can be used to defend traditional views of the role and function of women, but it can also be used to undermine these views and provide the basis for a liberating reading of tradition.

In her research, Walker found the meaning given to Mary by readers to be ambiguous and in some ways contradictory. There were also signs of differences between clergy and laity, the latter venerating statues and images in a way not intended by the priests, but to which they could relate better, while the popular Marian devotion was played down by certain representatives of the official Church. The same ambiguity applies to the role of popular religion, which can have both an oppressive or liberatory function. The important contribution of this form of theology is that it constitutes a crucial aspect of the ordinary reader's identity and that it supports and sustains this identity over and against those who would seek to undermine it.

What Walker shows is that a traditional doctrine and practice can and is being used to develop an alternative understanding of that tradition. The discrepancy between official doctrine and what (ordinary) people think and do, has long been noticed. But, and that is the important point, it can form the basis for an alternative strategy, subverting the official position. Exactly because it is already part of the accepted tradition, it serves as a very effective springboard to launch an alternative understanding. Walker herself, in her quest to establish the meaning of this tradition in the worlds which Mary opens for contemporary victims of history, provides a convincing outline for an alternative way to theologize about Mary, a Mary who identifies with the poor, reveals the reign of God and the truth about humanity. She demonstrates that, with all the ambiguity and negative aspects of the tradition, texts of faith can transcend the oppressive world out of which they arose and that ordinary readers are ingenious enough to develop their own alternative readings of these texts.

Nolan makes a different move. His novel proposal concerns the construction of a genuine theology of work. But this is not a task for professional theologians or biblical scholars. In order to be authentic, it must be constructed by workers themselves, born out of their experience as workers and their theological reflection on it. Experience of work in general, including intellectual work, can be of value, but Nolan has something much more specific in mind: "It is the experience of working for a wage, working for a boss, working with one's hands. It is the experience of being used as a unit of labor, a machine, of being exploited for profit. It is the experience of alienation from one's work, from the product of one's labor, and therefore of alienation from oneself and from other workers" (214).

The worker, like other kinds of ordinary readers, reads the Bible with different eyes. The experience of work alerts him or her to aspects hitherto neglected in the text, much as women readers do. Nolan is careful not to speak for workers, but gives glimpses of what might be themes in such a theology of work. He refers to a "worker strand" in the story of creation, where the making of heaven and earth is described in work-related metaphors. The image of God as worker (who also rests like a worker on the seventh day) is suggestive and can be augmented by many related images in the New Testament.

Nolan's stimulating proposal leaves the reader unsatisfied, because of the brevity of the outline presented here. But the brevity is the direct result of his insistence that workers themselves must construct this theology. Although his life-long involvement with workers makes him as qualified anyone for the task, he is convinced that the ideal situation for the construction of a theology of work is not that of the professional theologians *making use* of the insights of workers, but that workers *make use of* the expertise of academics. In doing so, he echoes the basic philosophy of the work of the Institute for the Study of the Bible, as explained by West is his introductory essay.

The readings of ordinary readers are of interest not only for Bible study groups. If taken seriously, they can results in new insights and rejuvenate other theological issues. As Ukpong indicates, it is a new way of doing theology, which cuts across all theological disciplines.

North/South

A final contrast to be singled out is what can be called a North/South interface. It could refer to specific relationship, like the Western/African Christianity dichotomy discussed by Pobee, but it forms part of a much broader experience, which involves also other countries and other histories of the North and the South.

In describing the goal to pass over from "the language of Euro-centred and Euro-constructed theology to an African-centred and African-constructed theology so as to speak effectively to Africans, body, soul and spirit so that they may repent and have life, and that in abundance," Pobee articulates an ideal shared by many in the South (176). But how is that to be achieved in concrete terms? Pobee refers to the need for a "plenum of hermeneutics" (176). Can one be more specific?

Ukpong's idea of an "inculturation biblical hermeneutic" and his exposition of the parable of the "unjust" manager provides a good illustration of the potential of such an approach. Ukpong's method has much in common with the methods followed by the ISB. It consciously and explicitly seeks to interpret the biblical text from the socio-cultural perspectives of different people. The plurivalence of the text is celebrated, not suppressed. Like Wittenberg, it wants to place exegesis and theology once again back in the socio-cultural context where it is generated. Without denying the historical setting of the text, the emphasis is very much on the appropriation in a contemporary context, that is, in the world opened up in front of the text. Priority does not belong to historically authoritative readings, but to new readings. The dynamic rereading of the text involves entering the into the text conscious of the present context, with critical awareness. The text is not merely an object of analysis, but requires the involvement of the interpreter in the dynamics of the text. This means an emphasis on the ordinary, contemporary, real reader.

Most important is the switch of subjects: "Inculturation hermeneutic seeks to promote the employment of different cultural perspectives in biblical interpretation, and to bring the contribution of various cultural resources to our reading the Bible. In other words, it seeks to make the different socio-cultural contexts the *subject* of interpretation" (my italics). Once the worm has turned in this way, a critique of the prevalent reading, however powerful, becomes possible. Ukpong's fascinating interpretation of the parable of the unjust manager—a parable which has puzzled and is still puzzling biblical scholars—illustrates this change effectively. The different context means different starting points and leads to different evaluations of role players and situations. Peasant farmers, traders, exploitative bonds and debts, and the experience of situations in West Africa, result in a reversal of roles. The manager is no longer the villain, but the hero. His action is one of restitutive justice, a critique of an exploitative economic system. Justice means sharing the earth's wealth in such a way that nobody is exploited. From this perspective, new light is shed on global economics, the modern debt situation affecting North and South, and the effects of growing internationalization. "In sum, therefore, this parable challenges Christians to be committed to work towards the *reversal* of oppressive structures of contemporary economic systems; and to take life crises as challenges to rise to the new heights in response to the demands of the kingdom" (208).

Conclusion

The multi-faceted investigation of the scholar/ordinary reader interface in this volume reveals that it is also the meeting point of a whole series of related contrasts, contrasts which must be taken into account if the role of the ordinary reader is to be understood adequately. The attention to the ordinary reader brings a neglected, but necessary, facet of the interpretation process into focus. Two aspects remain problematic. First, the structural imbalance between scholar and reader. Whatever precautions are being taken to strengthen the position of the reader, in practice it remains very difficult to ensure that the reader is operating on an equal basis. Nonetheless, the scholar can ignore the reader only at his or her own peril. Second, methods of empirical research are in need of further refinement. Both qualitative and quantitative research in this volume is of varying depth and quality, but nonetheless essential for gaining a better understanding of the assumptions, attitudes, and conduct of real readers.

The ordinary reader remains a pivotal point in the process of interpretation and in the balance of power which accompanies this process. Whatever the authority of the dominant tradition may be, it can always be challenged from the perspective of the reader. But furthermore, in order to vindicate its claim to universal validity, the biblical text is dependent on the appropriation of readers with different orientations in different contexts. The ongoing process of interpretation safeguards the role of the reader, but also the promise of innovative, healing, liberating, and restorative readings.

WORKS CONSULTED

Fowler, Robert M.
    1992   *Let the Reader Understand: Reader-Response Criticism and the Gospel of Mark*. Minneapolis: Fortress.

Groeben, N.
    1977   *Rezeptionsforschung als empirischen Literaturwissenschaft*. Kronberg: Athenäum.

Schmidt, S. J.
    1982   *Grundriss der empirischen Literaturwissenschaft II*. Braunschweig: Vieweg.

Lategan, Bernard C., ed.
    1992   *The Reader and Beyond: Theory and Practice in South African Reception Studies*. Pretoria: HSRC.

Segers, R. T.
    1980   *Het lezen van literatuur*. Baarn: Ambo.

Smit, Dirk J.
    1994   "The Story of Contextual Hermeneutics and the Integrity of New Testament Interpretation in South Africa." *Neotestamentica* 28:265–89.

Steinberg, H.
    1983   "Socio-empirical Reading Research: A Critical Report about Some Revealing Surveys." *Poetics* 9: 119–46.

Steiner, George
    1979   "'Critic'/'Reader.'" *New Literary History* 10:423–52.

Van Gorp, H., R. Ghesquire, and R. T. Segers, eds.
    1981   *Receptie-Onderzoek: Mogelijkheden en Grenzen*. Leuven: Acco.

Society of Biblical Literature

The New Testament in the Greek Fathers

The New Testament Text of Cyril of Jerusalem
Roderic L. Mullen

This work presents Greek text from the works of Cyril of Jerusalem (ca. 315–386 C.E.), as well as an analysis of the text that shows the affinity of many of Cyril's readings with readings from New Testament manuscripts of Alexandrian text-type. The study demonstrates that Cyril was more interested in the meaning of a text than in textual analysis, and illustrates the trajectory of the New Testament text in Roman Palestine. This work will be of interest to advanced students of New Testament textual criticism and patristics.

Code: 06 30 07   448 pages
Cloth: $39.95   ISBN: 0-7885-0339-1

SBL Dissertation Series

The Jewish Heroes of Christian History
Hebrews 11 in Literary Context
Pamela Michelle Eisenbaum

By comparing the catalog of biblical heroes found in Hebrews 11 with other hero lists and retellings of biblical history, and by placing it within the context of Hebrews' hermeneutical perspective, the ideology implicit in the text emerges. Eisenbaum concludes that the heroes of Hebrews are not described as national leaders—as was more typical with hero lists—but rather as marginalized characters who are situated outside the national destiny of Israel. By portraying the biblical heroes as marginalized, the author of Hebrews constructs a radical, denationalized reading of Jewish scripture. Such a reading, in turn, became significant for the use of Jewish scripture by early Christianity.

Code: 06 21 56   264 pages
Cloth: $39.95   ISBN: 0-7885-0246-8

The Text of I Corinthians in the Writings of Origen
Darrell D. Hannah

This book reconstructs as much of Origen's text of 1 Corinthians as is possible by collecting all the citations, allusions and adaptations of the epistle from Origen's works. The analysis of these variant readings demonstrates that Origen's text is closely related to that of the Alexandrian witnesses, especially codices Vaticanus, Sinaiticus, and Ephraemi. Origen demonstrably gave little if any preference to the so called "primary Alexandrians" over the "secondary Alexandrians" and, further, his text is a great deal closer to the Byzantine text-type than to the Western text-type. This Byzantine element of Origen's text, the author argues, most probably arises from those readings which the Byzantine text-type shares with the Alexandrian. In addition to its other contributions, Hannah's painstaking work suggests that scholars need to re-examine the widespread use of the sub-categories "primary" and "secondary" Alexandrians.

Code: 06 30 04   320 pages
Cloth: $44.95   ISBN: 0-7885-0338-3

Scholars Press
P.O. Box 6996, Alpharetta, GA 30239-6996
Phone: 800-437-6692; Fax: 770-442-9742

Response to "'Reading With': An Exploration of the Interface between Critical and Ordinary Readings of the Bible"

Renita J. Weems
Vanderbilt Divinity School
United States of America

"What happens when ordinary readers from poor and marginalized communities call on biblical scholars to serve them in their reading of the Bible? What role is there for the socially engaged biblical scholar?" These questions, asked by Gerald West from the School of Theology at the University of Natal, are an apt frame for viewing the entire volume. The editors, Gerald West and Musa Dube, along with an array of colleagues, both academic and clergy (all academically trained), take it upon themselves to build a bridge of partnership across the vast chasm that has been set up to differentiate the reading strategies of the scholar from those of the ordinary reader. Contributors to this volume explore in a variety of ways the unique resources and skills that scholars and ordinary readers bring to interpretation and the possible transformations that can take place when the two collaborate in reading. While they draw on the gamut of critical reading theories to shed light on what it means to read the Bible with postcolonial and liberationist commitments, the contributors are all too well aware of the contradictory role the Bible has played in South African politics, both as an obstructive force and as a catalyzing resource in the struggle for justice and liberation. And it is precisely because it can and had been read in ways that declaim the rights of the Other that the contributors to this volume make explicit their commitments to read the Bible, not only *on behalf of*, but *with* the poor and marginalized. By making explicit such a commitment they have already radically challenged one of the most important tenets of their socialization as academics and intellectuals. Southern African academicians refuse to be neutral readers. These scholars expose their commitments, their interests, and their reading strategies to the scrutiny of the poor and the marginalized. And they expose them to us, their colleagues in the West, for scrutiny and example.

The real flesh and blood readers of this North American journal of experimental biblical criticism *Semeia* have rarely had an opportunity since the journal's inception to encounter other real flesh and blood readers in these pages. We have preferred the anonymity, objectivity, and respectability that comes with talk about hypothetical readers, mock readers, ideal readers, intended readers, informed readers, and super readers — those intratextual readers who are believed to be somehow inscribed within and constructed by the text itself — to the vulnerability, accountability, and vulgarity of talking about the self and one's own social situatedness. The scholars who have consistently acknowledged the role that their social and political contexts have played in shaping their reading strategies, and who have insisted the loudest and the most consistently upon the contextual character of all scholarship, have been those on the margins of mainstream circles of biblical discourse (e.g. women, North American minorities, readers and scholars from the Two-Thirds World). Our colleagues from Southern Africa argue here that the time has come for all biblical scholars to take responsibility for their scholarship and for the world in which to live. To acknowledge one's social location means more than to itemize one's vital statistics. It means also to scrutinize and talk openly about how one's scholarship interfaces with one's larger social and political hopes for the world.

For those of us in North America Gerald West's question about the role of the socially engaged scholar is so shocking in its relevance, immediacy, and practicality that we have hardly known how to address such matters in our academic journals. The very notion that our work might be of use to the ordinary reader, the thought that our scholarship has implications for the larger social and political projects of our era, the possibility that what we do in our ivory towers can and ought be understood by common peasant readers — these ideas are contrary both to some of the organizing principles of our discipline and to our socialization as academics. Despite the postmodern and poststructuralist orientation of much of our scholarship with its emphasis upon subjectivity, agency, and the rights of readers, biblical scholars in the West have not been willing in our scholarship to confront our own complex interests and locations as real flesh and blood readers. Western scholasticism has trained us well to avoid self-disclosure at all costs and to ignore (deny, is more accurate) the implications of our own political perspective upon our work.

It is both surprising and unsurprising, then, that one of the best models for how to discuss our commitments and engagements as real flesh and blood readers should come to us from our colleagues in South Africa (see Gerald West). Having to imagine and to build for themselves a new multi-racial, egalitarian society, one no longer based upon domination, oppression, racial polarization, and racial violence, and having to confess that theirs is a society where (scholarly) biblical interpretations do matter and do shape their society (where past biblical scholarship played its part in upholding apartheid, if by doing nothing else than leaving its assumptions unquestioned), South Africa scholars, or at least some of them, are in search of new ways for not only reading the Bible. South African biblical scholars are searching for new ways of conceiving, doing, and discussing their work as real flesh and blood scholars. What we have before us in this volume largely reflects the efforts of South African biblical scholars to construct for themselves a new identity and to take responsibility for their role in helping to shape a new South Africa.

Whereas we have already encountered scholarship interested in reading *on behalf of* previously unheard from communities of readers, this collection of articles describes in various ways what happens when scholars read *with* previously unheard from communities of readers. The difference is all the difference in the world. Here real flesh and blood Southern African scholars make themselves and their scholarship available to real flesh and blood Southern African poor and marginalized communities (women's Bible study circles, labor workers, grass root movements, popular religious sects). More importantly, here real flesh and blood Southern African scholars open themselves up for scrutiny as many of them attempt a critical analysis of their own multiply situated location as readers, scholars, ministers, activists, students, privileged citizens, white/black/colored/other, male/female. In short, this volume is about real readers reading the Bible in real situations.

In many respects "Reading With" is representative of a stream of publications produced by scholars from the Two Thirds World that describe the creativity, legitimacy, and subversive ingenuity of readings by indigenous people of color who read the Bible (R. S. Sugirtharajah; Kwok Pui-lan; Mercy Oduyoye; Fernando F. Segovia and Mary Ann Tolbert). Such publications are the rumblings of a not so subtle protest against the tendency of those in power to essentialize and homogenize the thoughts, words, and contributions of the Other. Reading *with* the Other means to allow the poor and the marginalized, for example, to describe for themselves and in their own words their reading tastes and habits. It also means no longer seeing scholars with ethnic, political, and ideological ties and roots in these communities as the surrogate reader for all poor and marginalized readers all over the world.

This volume permits us to see how scholars and intellectuals from across the racial, social, and economic divide in South Africa come together to both lend their academic expertise to the struggle and to lay open that same training to criticism and reformulation. For those contributors not born belonging to poor and marginalized classes in South Africa, the commitment to read with the poor and marginalized is surely a courageous and laudable one. But for those contributors in this volume who are descendants of poor and marginalized classes in South Africa, the commitment to read with one's own is fraught with ambivalence. Reading *on behalf of* ordinary readers not only means recognizing the right of the poor, the illiterate, and the colonized to describe and discuss their own reading strategies.

It also means to acknowledge the ways in which some of us have been indelibly shaped by our backgrounds. We see how much we remain indebted to members of our communities for our insights, our creativity, our subversive strategies, and for our passion for our work. More important, however, reading *with* them means for us who are both scholars and products of these communities to confront the ways in which we have been permanently changed by our academic training and new class privileges. Returning home and reading *with* our ancestors forces us to observe on a personal level the way education has altered our relationship to power in the society. We are forced to consider then that reading *with* poor and marginalized readers, or with any other ordinary reader for that matter, is potentially dangerous work. It is dangerous because it exposes scholars—and it exposes scholarship—to the those elements of human interpretation that defy scholasticism and forces us to examine the concrete ways in which our scholarship and our privileges as scholars rely upon the status quo.

For example, as a North American woman scholar of African ancestry teaching Bible in a Southern university, I find the inspiring words of the "illiterate" women of Gaborone, Mpophomeni, and Pedi and the manifest aspirations of African Independent Churches, to name a few, both familiar and haunting. Their words remind me as a scholar, woman, and person of color of readers I know only too well from my own community whose voices remind me constantly of my origins and my contradictions. They are the real readers who demand from me scholarship that is done on behalf of real people. When Bishop Virginia Lucas, founding member of the Glory Healing Church in Mogoditshane, Gaborone, responds to requests to defend her ministry in the face of the Bible's numerous interdictions against women with the comment, "When God spoke to me through the Spirit, God never opened the Bible to me. Instead, God's Spirit told me to begin a church and heal God's people, which is what I am doing," Lucas forces the academic reading with her to grapple with those hidden, irrecoverable elements of reading, those extratextual or supratextual reading strategies readers employ to negotiate meaning from the Bible (114).

The academic reading partner is forced to confront the integrity of real readers, illiterate though some may be. We are forced to see them as illiterate, but also intelligent people who know what they know about God, about faith, and about justice without ever having to read a page on the topics. In other words, readers like Bishop Virginia Lucas remind scholars of the limitations of science to account for everything that takes place when real readers encounter texts. We are reminded of the inadequacies of our metatheories to account for the complexity and diversity of human activities. We are also reminded of the irrecoverable, elusive, intractable part of the reading process which all readers make use of, and which poor and marginalized readers draw upon freely, when encountering the counterliberation impulses of biblical texts.

Finally, it should be pointed out that the academic is not the only one to gain from reading with the ordinary reader, as this volume amply attests. The ordinary reader gains from reading with the academic. One can only wonder what would happen if North American biblical scholars, for example, were to follow the lead of their Southern African colleagues and read with ordinary readers? What would happen if scholars of this learned journal read with religious right wing, conservatives in this country? What would happen if North American biblical scholars took it upon themselves to seek out Bible study groups with the militant millenialist sects scattered throughout its borders? What would happen if we actively pursued conversations with demagogues of hate, inviting them to join us in reading the Bible, listening intently to their strategies and rationalizations for interpretation and offering them new lens through which to view the Bible and themselves?

These can be admittedly odious tasks to take on. One can hardly imagine anything fruitful to be gained on the part of scholars from such a dialogue. But our own gain is not the point. The point is to acknowledge that through our silence, through our failure to declare our political commitments, and through our fictive objectivity, we have conspired with those pockets of apartheid hate and violence lodged within our own borders. We have hidden behind fictive readers in our scholarship to camouflage our own reading interests, refusing to acknowledge the role our scholarship plays in upholding or dismantling the status quo. By reading *with* those who, for some of us, are the most objectionable ordinary readers imaginable, we step from behind the safety of our ivory desks and do our part in repairing the world where real people use the Bible as their manifesto for living, dying, fighting, dreaming, struggling, and maiming each other. This present volume warrants our careful attention because it forces us to take responsibility for the world in which we live and it shows us how to take responsibility for the world which our scholarship creates.

BIBLICAL SCHOLARS AT THE INTERFACE BETWEEN CRITICAL AND ORDINARY READINGS: A RESPONSE

Daniel Patte
Vanderbilt University
United States of America

THE CHALLENGE OF THIS VOLUME

As I read the articles of this volume, many explicit references and allusions constantly remind me that all, except John Riches's, originate in one or another African contexts. By its very existence, this volume calls me and any other European–American biblical scholars to acknowledge that our own critical work originates in quite different cultural, social, and political contexts.

The more specific challenge which this volume is for us becomes clearer when we note that its title and topic, "Reading With," is derived from Gyatri Spivak's efforts to empower subalterns to speak (cf. West), and is born out of post-colonial reflections (as Dube underscores). Envisioning critical biblical studies in diverse African contexts, our colleagues found that they had to re-examine "The Interface Between Critical and Ordinary Readings"—a relationship which for us is commonly posited by practices of biblical scholarship born out of European-American hermeneutical reflections, derived from cultures which were and still are marked by colonialism and imperialism (as several of the authors would readily say). Thus, one of the questions implicitly raised by this volume is: Are our practices of critical biblical studies tainted by colonialism?

For us, European-American biblical scholars, this question is so unexpected and so broad that it is almost nonsensical. But we can not escape it when the more concrete question of the interface between critical and ordinary readings is raised. When it is considered in the African contexts, it appears that the traditional view of the relationship between critical and ordinary readings is problematic, because its shape is reminiscent of colonialist relationships (as Dube suggests). We, European-American biblical scholars, too often take this relationship for granted, as if it were "natural," and do not even imagine that our perception of this relationship might be problematic. A broad contribution of this volume is that it opens this question for us, or reopens it in new ways for those who are already aware of these issues—especially, feminists and other advocacy scholars.

As we read these essays, we cannot but reconsider the relationship between critical and ordinary readings, and thus how we behave as critical readers toward ordinary readers (e.g. students) in our actual *practices* of critical biblical studies, for instance, when we teach either in the classroom or through our writing. According to the traditional conception, propagated by male European-American scholars, critical readers tend to present themselves as possessors of a knowledge (about the Bible and how to interpret it) which they impart to ordinary readers who lack such a knowledge and are therefore bound to have improper readings of the Bible as long as they are not properly instructed. In such common practices,[1] critical readers convey the right way of reading to ordinary readers who presumably have wrong ways of reading that they should abandon. The problematic character of this pattern of relationship is shown by this volume which posits critical readers with European-American training and African ordinary readers. The colonialist, paternalistic attitudes and their inequity are then as clear as the injustice of economic imperialist exploitation (discussed by Ukpong who refers to the exploitation of Nigerian farmers).

From the outset, this volume of *Semeia* identifies the relationship between critical and ordinary readings as a problem area—as the origin of a generalized infection. Yet, this volume seeks to go farther by attempting to diagnose the exact nature of the problem. But, in view of the complexity of the issue, it appropriately sees itself as "an exploration" of the problem. Its different essays reflect disparate assessments of the problem. Regarding one issue or another, as readers, we are repeatedly called to take sides with certain authors against the others. The cumulative effect of these different articles and of the discrete choices they ask us to make is most appropriate. This volume does not provide a definite conclusion regarding the way in which the relationship between critical and ordinary readings of the Bible should be understood and practiced—a definite conclusion which all readers would have been expected to appropriate. Rather, it calls each of its readers to draw the conclusion which is appropriate for her or his specific context.

In this response, I propose to play the role that this volume asks me to play as its reader: I summarize how this volume helps me, a Protestant

---

[1] We often keep this pattern in our practices even though we have much more sophisticated theoretical views of this relationship, which we base upon hermeneutical theories.

male European-American critical reader of the Bible, to further rethink my relationship with ordinary readers of the Bible.

What I Seek to Accomplish by This Response or My View of the Interface between Critical and Ordinary Readers after Studying These Essays

I must clarify my position. As compared with most "ordinary" readers of this volume, I am an "expert" (a term used as equivalent to "critical reader" by Nolan). Why do I conceive of myself as an expert? For two reasons. On the one hand, I have a certain expertise in semiotic theory, which includes theories about the process of reading as one instance of communication.[2] On the other hand, and more importantly, I have "insider's knowledge." As I reported elsewhere,[3] I became aware that there was a fundamental problem in my practices of critical biblical studies when I was confronted with the pervading reality of apartheid in South African life and with the difficulties which colleagues had as they sought to transform their teaching of critical biblical studies for a post-apartheid society. In the process, I had the chance to meet and dialogue with several of the authors and/or to read their earlier works on this and related topics. I already had the opportunity to reflect on these issues, which are quite important for me. Since I could appropriately conceive of myself as an "expert-critical reader" of this volume, I accepted to write this response, which I, an expert-critical reader, write for the "ordinary" readers of this volume.

The question is then: How should I conceive my role toward you, my readers? As I answer this question, I also express the conclusions I drew as I read this volume,[4] regarding the way in which the relationship between critical and ordinary readings of the Bible should be understood and practiced by a Protestant male European-American.

Before going further I need to clarify who is the "you" to whom I write. "You" is a reader of this volume who, I presuppose, reads it as an "ordinary reader." By this, I simply mean that I expect that you are pressed by time; therefore when you receive this volume you read it quickly, as an ordinary reader would—instead of taking the time to ana-

---

[2] See especially, Daniel Patte, *The Religious Dimensions of Biblical Texts: Greimas's Structural Semiotics and Biblical Exegesis* (Atlanta: Scholars Press, 1990).

[3] See Daniel Patte, *Ethics of Biblical Interpretation: A Reevaluation* (Louisville: Westminster/John Knox, 1995).

[4] With the exceptions of the Introduction and of the other Responses which, of course, were not available to me as I write my own response.

lyze it in some detail, as I had to do as a critical reader preparing this response.

Of course, my presupposition might be wrong. It is quite possible that you are actually taking the time to study this volume carefully as an expert-critical reader. In this later case, please kindly play along, even though the "you" might not refer to you.

> Note the implication of this remark: *the same person can be at any given moment an "expert-critical reader" or an "ordinary reader"* of the Bible. It is a matter of attitude, not of person.

How should I conceive my role as a critical reader toward "you," an ordinary reader? In one word: as a facilitator (as suggested by West). Facilitating what? Am I to facilitate your reading of this volume? Yes, in a way. But, only in a very limited sense. As the General Editor of *Semeia*, I am one of those who contribute to make this text available to you.

> This is also a part of our role as critical biblical scholars: making the biblical text available through the technical procedures of textual criticism and of translations in the various vernaculars.

But, beyond this, I will NOT facilitate your reading *per se*. In his description of his work with a group, West underscores that "critical resources were not used as the way into the text." Why? Because, in West's example, "the generative theme determined by the group provided an initial entry into the reading process." I want to generalize these remarks and underscore that critical resources and critical readings are not, and have never been, the initial entry into the reading process. In most instances (if not always), an ordinary reading precedes a critical reading. This is clear in the case of my critical reading of this volume. It presupposes an ordinary reading of it on my part, and also presupposes that you, an ordinary reader, performed an ordinary reading. Consequently, my critical reading will NOT facilitate your reading of this volume, because you have already performed this reading. Furthermore, you understood your reading of it, and consequently you reached certain conclusions regarding the significance of this volume for you. I presuppose that when you opened it you were already a competent and interested reader.[5]

(1) By reading these essays, you have shown that you knew how to read and how to make sense of these pages—as any ordinary reader does when reading a text. This is to say that, together with a general linguistic competence, you had the use of certain semantic categories by means of

---

[5] The order between competence and interest, and consequently between epistemological judgments and value judgments, is arbitrary. In actual readings, these take place in either order or simultaneously.

which you recognized that these essays deal with certain issues, themes, topics. Your first set of conclusions (which might be quite general or quite specific) resulted from a series of epistemological judgments, through which you identified in each essay, and possibly, in the entire volume, what makes sense for you, as well as what does not make sense for you. But, as an ordinary reader pressed by time, you just did all this as you read, without taking the time of being self-conscious about each of your epistemological decisions (as a critical reader should).

(2) Your reading also includes assessing the relative value or significance for you of "what makes sense for you" in the text.[6] Since you picked up the volume, you were at the very least interested by *Semeia*. Since you took the time to read the issue after opening it and consulting the title and the table of contents, I can also say that you anticipated that you would find in these essays something which is of interest to you. Otherwise, why would you read them? And why, after beginning, would you continue reading them? Whatever might be your specific "interest" (or stake)[7] in these essays—whether your interest was in finding the weak points of the arguments, so as to dismiss the whole question as meaningless, or whether it was in identifying a better way of understanding and performing your work as a biblical scholar, or something else, you anticipated that there would be "something significant for you" in these pages. By the end of your reading, and thus after identifying what makes or does not make sense for you, you reached conclusions regarding the significance of this volume for you. Whether these are positive or negative does not make any difference at this point (although my personal conclusions are very positive). Here, I simply want to emphasize that any reading ends up with conclusions regarding the significance of the text for the readers, even when it pretends to be disinterested,[8] and that any reading reaches such conclusions by performing a series of value judgments re-

---

[6] Once again, the order between these two processes varies. I do not mean to exclude the possibility that you responded emotionally to this text (perceiving value in it), before making sense of it. But, this emotional response is usually reserved by most readers of *Semeia* for more poetic or symbolic texts.

[7] I use the term "interest" in a very general sense to designate all kinds of motivation, including coercion (being forced by someone else to do it, and doing it in order to avoid certain penalties), obligation (doing it out of a sense of duty, because reading these essays serves a broader purpose), as well as free-will (doing it, because one has something at stake in this reading, or simply because one expects pleasure from it). In all these cases, directly or indirectly, it is in our "interest" to perform the action (reading).

[8] I should perhaps have written "especially when it pretends to be disinterested"!

garding the relative positive or negative significance for the readers of what they identified as "making sense."[9]

Since I, the expert-critical reader, need neither to convince you, the ordinary readers, to read this volume (you were already convinced to do so), nor to teach you how to read it (you already knew how to read and how to make sense out of it), what then is my role as facilitator?

In order to understand it, let us remember that I had to presuppose that "you were pressed by time, and that therefore you read this text quite quickly, as ordinary readers would." This statement defines an "ordinary reader" as someone who has not taken the time to be self-conscious about the process of reading which he or she performs. As an ordinary reader, you lack neither interest nor competence. You are exclusively concerned to get at "what makes sense for you" (or "what does not make sense" for you) in the text and to reach conclusions concerning the significance of these findings for you. In your hurry, you are concerned neither with "how you made sense (or not) of the text" nor with "why this or that point is significant for you."

My role as a critical reader/facilitator (or expert) appears: it is simply a matter of helping you to bring to critical understanding *how* and *why* you read this volume as you did. In other words, it is a matter of facilitating your understanding of "how you made sense" (or did not make sense) of the text and of "why" you concluded that this or that point had a positive or negative significance for you, so that *you* might assess your own reading and its conclusions regarding the significance of this text for you.

How will I help you take notice of the choices you made throughout your reading? How will I help you recognize that in order to make sense of the text you have used certain (and not other) semantic categories which focused your attention on certain aspects of the text and hid other aspects from you? How will I help you recognize that the value judgments which help you identify what is significant for you had a similar effect for you (focusing your attention on certain aspects of the text and hiding others)? Obviously, I cannot point out to you what are the choices you made. To begin with, I do not know how you read this volume and what your conclusions are. But even if we were together and if you would tell me how you read it, I could merely propose wild guesses regarding how and why you reached such conclusions. I can only be a facilitator, by presenting some of the options I perceived in the text as I was reading it myself and identifying what is significant in it for me.

---

[9] Alternatively, if the order is reversed, it might be a matter of finding what makes sense among the things you have identified as significant for you.

By describing, as self-consciously as possible, some of the choices I made in the process of my own reading, I can hope to make you aware that your own reading involved choices among the options offered by this volume, and entice you to seek to identify how and why you reached specific conclusions regarding the significance (or lack of significance) of this volume for you as ordinary reader. By presenting to you my own critical reading, I hope to entice you to transform your ordinary reading into a critical reading. By becoming self-conscious of the choices we made in each of our readings, and thus by recognizing the possibility and plausibility of other readings, we put yourself in a position of assessing the relative value of our own conclusions about the significance of this volume for us in the present.

In what follows, I briefly explain my conclusions (regarding what I see to be the particularly significant contributions of this volume for understanding the relationship between critical and ordinary readings, namely certain epistemological and value judgments) by making explicit some of the epistemological and value judgments which led me to these conclusions. If this presentation seems circular, it is because it actually is! How else can I self-consciously present the process of being self-conscious (in the process of reading)!

READING AS CHOOSING PARTICULARLY SIGNIFICANT VOICE(S) OF THE TEXT

I have concluded from my own reading of this volume that it makes two significant general points. This volume conveys: (1) that any reading process, be it critical or ordinary, involves making choices among various options offered by a text so as to identify what is particularly significant for the reader(s) in a specific context; and (2) that different cultures have different conceptualizations of the way in which readers choose among these options.

The very fact that each of the essays deals with the interface between two different but appropriate kinds of reading (critical and ordinary readings) already expresses that any reader has a choice among several potential readings of a given text. This first point expresses how I perceive the unity of this volume; this is how, for me, these essays make sense together. Regarding the second point, the great differences among the articles make explicit that there are different ways of conceiving of how and why a reader chooses a certain reading.[10]

It is particularly significant for me that this volume makes these two interrelated points, because it is an invitation to ponder how and why

---

[10] This is, in brief, the twin epistemological judgment which led me to select these two points as particularly meaningful.

readers choose among potential readings of a text. It is important for us to do so, because our conceptualization of the relationship between critical and ordinary readings, and thus whether it is or not colonialist, depends upon our conception of these choices and of the way they are made.[11]

As I sought to make sense of this volume and to identify what is significant in it for me, it soon became clear that I had to pick and choose among its different essays. They represent quite different "voices" which express quite different views on certain themes or topics. By confronting us with a choice among these views, this volume suggests a broad cognitive framework and a metaphor for understanding the phenomenon of multiple readings: a text as having a plurality of voices.

This metaphor seems helpful.[12] The authors of these essays are not speaking with one voice; their voices have quite distinctive sounds, because they echo debates, dialogues, and conversations taking place in different milieux.

In the case of this collection of essays, there is no doubt that the text before me (the volume) involves a plurality of discrete voices—represented by the discrete essays—among which I have to make a choice, since they are discordant. Yet, the case of a text written by a single author is similar. Any given text (including a biblical text) involves several voices, even if they are not as clearly separated as in a collection of essays, and thus the reading of any text involves making a similar choice among its voices.[13] Why? Long's essay indirectly provides us with a very appropriate answer: because the "real" author of the text could not but speak/write with different voices. In saying so, I apply to the real author what Long says about the real reader.

As Long analyzes his own reading, he describes himself as being several readers at once: a South African political/reader, a priest/reader, a pray–er/reader, a suspicious/reader, a pastor/reader, an institutional-church/reader, a middle-class white/reader, a male/reader, a church/Academy/reader. As any given real reader is not one but several readers, so also any given author is someone who necessarily has multiple personae and thus is someone who speaks with different voices. For instance, in a text might include the voices of the author: as addressing a specific audience in time and space with a specific goal; as a polemicist

---

[11] This is a brief sketch of the value judgment involved in my conclusions.

[12] The metaphor of a text as having multiple voices as a representation of its polysemy is similar to the metaphors of the multi-dimensionality of the text (which I use in Patte, *Ethics of Biblical Interpretation*) and of the multiple codes of the text (which Bal uses in Mieke Bal, *Murder and Difference: Gender, Genre, and Scholarship on Sisera's Death*. Trans. M. Gumpert. Bloomington: Indiana University Press, 1988).

[13] This of course means that each of the essays also has several voices. But, in this brief response I cannot discuss these.

against opponents; as a person trained to use the literary and/or rhetorical conventions of his or her time; as knowledgeable about certain traditions; as a member of a family and/or a community (or several!); as a believer sharing the convictions of a community; as a believer with idiosyncratic convictions; as a man or a woman; as a person with a certain status in a society and belonging to a certain class; as a member of a society and of a culture, etc., etc. As we well know from our own experience of role playing, we do not say the same thing when we speak with the voices of different personae. In some instances, we even say contradictory things-e.g. when we express our personal idiosyncratic convictions and those of the community to which we belong. Nevertheless, in actual experience, we cannot help but to be, to live as, to speak as a person with a multiplicity of personae. So it is with any *real* author. When speaking or writing, this author cannot help but to express himself or herself with a multiplicity of voices, which might at times be contradictory.

With the help of this metaphor, I can begin to conceptualize in a general way how reading-choices take place according to this volume as a whole. As a real ordinary reader, with multiple personae (like Long) and thus multiple inner voices, each time I read a given text, I perceive as making sense (or not) certain voices of the text which resonate with some of my inner voices, and among these I further select those which sound more significant than others for me/us.

CHOOSING THE GROUND FOR OUR EPISTEMOLOGICAL JUDGMENTS: HERMENEUTICAL THEORIES OR POPULAR RELIGIOUS AND CULTURAL EXPERIENCES

As I further consider this volume, the juxtaposition of these essays makes a very important point for me and other European-American biblical scholars by underscoring the surprising way in which certain essays implicitly or explicitly ground their conclusions.[14]

No surprises for me in Long's essay: following traditional European-American scholarship, he grounds the conclusions of his (critical) reading of a text (and the critical argument which supports these conclusions) in a basic epistemological judgment formulated out of reflection about existing hermeneutical theories. Thus, Long grounds his epistemological judgment (which ultimately allows him to argue for a type of critical readings which would be as contextual as ordinary readings) in a remarkably clear discussion of Gadamer, Derrida, and Ricoeur. A plausible reading is a reading which abides by the epistemology established in

---

[14] Of course, my training in semiotics led me to pay attention to these aspects (or voices) of the essays.

European hermeneutical theories. The contextual reading which Long proposes makes sense, because one can show that it abides by this epistemology. Similar comments could be made about Wittenberg's paper.[15]

But, I should say that, at first, I was quite surprised to find these papers in this volume. What is Long's typically European-American essay doing in this volume? But soon I saw that, along with Wittenberg's, it played an essential role. It made me aware of the fact that several of the other essays ground their epistemological judgments in quite different ways: no longer on reflections on hermeneutical theories, but on reflections on the popular religious and cultural experiences of African people.

For Pobee, where does one find the semantic categories which will allow us to assess which biblical interpretations make sense? In the popular uses of the Bible. Indeed in the most popular uses one can find: the magical uses of the Bible; the uses of the Bible in political rhetoric; a simple woman always carrying a Bible with her, because it is the only "book which reads me!" In sum, as Pobee emphasizes, popular African religions and cultures should be viewed not merely as "contexts" in which the interpretation of the Bible should be conceptualized, but as the "hermeneutic" which provides the epistemology (and ontology) for African readings of the Bible—and, I should underscore, an appropriate epistemology for these readings.

A similar point (although with various nuances) is made by Draper (who emphasizes the distinctiveness and legitimacy of "oral hermeneutics"), by Dube (who identifies what I would call the "epistemological" framework of actual readings of the Bible in AICs as a *"Semoya* framework"), by Nolan (note his grounding of the "theology of work" in the experience, faith, biblical interpretations, and interests of workers), by Ukpong (who calls for the reading of biblical texts "from an inculturation biblical hermeneutic," which in his example finds an epistemology in the social and economic situation of West African farmers), and by Walker (who emphasizes the epistemological privilege of the poor, and therefore the epistemology of popular religion expressed in Marian devotion).

As I read each of these papers on its own, none made for me the point which Pobee's paper made, namely that popular African religions and cultures should be viewed as the "hermeneutic" which provides the le-

---

[15] At first, *Wittenberg's* search for a "good" epistemology seems quite far from Long's, since it involves the rejection of an epistemology "from above" (out of the Enlightenment) in favor of a different epistemology, "from below." Yet, one soon discovers that this epistemology "from below" is coming from the biblical text read in social scientific terms (i.e. in terms of European-American methodologies, as the footnotes clarify) *for* the poor and the oppressed, rather than coming from the poor and the oppressed among whom the epistemology would be found and *with* whom the biblical text would then be read.

gitimate epistemology for African readings. Yet, when I read these other papers in juxtaposition with Long's and Wittenberg's essays, they make for me the same point, all the more forcefully that they do not state it in a direct way, namely that:

> Popular African religions and cultures (including their socio-economic dimensions) have the same status as European-American hermeneutical theories, in that all of them provide appropriate epistemologies—that is, epistemologies on the basis of which readers can appropriately make sense of a text.

The different ways of making sense of the text in terms of these epistemologies can be understood in the perspective of the above discussion of the multiple voices of a text. Different epistemologies (be they African, European, or American) tune the readers to different voices.

Of course, a European epistemology can be used to assess African (ordinary) readings of the Bible. Yet, one should not be surprised to find that this epistemology is not operative in the African reading as Mosala's paper demonstrates in an exemplary way. Using hermeneutical categories developed in theories which reflect a European epistemology, the categories of "race, class, and gender," to investigate African Independent Churches, Mosala carefully avoided to force these categories upon the use of the Bible by these churches, and therefore reach the important conclusion that "they play no distinctively sub-cultural role among the AICs." The hermeneutical and epistemological categories which are really operative are African ones, such as those which Dube's research begins to identify.

What then is the role of a critical reading vis-à-vis ordinary readings of text? It is not to urge readers to produce contextual or inculturated readings (as seems to be advocated by West, Ukpong, and others), but simply to bring to light ("bring to critical understanding," as I like to say) which epistemology and hermeneutical categories ordinary readings have used—with the understanding that one epistemology is as appropriate as another. Consequently, a given critical reading should bring to light the culturally-marked epistemology of the ordinary reading it happens to bring to understanding. Thus, as Riches concludes:

> There is no sharp division between cultural readings of the Bible and "purely historical" readings, or indeed any other kind of readings. European academic readings have been as much driven by major cultural questions and perspectives as any other.

In sum, there is no real division between critical and ordinary readings in terms of inculturation. The difference is simply that critical readings make explicit their choices of (cultural) categories, while ordinary readings make a spontaneous (or sub-conscious) use of these categories.

Showing the Legitimacy of Ordinary Readings and the Authority/Power of the Biblical Text

Beyond making explicit the epistemological categories used in a given reading of the text, the task of critical readings includes showing the specific voice (set of features, dimension, or code) of the text which becomes the focus when the text is read in terms of these categories. This amounts to showing the *legitimacy* of a certain kind of ordinary readings, that is, showing that these readings reflect one of the ways in which the text actually affects certain readers—while other readers are attuned to (affected by) other voices of the text, because they have heard it in terms of different epistemological categories.

The articles of this volume suggest that African ordinary readings (and other ordinary readings) are, in most instances, legitimate. I agree. Although they are different from European-American readings, they are legitimate because they use a different epistemology (as emphasized by several authors and as discussed above). Yet, for me, it is also because African readers believe in the authority and power of the Bible as Scripture (or even as magical text; cf. Pobee). Let us remember that an ordinary reading expresses the way in which readers are *affected* by a text. Since most African readers of the Bible are people who have a strong sense of the religious authority of this text (even if it is an oral authority), and thus people who believe in the power of this text to affect their lives, one can be confident that their readings (their conclusions about the teaching of this text for them) reflect in each instance an actual voice, or dimension, or code of the text. In sum, even though ordinary readings (as any readings) are always in need of refinements, as faith-interpretations (or *pro me/nobis* interpretations) they can be said to be basically legitimate, even before critical readings make it explicit.

Ukpong's study of the inculturation of the parable of the shrewd manager (Luke 16:1–13) is the only article of this volume which undertakes to make explicit the legitimacy of an ordinary reading. The author must be applauded for showing that the reading of the parable inculturated in terms of the situation of Western African farmers is *legitimate*, that is, properly grounded in the text and its context. This is what, according to the overall message of this volume, one should and can demonstrate regarding each ordinary African reading. Yet, the author goes against the overall message of the volume and against his own repeated rejection of "the idea of one and universally valid interpretation of the biblical text" by involuntarily adopting the traditional attitude of male European-American scholars, as he seeks to demonstrate that readings which have different conclusions are illegitimate (are incorrectly or inappropriately grounded in the textual evidence). In terms of the above discussion, in order to establish the legitimacy of this inculturated reading, it was enough to show that it is based upon a specific dimension of the text, or that it accounts for a specific code, or again that it is attuned to a specific voice of the text—and that the other and different (European-American) readings are related to different dimensions, codes, or voices. In sum, the polemical arguments of this essay are not necessary, and even counterproductive.

Draper's article makes an essential point through its insistence upon the orality of African interpretations. As one seeks to bring to understanding the textual voice (or dimension or code) which is the focus of a given African interpretation, it is certainly important to take into account the oral (or residual-oral) character of the biblical text. By saying so, I simply underscore that Draper's paper and the works on orality he mentions call for the development of a critical method of "oral exegesis." Such a method would quite certainly help in showing the legitimacy of many African interpretations, especially those found in the African Independent Churches.

Through the use of existing critical methods or of newly developed ones better adapted to the epistemologies found in African popular religions and cultures (such as an eventual "oral critical exegesis"), critical readings will show the legitimacy of quite different African readings, alongside European-American readings. Yet, this does not mean that all readings and all epistemologies have the same value.

Choosing the Ground for Our Value Judgments: The Privileged Option for the Poor

Several articles of this volume strongly emphasizes the need to choose among potential readings of biblical texts on the basis of a specific value judgment. This point is clearly made by West's as well as by Dube's, Nolan's, Pobee's, and Ukpong's articles. I can therefore be brief. Such a value judgment is practiced when one affirms the privileged option for the poor and oppressed. At this point it is no longer a matter of the privileged epistemology of the poor (cf. Walker), that is, of recognizing the legitimacy of the epistemologies of popular religions and cultures. Such epistemologies bring about readings of the Bible which affect people in quite different ways: readings which are oppressive (or support the continuation of oppression) as well as readings which are liberating. Passing a value judgment in terms of the privileged option for the poor is opting for the readings which promote justice and true liberation and rejecting as evil readings which prolong the oppression of the poor.

The questions raised by the choice of a reading in terms of such a value judgment are, of course: How does one define justice and decide what is "truly liberating"? Who will provide such a definition? Who will make such a decision?

Dube's article presents what is, for me, a most fascinating and appropriate answer, when she describes the *Semoya* readings of the Bible in worship services of African Independent Churches. It is the community as moved by *Moya*, the African inculturated Spirit, which in its wisdom is alone in a position of discerning those readings which are truly free from colonialism and thus truly liberating. This "community moved by *Moya*" is, in my mind, not to be limited to the AICs' communities (nor to be necessarily identified with them). I expect that it will be delimited and defined in different ways in the various regions of Africa (and according to church affiliations). My point is simply that the value judgment which ultimately allows people to discern among the diverse inculturated readings which one is the liberating Word of God (as good news) is not a judgment that critical readers pass upon ordinary readings. Critical readers can do nothing more than show the diversity of legitimate readings in terms of diverse cultural epistemologies. It is the community of ordinary readers which has the last word, as it had the first words. It is the community of ordinary readers which had the first words, as it proffered the ordinary readings. Critical readers as facilitators help ordinary readers to bring to critical understanding these readings; then it becomes clear that one has a choice among several legitimate interpretations. But it is the community of ordinary readers which has the last word, when it discerns and proclaims which of these interpretations is Word of God, as the communal sermons of the African Independent Churches do.

"READING WITH": AN EXPLORATION OF THE INTERFACE BETWEEN "CRITICAL" AND "ORDINARY"[1] READINGS OF THE BIBLE: A RESPONSE

Teresia M. Hinga
De Paul University
United States of America

Ever since the introduction of Christianity in Africa, the Bible has fascinated many Africans and has been a resource for inspiration and a frame of reference for living. The fact that African cultures are typically oral rather than literate cultures has not deterred Africans from "reading" the Bible diligently, seeking the word of God for themselves and their circumstances.

Meanwhile, down the ages, the Bible has also been the focus of scholarly attention as academics seek to present the Bible in its own terms by seeking to analyze the Bible as literature (literary criticism) and as history (historical criticism).

For a long time, these two ways of reading the Bible have pursued their own independent and often parallel paths. At times however, the "academic readers" of the Bible have often been prescriptive and suspicious of "ordinary" readings, which they suspect of not being rigorous enough and possibly constituting erroneous interpretations.

It is against this background, that this special issue of *Semeia* entitled "Reading With" has set out to explore the intersection or interface between "academic critical biblical" readings and "ordinary" readings of the Bible. Categorizing themselves as "critical readers," writers in this volume express their wish to participate in a "reading with" *"ordinary readers"* whom they identify as the poor and oppressed, the victims of various injustices and conditions of domination prevailing in Africa. Thus, the volume presents writers who are engaged in bridging the gap

---

[1] The use of inverted commas on the terms "critical" and "Ordinary" in this essay is meant to draw attention to the fact that the choice of these terms is not mine and that, as I comment later in the essay, the use of these terms is itself in need of critical analysis.

between biblical studies as an academic enterprise and the study of the Bible as a resource for personal guidance in life. Their frame of reference seems to be that of liberation hermeneutics whose starting point, as West indicates, is "the epistemological privilege of the poor."

Such a committed "reading with" the poor is in my view long overdue. In the past, the academic enterprise, not only in theology and religion but in all spheres of scholarship, has tended to be elitist and to function, howbeit sometimes unwittingly, in the service of dominant cultures. One recalls here the role that anthropological discourse played as a precursor of imperialism in Africa in so far as it created the myth of "primitive" people and "dark continent" which had to be redeemed from its "pagan," "savage," and "uncivilized" ways.[2] The Bible in particular has been coopted and pressed into the service of the oppressors.[3] At its best academic scholarship has been indifferent to the plight of the poor, hiding behind the subtly fallacious idea that academic studies demand objectivity. Fortunately, an increasing number of scholars are realizing that there is a fallacy implicit in claiming objectivity in discourse, since no discourse is entirely free from ideological and other presuppositions. A more authentic approach is to acknowledge one's biases, analytical starting points, and hermeneutical principles. The writers in this volume have by and large been conscious of the need to articulate their ideological starting points and have persuasively argued that this does not necessarily detract from the rigor of their scholarship. Instead, this acknowledgement enriches and challenges them as scholars to be accountable not only to the academy but also to the people and contexts in which they do their scholarship. They have consciously chosen to follow the path of an *engaged* study of the Bible which is deliberately oriented to the service of the oppressed.

Within the African context, however, situations of specific oppressions and dominations prevail. Colonization, sexism, and racism operate in an intersecting way to create painful situations for people. A reading with Africa, therefore, must necessarily take into consideration the multiple and intersecting oppressions that prevail on the continent.

The writers have, in my view and to a significant extent, succeeded in their efforts to read with the "poor" for several reasons. First, all the papers focus on the African context. They therefore constitute a "reading with Africa," a continent which has been at the bottom of the heap in re-

---

[2] See, for example, "Victorians and The Africans: The Genealogy of the Myth of The Dark Continent," Pp. 185–222 in Henry Louis Gates, ed. *Race Writing And Difference:* University of Chicago Press, 1986.

[3] See, for example, the Kairos Document (1985:3ff), produced by Black Theologians in South Africa and its critique of the use of Romans 13 to justify Apartheid.

lation to Western centers and epistemology. For a long time designated "The Dark Continent" and its peoples "primitive" and untutored, Africa in general has suffered radical peripheralisation even in comparison with other parts of the Two-Thirds world. With reference to "critical" biblical scholarship, the epistemological center has been Europe. Most of the so-called "critical readers" of the Bible have been European. European perspectives were imported into the continent, and efforts were made to force Africans to adopt these since was assumed that Africans had nothing to offer the rest of the world. The ensuing "epistemological ethnocentricism" is one of the issues that Pobee addresses. He argues for the "Passover of Language," a shifting of epistemological centers so that biblical scholarship is done in a language that takes into consideration the cultural, historical, social, and political context as hermeneutically relevant. Such a shift in method would take the critical scholars closer to the long overdue goal of "reading with" those who have been historically marginalised. The focus on Africa in these essays, then, is in itself a "Reading With" the marginalised and with the oppressed.

While all the papers presented here participate in this shift in methods and objectives of doing biblical scholarship, three papers exemplify the ethos of this volume: namely, those by Pobee, West, and Dube.

Addressing himself largely to scholarly readers, Pobee argues for a shift in method from Eurocentricism and its attendant text-centricism, to a people-centered and context-centered biblical scholarship. He argues that, particularly in Africa, scholarship (biblical or otherwise) cannot afford to be an ivory-tower exercise. Scholarship for the sake of scholarship is a luxury that is yet to be achieved and whose desirability is questionable.

Pobee clearly states that scholarship in Africa must be answerable to the hopes, dreams, and fears of the society in which it is done. Pobee's paper emerges as a call to biblical scholars to participate in a socially engaged biblical scholarship. As Pobee sees it, part of the task for the academic scholars of the Bible is to facilitate the creation of a "Passover" of language, a translation of the Bible so that it speaks the language of the people. In this process of "Passover," the "critical reader" seeking hermeneutical strategies suitable for the African situation would have to address the cultural and social-political context of Africa. This is a context that is simultaneously one of pluralism and which therefore deserves what Pobee calls the "hermeneutics of pluralism."

While Pobee addresses the "academic critical readers" and puts up sign posts indicating the direction that biblical studies in Africa should take, West and Dube (among others) attempt to practice the hermeneutical principles of reading the Bible for liberation.

West focuses on the implications of biblical studies in the South African context, a context, which until recently has been characterized by unmitigated oppression of the majority black people. In this context "ordinary readers" of the Bible abound and a variety of interpretations prevail. As West puts it, the context of apartheid "demanded new readers and new theologies," and he laments that these readings "that resolved the struggle against apartheid are in danger of being forgotten."

West tests the theory of liberative hermeneutics and reading as a biblical scholar among those who have struggled under apartheid and whose struggle is not yet over. A few noteworthy points emerge from his attempt to implement the principle of "reading with."

First, an authentic "reading with" must take into consideration, not only the "text" of the Bible, but also the "context" of the readers. The innovative readings of the Bible by the oppressed often seem to spring not only from the hearing of the "words" of the Bible, but also from a sense of resonance between their "contexts" and those which gave which gave the biblical "texts" birth. For example, the black South Africans' experience of oppression under apartheid resonates with that of the Israelites under Pharaoh. The Africans' sense of injustice and longing for liberation from apartheid significantly echoed that of the Israelites under the Egyptian oppression. For the black people in South Africa however, a knowledge of the "text" alone is not adequate. The burning question for them is: What, if anything has the biblical "text," for example, the story of the Exodus, got to do with their immediate context. For such oppressed readers the study of the Bible is an applied discipline, since it is done to address specific day-to-day experiences in the readers' lives.

Second, West identifies at least two issues that face the "critical reader" in the process of trying to read with the "ordinary reader":

To what extent does the academic reader avoid usurping the voice of the poor when presuming to speak on behalf of the poor?

To what extent does she/he avoid romanticizing their views by claiming only to listen to the poor, while failing to engage in serious conversation with the poor for mutual enrichment?

West points out that while "listening" to the poor is an improvement on earlier strategies, which palpably ignored or derided the voice of the poor, "engaging" in conversation with the poor is demanded by the long-standing fact that "ordinary people" are also subjects, and to refuse to take this subjectivity and agency into account is to submerge them further into a quagmire of domination. One of the strengths of West's article lies in his recognition of the need to go beyond mere listening to the poor to a serious engagement with them in mutually enriching analysis of biblical texts and African contexts. Such an attempt to engage the poor in analytical discourse is largely unprecedented and is highly commendable.

What is even more commendable is West's recognition that the willingness to speak with the oppressed may be a necessary but not sufficient condition for a successful "reading with" them, because the participants start from unequal social locations. The "academic scholar" already comes from a privileged position while the "ordinary reader" comes from an oppressed position of racial discrimination. Indeed, the very fact of being dominated has led the oppressed to develop a coded way of reading the texts: to respond to their contexts by articulating themselves theologically. Taking such coded readings and self-articulations at face value may miss the real message of the "ordinary readers." Some scholars have fallen into the trap of thinking that the poor are so oppressed that they have completely lost their voice and that they can only speak a language of the "master." In such cases the "academic critical readers" see their role as that of helping the oppressed break the silence and create their own language. The strength of West's paper is in his recognition that the poor have not entirely lost their voice—that indeed they may have already found it necessary to create a language that is consistent with their struggles for survival and resistance. The language is necessarily coded, often oblique, but nonetheless it constitutes a powerful critique of the dominant cultures. It simultaneously speaks of the oppressed's awareness of their oppression and their will to struggle and survive the oppression. The discovery that "ordinary readers" are in effect "critical" readers in their contexts of oppression and that they critically respond to oppression is an important stance for an "academic reader" who wishes to participate in a genuine reading with the oppressed. Only then can the "critical (academic) reader," become an ally, rather than a liability, to the "ordinary reader." According to West, the scholar becomes an ally by becoming a participant and a facilitator in a process through which the ordinary readers' hidden meaning can be articulated and ultimately owned.

I was specially drawn to Dube's article since it resonated with my research attempts ten years ago when I sought to "read," not on behalf of, but "with" the members of the Legio Maria Church, one of the many independent churches in Kenya. I was concerned to foreground the women in this church who have been doubly left out of the picture by the dominant culture and the colonial missionary churches.[4]

Dube discusses the contextual nature of the Bible reading in Botswana. She points out that neither the text nor the context alone are relevant to the academic reader who wishes to read with the oppressed. Us-

---

[4] See T. M. Hinga, "Women, Power, and Liberation in an African Church." Unpublished Ph.D. Thesis. University of Lancaster, 1990.

ing the case of "ordinary" Batswana women's reading of the Bible, Dube notes that the women claim to read the text and their context from the perspective of *Semoya* (Of the Spirit). They therefore do not consider their readings to be "ordinary," since they are readings of a people empowered, energized, and enlightened by *Moya*, Spirit! In this process of reading an academic reader of the Bible would have to reckon with the people's self-understanding. What are the analytical implications of the people's claim to be reading the Bible "through the power of the Spirit"?

Several points are pertinent here.

First of all, the self-description of the Batswana women as a people driven and enlightened by the spirit reflects the African cultural context which refuses to accept the dichotomy between matter and spirit. In the perspective of these African readers and context, the written "text" is considered dead unless it is energized by the Spirit of God. It is only then that it becomes the "life giving and empowering Word of God." Reading with *Semoya* is, at one level, a point of contact between the world view of the Bible, which also features the centrality of the Spirit and, on another level, to be in contact with African religious views. Second, for African people, the Bible is not just text, it is potent precisely because it is charged with *Moya*. Ordinary African readers go to the Bible, as Pobee also points out, to tap this potency, this life-giving power. This reality raises a crucial question for the "critical" reader who desires to read with such Africans. To what extent is the "critical reader" willing to surrender to *Moya* and, along with ordinary reader, follow the prompting of *Semoya* in the attempt to bring to life the rigid texts written long ago for other people and other contexts? The answer to this question may well be a significant measure of the "academic reader's capacity to read with the so called "ordinary readers" who, living in life-sapping and paralysing situations of oppression, necessarily view the Bible as a life-giving and empowering resource.

Third, the significance of *Semoya* in African biblical hermeneutics is also apparent when we consider that African people have been rendered voiceless by the discourse and praxis of domination. In such contexts the Spirit becomes the voice of those who are muted by the silencing processes inherent in their condition of oppression. The Spirit literally becomes the voice of the voiceless (Hinga,1990:267ff.).

For a people who are also rendered powerless by oppression, the Spirit is their source of power *par excellence*. For a people who have been treated unjustly and unfairly, the experience of *Moya*, Spirit, that blows where it wills and is no respecter of persons becomes a source of their confidence that justice will eventually prevail. The realization of the symbolic significance of *Semoya* in the theological self-understanding of the

African Christians helps one understand the rather unexpected interpretations that the women in Dube interviewed give to the story of the Canaanite woman and her encounter with Jesus.

According to these women, the story of the Canaanite woman reveals God's willingness to vindicate the oppressed. They consider Jesus was empowered by *Moya* to seek out this woman in order to bring her the benefits of the kingdom, which include for them healing and restoration of life. As far as they are concerned, the central actor is God's Spirit, working through Jesus to show impartiality and willingness to vindicate the victims of injustice. Consequently, according to Dube, all of her respondents insisted that Jesus "came for all people" (Dube, 119).

The strength of Dube's reading with "ordinary" Batswana women, as with West, lies in her willingness to acknowledge her social-political location in the discourse. In spite of being a Motswana woman herself, Dube acknowledges that her hermeneutical glasses have significantly been influenced by her Western academic training. She avoids usurping the voice and agency of "ordinary" Batswana women. She acknowledges her text-centeredness born out of her academic training in the West. She foregrounds and privileges the voice of ordinary women and avoids putting words in their mouths. At the same time, however, Dube is an "ordinary reader;" compared to European women, her voice is an "ordinary voice" in so far as it seeks to address the context of colonialism from which African women, including herself, must read the Bible.

The case of Dube illustrates that to read with the oppressed and the poor is simultaneously to read in critique of oppressors and those who dominate. It also illustrates that the dichotomy between the "ordinary reading" and "critical reading" in Africa is ultimately a false one, since African scholars like Pobee and Dube are simultaneously "ordinary readers." They share and participate in the contexts of struggle that necessitate the birth of a liberative hermeneutics in the first place. The commitment of such academics to do socially engaged scholarship is simultaneously self-liberative in so far as they too are claiming the space for their own ordinary readings, which are in continuity with those of the people for whom and among whom they struggle. The recognition by academic scholars that ultimately they themselves are "ordinary" (differing with others only in so far as they have different but not necessarily better resources for reading) will go along way in eliminating the problem of elitism and the hubris implicit even in African scholars who may, at times, not be able to resist to speak for the "Other." Realizing that the "Other" is ultimately the self will help bridge the gap between the academics and non-academics, between "ordinary" and the so-called critical readers. This realization may eventually necessitate a reexamination of the very language that we use to describe the "poor" even in the context of liberative hermeneutics. When scholars claim to make an option for the poor, what are they saying about their relationship with the poor? In what sense are ordinary people poor and in what sense are scholars rich? Does material poverty reflect intellectual poverty? Why do we describe ourselves as "critical" and the poor as "ordinary"? In my view these are crucial questions if we are ultimately to get rid of hierarchical and dualistic thinking, which has been the bane in discourse about Africa and its peoples. This is one of the problems that this volume seeks to address in a commendable way. The process of "reading with" the "poor" is simultaneously a privilege and a task which has hardly began and which must be sustained consistently in all areas of scholarship, including of course biblical scholarship.

www.ingramcontent.com/pod-product-compliance
Lightning Source LLC
Chambersburg PA
CBHW031309150426
43191CB00005B/149